Responsible Citizens, Irresponsible States

Responsible Citizens, Irresponsible States

Should Citizens Pay for Their State's Wrongdoings?

AVIA PASTERNAK

OXFORD
UNIVERSITY PRESS

OXFORD
UNIVERSITY PRESS

Oxford University Press is a department of the University of Oxford. It furthers
the University's objective of excellence in research, scholarship, and education
by publishing worldwide. Oxford is a registered trade mark of Oxford University
Press in the UK and certain other countries.

Published in the United States of America by Oxford University Press
198 Madison Avenue, New York, NY 10016, United States of America.

Library of Congress Cataloging-in-Publication Data
Names: Pasternak, Avia, 1975– author.
Title: Responsible citizens, irresponsible states:
should citizens pay for their state's wrongdoings? / Avia Pasternak.
Description: New York, NY, United States of America :
Oxford University Press, [2021] |
Includes bibliographical references and index.
Identifiers: LCCN 2021013666 (print) | LCCN 2021013667 (ebook) |
ISBN 9780197541036 (hardback) | ISBN 9780197541050 (epub)
Subjects: LCSH: Progress—Moral and ethical aspects. | Social change—Moral
and ethical aspects. | Citizenship—Moral and ethical aspects. |
State, The—Moral and ethical aspects. | Moral conditions.
Classification: LCC HM891 .P37 2021 (print) |
LCC HM891 (ebook) | DDC 303.44—dc23
LC record available at https://lccn.loc.gov/2021013666
LC ebook record available at https://lccn.loc.gov/2021013667

DOI: 10.1093/oso/9780197541036.001.0001

1 3 5 7 9 8 6 4 2

Printed by Integrated Books International, United States of America

To my parents,
Nurit and Ehud

Contents

Acknowledgments

The ideas presented in this book have been accompanying me for a long time. I started thinking about the question of citizens' responsibility for their state's injustice as a young political activist in Israel. I turned to examine it more systematically during my doctoral studies at Nuffield College, Oxford, and have been working and thinking about it ever since. In the course of these years I accumulated many intellectual debts to both individuals and institutions.

I'll start with institutions. I am grateful to the British Academy for granting me the British Academy Senior Research Award, which allowed me to dedicate a whole year to this project and to bring it to completion. I am also grateful to my Department at University College London, which offers a wonderful research environment. I have had countless conversations on this work with my political philosophy colleagues in the Department—Jeff Howard, Emily McTernan, Saladin Meckled-Garcia, Adam Swift, and Albert Weale—as well as with many of my political science colleagues. These conversations taught me how closely intertwined political science and political philosophy are.

I have a long-standing intellectual debt to the Nuffield Political Theory Workshop. The Workshop was the hub around which my intellectual life as a DPhil student revolved and where many of my early thoughts about citizens' responsibility were formed. Over the years, I was invited back to the Workshop to present drafts chapters. The Workshop was also where I met several brilliant female political philosophers, who, over the years, would become my friends and intellectual sounding board. I am deeply grateful to David Miller, who created this institution and chaired it during my time in Oxford.

There are many individuals to whom I owe a debt of gratitude. Over the years I have had incredibly valuable exchanges with colleagues about the ideas developed in this book: Bob Goodin, who was also working on questions of complicity and compromise while we were colleagues at the Department of Government at the University of Essex; Lucas Leeman, my colleague at UCL who helped me understand the data on citizens' attitudes to their state; Jinyu Sun, whose doctoral dissertation I had the pleasure to supervise at UCL and who offered invaluable insights about citizens' involvement in their state in authoritarian regimes. I am also grateful to Natasha Esrow, Jeff King, Melissa Lane, Christian List, Roland Meeks, and Dorota Mokrosinska, and to Cecile Fabre, Cecile Laborde, and Anna Stilz for their support and their insights, not just about collective responsibility but about writing monographs in general.

I have presented draft chapters of this book at several workshops and research seminars and am thankful to the organizers and to the participants and audiences for their comments and suggestions. These included a workshop on artificial intelligence at the University of Cambridge, a workshop on collectivity and responsibility at Lund University, a workshop on political philosophy and social ontology at the London School of Economics, a workshop on responsibility in complex systems at Umeå University, a workshop on collective state responsibility at the Centre for Ethics at Zurich, a workshop on state agency and citizens' complicity at Princeton's Center for Human Values, the Princeton University Normative Methods Philosophy Seminar, the University of Richmond Political Theory Forum, the Oxford Political Theory Research Seminar, and the American political Science Association 2019 Annual Conference.

My deepest gratitude goes to colleagues and friends who took the time to read draft chapters and who sent me invaluable written comments: Stephanie Collins, Rob Jubb, Holly Lawford-Smith, David Lefkowitz, David Schweikard, and an anonymous referee for Oxford University Press. Zosia Stemplowska organized with incredible efficiency a manuscript workshop with Daniel Butt, Cecile Fabre, Sarah Fine, Tom Parr, David Miller, Zofia Stemplowska, and Victor Tadros. Christian Barry also read the whole manuscript as a referee for Oxford University Press. I am incredibly grateful to these colleagues for their generosity and their insights.

Finally, there are few individuals whose ongoing support made this book possible. I am grateful to my parents, Nurit and Ehud Pasternak, for teaching me to care about citizens' collective responsibility in the first place, and for their infinite love and support. To Zofia Stemplowska and Sarah Fine—brilliant political philosophers, fellow working moms and close friends—for their humor, support, and encouragement. To my children, Eli and Yann, for everything they have given me. And lastly, to Roland Meeks, for his patience, wit, and IT skills, and for providing a proper cup of tea at just the right moments.

Introduction

Holding states responsible for their wrongdoings is a common practice. At the international level, states routinely pay compensation and other forms of reparation for wrongs they inflicted on other states and individuals. Consider, for example, the reparations scheme for the victims of the Holocaust, which West Germany took upon itself in the aftermath of the Second World War. By 2001, Germany had paid a total of approximately US$61.5 billion into this scheme.[1] Or consider the United Nations Compensation Commission (UNCC). Established by the United Nations Security Council in 1991, its mission was to process claims against Iraq for the damage and loss it had caused during its invasion of Kuwait and the war that ensued. By 2005 the fund had awarded a total of US$52.4 billion.[2] In contrast, no country has paid compensation to Iraq and to Iraqi citizens for the harm inflicted on them in the course of the 2003 US-led invasion. However, in 2017 Haider al-Abadi, the Iraqi prime minister, argued that the US and Britain owed his country such compensation, given the chaos and destruction that their actions had inflicted on it.[3]

States also take upon themselves domestic compensation schemes. For example, in the decades that followed the fall of the

---

[1] Ariel Colonomos and Andrea Armstrong, "German Reparations to the Jews after World War II: A Turning Point in the History of Reparation," in *The Handbook of Reparations*, ed. Pablo de Greiff (Oxford: Oxford University Press 2006), 408.

[2] Hans van Houtte, Hans Das, and Bart Delmartino, "The United Nations Compensation Commission," in *The Handbook of Reparations*, ed. Pablo de Greiff (Oxford: Oxford University Press, 2006), 321–89 .

[3] "Iraq Demands America, Britain Pay Reparations for 2003 Invasion," *The New Arab*, January 19, 2017, https://english.alaraby.co.uk/english/news/2017/1/19/iraq-demands-america-britain-pay-reparations-for-2003-invasion.

Responsible Citizens, Irresponsible States. Avia Pasternak, Oxford University Press. © Oxford University Press 2021. DOI: 10.1093/oso/9780197541036.003.0001

dictatorial regimes in Argenita (1983) and Chile (1990), the newly established democratic governments implemented reparations programs for the victims of the grave human rights violations committed by their predecessors.[4] In 2008 the Canadian government set up a reparations program for individuals who were forcibly removed as children from their indigenous communities to "residential schools." As well as apologizing for its support of this policy, the Canadian government paid over CAN$5 billion in compensation and toward rehabilitation and commemorative projects.[5]

These few examples do not suggest, of course, that states always address the wrongs they committed in their distant or recent past. In the world as we know it, and given the lack of effective enforcement mechanisms at the international level, all too often states blatantly refuse or fail to address their remedial obligations. Nevertheless, it does happen, at least occasionally, that states are forced to address such obligations, or even do so willingly.

In the five cases mentioned above, the state itself was found responsible for the wrongdoings in question. Holding states responsible is a core feature of international law, the main purpose of which is to regulate the behavior of states. In international law, states are legal entities with their own legal rights and duties.[6] But the idea of state responsibility can also be grounded in a deeper epistemological and ethical outlook, according to which the state itself is an institutional moral agent, acting in the world in the light of its own beliefs and desires. When moral agents wrong others,

---

[4] José Maria Guemba, "Economic Reparations for Grave Human Rights Violations," in *The Handbook of Reparations*, ed. Pablo de Greiff (Oxford: Oxford University Press, 2006), 22–51; Elisabeth Lira, "The Reparations Policy for Human Rights Violations in Chile," in *The Handbook of Reparations*, ed. Pablo de Greiff (Oxford: Oxford University Press, 2006), 56–101.

[5] Catherine Lu, *Justice and Reconciliation in World Politics* (Cambridge: Cambridge University Press, 2017), 6–7.

[6] A. Cassesse, *International Law in a Divided World* (Oxford: Oxford University Press, 1986), 3.

Are states moral agents?

we expect them to address the plight of their victims, as a way of making them whole again.

And yet, unlike individual moral agents, states are constituted of people, as well as of the decision-making and authority processes that bind them together.[7] And when we hold the state responsible, its citizens will be affected. When West Germany, Iraq, Canada, Argentina and Chile discharged their compensatory liabilities to their victims, the large sums of money that were needed to finance these compensation schemes came from the public purse. Their responsibility to address their wrongdoing was distributed, *de facto*, to their populations.[8] *PO @ extreme*

[Is this "distributive effect" of state responsibility, from the state to its population at large, normatively justified? Common intuitions do not provide a decisive answer on this complex question. On the one hand, the reparation schemes which I mentioned—including those undertaken by West Germany, Argentina, and Chile—are commonly regarded as laudable enterprises, despite their impact on the citizenry as a whole. Indeed, many would argue that West Germany's implementation of the 1952 scheme was a crucial step in paving its way back into the international community after World War II. But, on the other hand, another common intuition is that at least the oppressed subjects of dictatorial regimes should not be bearing the costs of their state's policies. This latter view is expressed, for example, in Naomi Klein's scathing critique of the UNCC, which, she argues, ended up imposing unacceptable

---

[7] Tracy Isaacs, "Collective Moral Responsibility and Collective Intention," *Midwest Studies in Philosophy* 30, no. 1 (2006): 59–73.

[8] For an analysis of how reparation schemes are financed, especially in transitional regimes, see Alexander Segovia, "Financing Reparations Programs," in *The Handbook of Reparations*, ed. Pablo de Greiff (Oxford: Oxford University Press, 2006), 651–73. This analysis demonstrates that the state typically uses its public budget. Admittedly this is a simplified account of how states finance their liabilities. In reality, public budgets are much more complex, as governments can, *inter alia*, borrow the money, or impose the obligation on future generations by deferring repayment. But for the purposes of the discussion here I leave such complications aside. I assume it is possible to draw some link between the state's compensatory liabilities and the resources it draws from its current population.

4 RESPONSIBLE CITIZENS, IRRESPONSIBLE STATES

burdens on the people of Iraq, who were "themselves Saddam's primary victims."[9]

Perhaps it could be argued that the distributive effect is more easily justified in democratic states, given that their citizens are served by their state and have various opportunities to take part in its decision-making process. But here too it is fairly easy to identify citizens who seem to have a valid argument against their state imposing on them a share of the burden. Consider citizens who were very young, or not even born, when the wrongs in question were committed. Or consider citizens who did all that was in their power to resist the implementation of these wrongful policies. Or consider the citizens who are burdened with compensation for wrongs that were hidden from them by their governments. In all these cases even democratic citizens find themselves encumbered with responsibilities for outcomes they tried to prevent or had no control over. Should they be the ones paying the price? There are reasons to doubt, Larry May tells us, the "fairness of a policy which creates the same penalty for all members . . . when these members had decidedly different contributions to the criminal result."[10] In a similar spirit James Crawford and Jeremy Watkins tell us that the distributive effect may seem

> as unfair and ethically backwards as the treatment meted out under primitive systems of collective responsibility in which whole tribes or nations are subject to reprisals: after all, in both set-ups innocent people are called upon to pay the price for the misdeeds and mistakes of their rulers.[11]

---

[9] Naomi Klein, "Why Is War-Torn Iraq Giving $190,000 to Toys R Us?," *The Guardian*, October 16, 2004, http://www.guardian.co.uk/world/2004/oct/16/iraq.comment.

[10] Larry May, *The Morality of Groups: Collective Responsibility, Group-Based Harm, and Corporate Rights* (Notre Dame, IN: University of Notre Dame Press, 1987), 104.

[11] James Crawford and Jeremy Watkins, "International Responsibility," in *The Philosophy of International Law*, ed. Samantha Besson and John Tasioulas (Oxford: Oxford University Press, 2010), 290.

Notice that the fact that state responsibility has a distributive effect is hardly surprising in and of itself. Indeed, a similar impact often occurs when an individual offender pays compensation, and those in their vicinity—e.g., family members, creditors, or employees—suffer as a result. But, as Crawford and Watkins indicate, in the case of state responsibility, the distributive effect is more striking, for various reasons. First, unlike in the case of individual wrongdoers, it is very hard to imagine a scenario where the state's corporate liabilities will not directly affect its citizenry. The distributive effect of state responsibility seems unavoidable, given the very corporate nature of the state. Second, as the ultimate policymaker and law enforcer of the land, the state has the capacity to decide upon the pattern of the distribution of its corporate liabilities, and to enforce it upon its citizens. Citizens have very little opportunity to avoid these costs. Third, given that the raison-d'être of the state is securing its citizens' rights and well-being, channeling its resources toward compensation schemes may come into conflict with its ability to provide for the needs of its citizens. It follows then that understanding when and how the distributive effect is justified matters, for several reasons. For one thing, it bears on the decisions made in international bodies, such as the United Nations Security Council, which have the authority to impose schemes of compensation on delinquent states. As we will see throughout this book, the way in which such schemes are designed can have a serious impact on the population of the target state, and that impact ought to be taken into account. Similarly, the discussion can help to shape state policies, and their own design of compensation schemes within the state. Finally, the question bears on citizens' assessment of their own state policies. After all, if citizens are not persuaded that there is a good enough justification for the burdens that fall on them as result of their state's reparatory commitments, they might be less inclined to support its compensation schemes.

The task of the present book is to explore how the distributive effect of the state's responsibility should be managed, across various regime types. The argument I develop does not support the current approach in both domestic and international politics, which by default lets the burden fall on the citizens of the wrongdoing state at large. But it also does not side with those who argue that the distribution of the burden should target those members of the state—such as government officials—who are more heavily involved in the state's policymaking. My account carves a middle ground between these two positions, and offers a solution that is sensitive to both pragmatic and normative considerations.

In the rest of the Introduction I will briefly describe the three core themes I develop in this book. First, I offer a novel justification of citizens' obligation to share in their state's remedial obligations, one that revolves around their participation in their state. Second, I examine the application of this justification to the citizens of both democratic and nondemocratic states. Third, I argue that the distribution of responsibility in the state should be case sensitive and informed by the nature of the state and its relationship with its citizens.

Before I turn to briefly present these themes, it's worth noting that the question of the distributive effect is distinct from another important debate in political theory, which concerns the source and scope of citizens' political obligations. It is a common view among political theorists (and citizens) that in reasonably just states, citizens have a general moral obligation to accept the authority of the state and to obey its laws. This commitment implies that, should the state implement a compensation scheme, its citizens ought to accept the burden it distributes on them, even if they think this burden cannot be justified. But our concern here is not with the question of whether citizens should comply with their state's decisions, but with the prior question of whether the distributive effect is justified in the first place. Not only that, as we shall see later on, the problem of the distributive effect arises also in states that are not reasonably just, and where, it is commonly thought, citizens do not have *prima facie* political obligations to accept their state's laws. Here too we would like to know whether the state or the international community are justified in demanding that citizens accept the burdens that result from their state's actions.

I.1 Intentional Citizenship

As I briefly mentioned, one approach to the problem of the distributive effect follows the commonly shared intuition that those who share the blame for bringing about a wrongful harm should be charged with the task of righting it. On this view, the distribution of the burden should aim to ensure that it falls on those people within the state who wrongly contributed to the planning and/or execution of its policies. Imagine, for example, that instead of using the revenues raised by Iraq's oil sales (under the sanctions regime that was imposed on it in the aftermath of the Gulf War), the designers of the UNCC would have targeted the assets of key officeholders in the Iraqi regime. Or imagine that instead of using its public budget to compensate Holocaust victims, West Germany would have sought to target the assets of former members of the Nazi Party. Wouldn't such schemes be better alternatives to those that Iraq and West Germany actually deployed?

I think that the answer to this question is negative. My objection to the blame-tracking distribution is pragmatic rather than principled. I think that, as a matter of practice, it is very unlikely that a blame-tracking distribution could be successfully implemented in states as we know them, given the complex structure of the state. In order to be able to successfully meet the needs of the victims, it is almost inevitable that a state would have to deviate from a blame-tracking model and implement a distribution that falls more or less equally on all the citizens. Can such a distribution be justified?

The first task of this book is to develop a new justification for the distribution of the burden among the population at large. The starting point of my justification is the observation that people commonly do feel that they are responsible, in a sense, for the actions of their state—even if they protested against them, and even if they had no control over them. Karl Jaspers expresses this sentiment in his famous essay on German Guilt, which he wrote for German audiences in the aftermath of the Second World War. There he invoked the idea of "political guilt," which, "involving the deeds of statesmen and of the citizenry of a state, results in my having to bear the consequences of the deeds of the state whose power governs me and under whose orders I live."[12] Jaspers's words seem to sit uneasily with the liberal individualist outlook that most Western contemporary political philosophers share. As we saw earlier, the concern here is that people should not be held liable for outcomes simply by virtue of some ascriptive property they had no control over—namely the state they happened to be born into and become a citizen of.

In the first chapters of this book I develop an argument that affirms people's common sentiments toward their state, but is also compatible with our liberal and individualist commitments. My core suggestion is that, typically, citizenship is not merely an ascriptive property. Rather, citizenship involves various volitional acts. Citizens act in their state, and their duty to share in their state's remedial responsibilities flows from their participation in it.

There is by now a very rich body of literature on the nature of collective action and on the duties that fall on individuals when they act together in groups. Typically, this literature focuses on small and intimate groups. It might seem implausible to suggest that the state—a complex, hierarchical, and compartmentalized institution, composed of a vast number of individuals, most of whom have no personal connection to each other, and who often disagree on how the state should be run—is a site of collective action. But I disagree. I develop the idea of what I call "intentional citizenship."

---

[12] Karl Jaspers, *The Question of German Guilt* (New York: Fordham University Press, 2000), 25.

Intentional citizens are citizens who perform the various roles
their state allocates to them (pay their taxes, obey the law, vote,
serve in the military, etc.). When they act so, they have a "participatory intention" to take part in their state. They see themselves
as contributing, or potentially contributing, to the general maintenance of the corporate agency of their state and to the execution of
its plans.[13] Intentional citizens, I suggest, are participating in a very
wide range of their state policies, including those they made marginal contributions to, those they disagree with, those they publicly
protested against, and those they did not know about. As long as
they intend to support their state itself, they are participating in the
policies its decision-making process generates. Finally, I argue that
as participants in their state's actions, citizens incur a special responsibility with regard to the outcomes of these actions. It is thus   *intentional*
permissible to demand that all of them contribute to the collective   *citizens*
effort of meeting the state's victims' demands, regardless of their
personal level of blame. In short, intentional citizenship can justify
the real-world practice of letting the burden fall on citizens at large.

However, there is an important caveat to this argument. I believe that the intentional-citizenship-based justification of the distributive effect applies only when citizens' participatory intentions
are *genuine*. Genuine participation requires that citizens are not   *but we*
forced against their will to take part in their state. Instead, they   *are!*
are motivated to act in it by their own reasons—for example, because they see their citizenship as constitutive of their self-identity,
or they enjoy the various opportunities it provides them with.
Citizens who are genuinely participants in their state are liable for
the costs of their state's wrongdoings. But citizens who see the state
as an alien force in their lives, and who would have left it, if only
they could, are not genuine participants in their state, and their

[13] I draw here on Christopher Kutz's theory of collective action. See Christopher Kutz,
Complicity: Ethics and Law for a Collective Age (Cambridge: Cambridge University
Press, 2000).

Not a western thing,
intentional participation

membership in it does not suffice, in itself, to justify the distributive effect being applied to them. The justification I develop for an equal distribution of the burden on the population at large relies then, to a great extent, on citizens' internal attitudes.

How to determine if someone is a genuine intentional citizen?

I.2 Intentional Citizenship in Democracies and in Autocracies

Given that the intentional citizenship argument relies on citizens' subjective attitudes, it is vulnerable to an immediate objection: How common is intentional citizenship in the real world, across various states and regime types? If the answer to this question is "not at all," then my argument, as theoretically sound as it may be, has no action-guiding implications.

This is an empirical objection, so the answer to it requires an empirical examination of people's attitudes to their citizenship and their state. It is fairly easy to carry out this examination in democratic states. Here I confirm the extent of intentional citizenship by looking at attitude surveys on people's views about their national identity and their state. The data suggests that in democracies, intentional citizenship is widespread among the population at large. There are some exceptions here. In democracies with strong secessionist minorities, there are those who see themselves as forced to live in a state that conflicts with their nationalist aspirations. And in most real-world democracies, imperfect as they are, there are groups of oppressed and disadvantaged citizens who are deeply alienated from their state. But, by and large, intentional citizenship is fairly widespread among democratic citizens. *but is it genuine!*

However, the picture is different in nondemocratic, or authoritarian, states. Such states receive little attention in mainstream political philosophy, which tends to focus its attention on the design of the just and democratic state, and on the rights and obligations of democratic citizens. The lack of attention to nondemocracies is perhaps surprising, given the fact that a quarter of the states in our world today are not democratic, and about a third of the world's population lives in nondemocratic states. Not only that, but nondemocratic states greatly differ from each other in their regime structure, the type and level of rights they grant their citizens, and the level of repression they deploy to ensure their citizens' compliance.

A second goal of this book, then, is to begin to fill this lacuna, by paying closer attention to the relationship between citizens and their state in nondemocratic regimes and the obligations that flow from it. I examine some of the modes of civic participation, state repression, and state manipulation that are deployed by nondemocratic states. I use this data in order to examine the extent of intentional citizenship in such states in general, and, following from this, the extent to which their citizens are liable for the remedial costs of their state's wrongdoing. I conclude that in most (but not all) types of nondemocracies, intentional citizenship is not prevalent, and that therefore it is harder to justify the distributive effect in those states.

I.3 Distributing State Responsibility: A Discriminatory Framework

The current legal framework of international affairs is blind to the internal structure of the state. All states are equal in the eyes of international law, regardless of their internal decision-making and authority mechanisms. Based on the empirical findings I mentioned above, the third core argument of this book challenges this nondiscriminatory framework. In doing that, it joins a long line of political philosophers and legal theorists who have raised similar concerns. Supporters of the "odious debt doctrine," for example, argue that debts that are incurred by repressive governments should not pass to their democratic successors.[14] Recent scholarship on trade in natural resources argues that oppressive governments should have the right to trade in the resources of their country, given that their true owner is the people.[15] Others question the rights of authoritarian states to exercise territorial sovereignty.[16] I make similar observations with regard to the practice of holding states remedially responsible for their wrongdoings. I reject the one-size-fits-all approach to state responsibility, which ignores the way it falls on the citizenry. The core problem with this approach, as we already saw, is that in some states, and with regard to some or all of their wrongdoings, the burden ought not to fall on the citizens at large. In those states, the harm that falls on citizens when their state is held accountable comes with a heavy moral price. In those states, then, alternative routes for the distribution of responsibility, which avoid this cost, should be explored.

My analysis suggests, then, that the way in which we hold states responsible for their wrongdoings at the international level, and the way in which states should internally distribute their remedial responsibilities, ought to be context-sensitive. To assess if and how the burden should fall on citizens, we must look into the regime type of the state in question, both at the time it committed the wrongdoing and at present, the extent of intentional citizenship in it, as well as other related factors that will be explored throughout the book (including the extent to which citizens have benefited from their state's wrongdoing and whether they have a special relation to its victims).[17] These factors shape the appropriate pattern

[14] Jeff King, "Odious Debt: The Terms of the Debate," *North Carolina Journal of International Law* 32, no. 4 (2006), 605–667.

[15] Leif Wenar, "Property Rights and the Resource Curse," *Philosophy and Public Affairs* 36, no. 1 (2008), 2–32.

[16] Anna Stilz, "Nations, States and Territory," *Ethics* 112, no. 3 (2011), 572–601.

[17] This conclusion is inspired by and follows the recommendations offered by David Miller, in his paper on the distribution of remedial responsibilities. Miller recommends a pluralist approach to the distribution question, one which first identifies the various agents who may be connected to the victim in some way, and then assesses the strength of that connection and apportions the responsibility accordingly. See David Miller, "Distributing Responsibilities," *Journal of Political Philosophy* 9, no. 4 (2001), 453–71.

of distribution in the state. States should be held remedially responsible for their wrongdoing, but the precise way in which we hold them responsible should be constrained by and sensitive to the impact on their citizens, and the extent to which they are liable to incur the burden.

I.4 Plan of the Book

The book proceeds in two stages. In the first four chapters I present the problem of the distributive effect and develop my justification for a distribution of the burden among the citizenship at large. In the last three chapters I build on this analysis to offer a comprehensive framework for the distribution of responsibility in the state, one that is context-dependent and sensitive to the various relevant factors at play. I also demonstrate some of the pragmatic implications of this model.

Chapter 1 sets the stage for the discussion, by presenting the problem of the distributive effect, and the literature around it. It first defends the idea that states are corporate moral agents, and as such morally responsible for their wrongdoings in at least two distinct senses: they may be blameworthy when they act wrongly, and they incur forward-looking responsibilities to address the wrong. Examining the existing literature on the distributive effect, I distinguish between two core views on how this distribution should be designed. The first approach, which I refer to as "proportional distribution," argues that the distribution should track the state's members' blameworthy contributions to their state's wrongdoings. The second approach—the "nonproportional distribution"—lets the burden fall on the population at large.

In Chapter 2 I begin to develop my justification for a nonproportional distribution. I present the theoretical model according to which people who intentionally participate in a collective act are liable, in some sense, for the outcomes of that collective act, and I explore the moral obligations that flow from participation in a collective activity. Specifically, I suggest that agents who genuinely participate in a group, with their participation not being forced on them against their will, are liable for a nonproportional share of their group's remedial obligations, in circumstances where a proportional distribution is not feasible or is very costly.

Chapter 3 applies the idea of intentional participation in the state. Here I show that being a citizen typically involves acting together in the state, and that citizens who act together in the state are taking part in a very wide range of their state's policies, including policies they object to or are unaware of. I then defend the claim that when participation in the state is genuine, it grounds citizens' obligation to accept a nonproportional share of their state's remedial obligations.

Chapter 4 turns to examine the application of the intentional citizenship framework to real-world states. I examine people's attitudes to their states, as they are reported in cross-national attitude surveys on national identity: the World Values Survey, the Eurobarometer, the International Social Programme on National Identity Survey, and the Afrobarometer. I conclude that in many countries, and certainly in most democratic countries, large majorities have a fairly strong attachment to their country or state and are intentional participants in their state. But I also identify groups who remain outside the model of intentional citizenship. I then turn to the literature in comparative politics on nondemocratic states, and draw conclusions on the extent of intentional citizenship in them, based on the patterns of civic participation, state oppression, and state manipulation.

In chapter 5 I build on these findings and develop a viable model for the distribution of the state's responsibility within the state. First, I examine alternative justifications for the nonproportional, or equal, distribution, which do not revolve around intentional participation. These include democratic authorization, benefiting from a wrongdoing, having a special capacity to address it, and having special associative obligations to the victims of the wrongdoing. I show that these factors have limited application in real-world cases of state wrongdoing. I then propose the process by which we should determine how a state's responsibility should be distributed between its citizens in specific cases. This process involves the examination of several factors: the extent to which we can determine the level of blame of key actors within the state, our assessment of the scope of intentional citizenship in the state, and the nature of the regime that perpetrates the wrongdoing. These factors will determine the shape of the distribution that is appropriate, given the specific circumstances at hand. In practical terms, this process is likely to lead to the conclusion that, by and large, in democratic states, an equal distribution will be overall justified, while in many authoritarian states it will not. When an equal distribution cannot be overall justified, alternative solutions should be weighed against the option of imposing the burden on the state's citizens: leaving the burden with the victims, or transferring some of it to the international community.

Chapter 6 considers the pragmatic implications of my proposed model for public international law. I first examine the way in which current practices in international law extract compensations from delinquent states. Here I focus in particular on the UNCC—a landmark and influential scheme—which extracted compensation from Iraq in the aftermath of the Gulf War. Given the design of the UNCC, the burden of compensation fell on ordinary Iraqis at large. I examine the impact, given the regime character of the Iraqi state under the rule of Saddam Hussein's Ba'ath Party. I then turn to assess the implications of my framework for the idea of state punishment. Here I focus on two influential justifications of punishment in general: the expressive view and the duties to victims view. I show that the idea of punishing states is plausible on both accounts. I then demonstrate how my proposed framework should shape the way we punish states.

In chapter 7 I turn to examine the question of responsibility for historical wrongs. It is a common view, both in political theory and practice, that present-day states have remedial obligations to the descendants of the victims of the wrongs they committed in the past. This view, too, faces the challenge of the distributive effect: Why should current generations be encumbered with the burden of repairing the wrongs of the past? I examine this question through the lens of the intentional participation framework. I argue that citizens who are intentional participants in their state can be expected to accept a nonproportional share of the burdens of their state remedial responsibilities even for historical wrongs that were committed before their lifetime. However, in line with my general model of the distribution of responsibility in the state, for that to be the case, the state's regime structure at the time it committed the wrongdoing will affect the scope of its liabilities, at that time and in the future. This restriction has important implications for how we hold states responsible in cases of state identity change, such as state secession and internal regime change. The common view in public international law and practice is that regime change does not affect the compensatory liabilities of the state. But my framework challenges this view, and suggests that present-day citizens are not necessarily liable for the wrongs committed by their state in the past, under the rule of a highly oppressive regime.

1

State Responsibility and Its Distributive Effect

When a state commits a serious wrong, it seems entirely appropriate to demand that it should repair the harm it has caused and compensate its victims. But, as we saw in the Introduction, the practice of holding states responsible for their crimes in this way has a troubling feature. Recall the examples I mentioned: when West Germany, Iraq, Argentina, Chile, and Canada accepted their compensatory liabilities to the victims of their wrongdoings, they turned to the public purse to discharge these obligations. In other words, they transferred the burdens of reparations and compensation to their populations, both directly, when they raised additional taxes in order to finance this expenditure, and indirectly, when they reduced their public spending in other areas. Either way, these states' responsibility for their wrongdoings had a "distributive effect" on their citizens. Is this effect justified?

My goal in this chapter is to explore this question and to review the extant literature on it. I will first explain the very idea of state responsibility. My understanding of this idea draws on recent literature on corporate agency, which—as we will see in Section 1.1—supports the claim that the state is a corporate moral agent, and as such is morally responsible for its actions. In what sense is the state morally responsible? I turn to examine this question in Section 1.2. Here I identify two meanings of the term, both of which will play an important role throughout the book: moral responsibility as culpability, and moral responsibility as a forward-looking remedial duty. The question of the distributive effect applies to the second type of

Responsible Citizens, Irresponsible States. Avia Pasternak, Oxford University Press. © Oxford University Press 2021. DOI: 10.1093/oso/9780197541036.003.0002

responsibility, in the sense that it asks whether, when the state itself is responsible, or duty-bound, to address its wrongdoings, its citizens are responsible to ensure it is able to discharge this task.

In the rest of the chapter I turn to review the literature on this question. I show that existing justifications for the distributive effect can be roughly divided into two models. The first model, which I discuss in Section 1.3, suggests that states may distribute the burden in proportion to their citizens' blameworthy contributions to the state wrongdoing. While this model caters to our individualist intuitions, it is hard to see how it can be implemented in real-world states. The second model, which I describe in Section 1.4, supports a more expansive distribution of the burden across the population at large and is typically deployed by states in the real world. My goal in the rest of the book is to examine under what conditions this model could be justified.

1.1 States as Corporate Agents

The states I am concerned with throughout the book share some core features:[1] they have a *defined territory* in which they exercise their authority; they have a *permanent population* over which they exercise their authority; and they have an *effective government*, which is able to make and to enforce the laws of the land. The state's governmental apparatus consists of various branches. For example, in democracies the governmental apparatus consists of a legislative

---

[1] For an analysis of the legal definition of the state, see James Crawford, *The Creation of States in International Law*, 2nd ed. (Oxford: Oxford University Press, 2006), chapter 2. For the more philosophical literature, see David Copp, "The Idea of a Legitimate State," *Philosophy & Public Affairs* 28, no. 1 (1999: 3–45); Toni Erskine, "Assigning Responsibilities to Institutional Moral Agents: The Case of States and Quasi States," *Ethics and International Affairs* 15, no. 1 (2001: 67–86); Holly Lawford-Smith, *Not in Their Name: Are Citizens Culpable for Their States' Actions?* (Cambridge: Cambridge University Press, 2019); Herbert Morris, *An Essay on the Modern State* (Cambridge: Cambridge University Press, 1998), 19–45; Alexander Wendt, "The State as Person in International Theory," *Review of International Studies* 30, no. 2 (2004): 289–316.

branch (e.g., a parliament), an executive branch (e.g., the cabinet, the government ministries and departments, and the various local authorities), a judiciary, a military, and a police force. These branches are distinct yet sufficiently coordinated to count as being part of the same organizational scheme.[2] Finally, and related to all that, states have an *independent* authority. By that I mean that they enjoy external sovereignty and can make their own laws (within the requirements of international law).[3]

The states that bear these features make up the vast majority of states in the world. These states are quite different from each other, in the size of their territory, the size of their population, their internal structures, and their regime type. But regardless of these differences, they are all *institutional* entities. By this I mean that they are complex, integrated systems of formal and informal rules that define the roles, duties, and interactions between their various members, and that enable coordinated decision-making and action across the state as a whole.[4]

A constitutive premise of international law is that states that bear these features are *legal* persons—i.e., they are entities that bear international legal rights and duties.[5] However our concern here is not so much with states' formal *legal* responsibilities, but rather with their *moral* responsibilities. At this point one might question the very idea that states have any moral responsibilities to speak

[2] Morris, *An Essay on the Modern State*, 45.

[3] Crawford, *The Creation of States*, 65. The Montevideo Convention on the Rights and Duties of States (1933), which provides the common legal definition of the state, does not include the condition of independence, and instead defines the state as having the capacity to enter into relations with other states. Following Crawford, I take it that the capacity to enter into interstate relations is better understood as a *consequence* of the state having an effective government and independence. See Crawford, *The Creation of States*, 61–62.

[4] Geoffrey M. Hodgson, "What Are Institutions?," *Journal of Economic Issues* 40, no. 1 (2006): 1–25. States that lack these features are "failed states," "quasi-states," or "puppet states." As Toni Erskine persuasively argues, the attribution of responsibility to such states is far more challenging. I leave such cases aside. See Erskine, "Assigning Responsibilities."

[5] Cassesse, "International Law in a Divided World," 4–7.

of. This objection rests on the assumption that the state—much like any other corporate body—is a mere legal fiction. Our national and international legal systems assign such bodies rights and responsibilities (e.g., the right to hold property, or tort liabilities), but they do so only for instrumental and pragmatic reasons—e.g., as a convenient and efficient way to promote international stability and economic growth. According to this view, then, there is no point in exploring the scope of states' moral duties and obligations. Whatever moral demands we make of states are actually demands we make of (some or all of) the individuals that comprise them.[6]

Those who adhere to this view would also be interested in the question of how the duties that result from state wrongdoing (understood as wrongs committed by individuals within the state) should be distributed among the state population, and the arguments I present in the next chapters may appeal to them as well. However, the more common conception of the state in the existing literature has a different outlook. On this view the state is a real moral agent, with its own moral responsibilities (and, some would argue, moral rights). One might think that this idea satisfactorily closes the debate on who bears the responsibility for the state's wrongdoing: it's the state, as the moral agent who perpetrated the wrongs. But, as we will shortly see, the problem of the distributive effect holds even if we accept the corporate moral agency thesis. Given the prevalence of this thesis in existing accounts of the state, I will take it as my starting point here.

There are various versions of the corporate moral agency thesis, but for the purposes of the discussion here we need not dwell on their differences in detail. Instead, I will briefly mention one influential version of this view, as developed by Christian

---

[6] See, e.g., John Dewey, "The Historic Background of Corporate Legal Personality," *Yale Law Journal* 35, no. 6 (1926): 655–73; cf. Edmund Wall, "The Problem of Group Agency," *Philosophical Forum* 31, no. 2 (2000): 187–97; David Rönnegard, *The Fallacy of Corporate Moral Agency* (Dordrecht: Springer, 2015).

List and Philip Pettit, and demonstrate its application to the state.[7]

List and Pettit define agents as entities that are capable of having representational states (such as beliefs) and motivational states (such as desires), can act upon their motivational states, and have the capacity for minimal rationality (i.e., the capacity to form beliefs and desires that are consistent over time and to act in ways that are consistent with these beliefs and desires).[8] Their core observation is that some groups—specifically those with central decision-making procedures and authority structures—can be agents. As they explain, many groups, and especially groups that are formed in order to execute complex, long-term goals, have a strong interest in meeting the demands of group-level rationality. But achieving group-level rationality can be quite difficult, given that groups' beliefs and preferences are constituted by their members' often conflicting beliefs and preferences. As rational choice theorists have long noted, aggregating group members' conflicting preferences through, say, simple majoritarianism inevitably leads to inconsistent results at the group level, and therefore to failures in group rationality (List and Pettit refer to this problem as "the discursive dilemma"). In order to achieve minimal rationality, the group members must find mechanisms that will generate synchronically and diachronically consistent beliefs and preferences at the group level. One way of doing this, as proposed by List and Pettit, is to adopt a group decision-making process that collects members' attitudes or beliefs on separate premises, rather than

like democracy?

[7] Christian List and Philip Pettit, *Group Agency: The Possibility, Design, and Status of Corporate Agents* (Oxford: Oxford University Press, 2011). Other important accounts of corporate agency include David Copp, "The Collective Moral Autonomy Thesis," *Journal of Social Philosophy* 38 (2007): 369–88; Peter French, *Collective and Corporate Responsibility* (New York: Columbia University Press, 1984); Tracy Isaacs, *Moral Responsibility in Collective Contexts* (Oxford: Oxford University Press, 2011). For a general review of this literature, see Deborah Tollefsen, *Groups as Agents* (Cambridge: Polity Press, 2015). For a review of the various accounts' application to the state, see Lawford-Smith, *Not in Their Name.*

[8] List and Pettit, *Group Agency*, 20–24.

their beliefs on the outcomes of these premises. This mechanism allows the group to "collectivize its reason" as a group-level view is formed from the logical combination of the results of the majoritarian aggregation of members' views on each separate premise.[9] Other ways of collectivizing the group's reasoning include ruling out aggregative outcomes that are not compatible with the group's previous decisions (e.g., submitting the group's decision to the authority of existing precedents), or requiring that these outcomes remain loyal to a core set of predetermined values (such as a constitution).[10] What these various mechanisms have in common is that they create a process in which the group's representational and motivational states (i.e., the outcomes of the decision-making process) depart from those of its members in a way that allows consistency over time. As a result, what the majority (or even all) of the members believe need not be the same as, and is not reducible to, the beliefs that are formed at the group level.[11] Groups that adopt such measures have what Pettit and List famously refer to as a "mind of their own," or "a way of being minded that is starkly discontinuous with the mentality of their members."[12]

Let's return to the case of states. States are often considered to be the prime examples of groups that can achieve corporate agency.[13] In order to function successfully over time and to execute the complex tasks they have, they must adopt some mechanisms to ensure long-term consistency in the formation of their collective beliefs and goals. These can include democratic measures such as constitutional commitments, systems of checks and balances between the

---

[9] Philip Pettit, "Groups with Minds of Their Own," in *Socializing Metaphysics: The Nature of Social Reality*, ed. Frederick F. Schmitt (Lanham, MD: Rowman & Littlefield, 2003), 171.

[10] Christian List, "The Logical Space of Democracy," *Philosophy & Public Affairs* 39, no. 3 (2011): 262–97.

[11] List and Pettit, *Group Agency*, chapter 3.

[12] Pettit, "Groups with Minds of Their Own," 167.

[13] List and Pettit, *Group Agency*, 40. Cf. Erskine, "Assigning Responsibilities"; Francois Tanguay-Renaud, "Criminalizing the State," *Criminal Law and Philosophy* 7, no. 2 (2013): 255–84; Wendt, "The State as Person in International Theory."

various branches of government, systems of judicial reviews, and multilayered decision-making processes. And they can include dictatorial measures, such as highly restricting the number of people who can take part in the state's decision-making process, and using repression and ideology in order to create a more unified set of preferences that is committed to a single goal. Whether democratic or dictatorial, such mechanisms enable the state, as a unified agent, to form a consistent set of goals over time and to ensure adherence to these goals across the various state branches.[14]

As corporate agents, states act in the world. Of course, given that they are not physical persons, they act through their members. These members are flesh and blood persons, and not all their actions are the actions of the state. But when they act on behalf of the state, or in their official capacity, their actions are the actions of the state. Thus, when a police officer makes an arrest, it is also the case that the state made an arrest. Notice, further, that it is not necessarily the case that an officeholder acts on specific instructions, or within narrowly and formally defined role obligations for the action to be that of the state. We commonly think that groups, and especially incorporated groups, can develop an informal corporate culture, or corporate ethos, expressed through the group's "values, heroes, rites and rituals."[15] This informal code shapes its members' understanding of their role, sometimes more so than a formal code. For example, a business corporation can have a sexist cultural ethos even if none of its formal codes and rules are sexist. States, too, develop a state-level culture or ethos, which informally sanctions certain modes of behavior among its members. A state can be racist, xenophobic, or sexist when it has a distinct ethos that allows for and supports its members' racist, xenophobic, or sexist behaviors in their capacities as role-holders. Finally, and related to this, the state

---

[14] Tanguay-Renaud, "Criminalizing the State." Cf. Lawford-Smith, *Not in Their Name*, 63–65.
[15] Pamela H. Bucy, "Corporate Criminal Liability: When Does It Make Sense," *American Criminal Law Review* 46 (2009): 1124.

can also be *omitting* to act. If, for example, the state has an obligation to rid itself of its racist ethos, yet its decision-making process fails to produce the policies that will move the state in this direction, then the state fails to meet its obligations and does wrong in that sense.[16]

But notice that not every act of a state official is also the act of the state. Not only do state officials also act as private individuals, they can also act outside the scope of their authority while performing their official duties. A police officer can exhibit racist behavior that is in violation of the Police Department's formal rules and informal ethos, for example. Assuming that the officer's displayed attitudes really are violations of the state's policies and rules, and also are not the product of the state's informal ethos, then they are not those of the state as such.[17]

1.2 The Moral Responsibilities of States

In the previous section, I discussed the idea of state agency. But agency in itself is not enough for an entity to be the appropriate subject of *moral* responsibilities. A sophisticated cleaning robot

---

[16] Gordon A. Christenson, "Attributing Acts of Omission to the State," *Michigan Journal of International Law* 12. No. 2 (1990): 312–70.

[17] Clearly it will not always be easy to determine when an officeholder acts *ultra vires*. In chapter 3, I return to this question. If officeholders act *ultra vires*, is the state responsible for their actions? According to Article 7 of *The International Law Commission's Articles on State Responsibility*, the answer to this question is positive: It considers the behavior of any organ of the state as an act of the state, "even if it exceeds its authority or contravenes instructions" (James Crawford, *The International Law Commission's Articles on State Responsibility: Introduction, Text and Commentaries* [Cambridge: Cambridge University Press, 2007], 106.) This statement does not sit comfortably with my account, according to which activities performed outside the scope of authority and against explicit instructions or informal ethos are not actions of the state. Nevertheless, I don't rule out that it can make sense to adopt a legal rule that assigns the state *vicarious* liability for the conduct of all its agents, even when they exceed their authority, given that the state can afterward hold the rogue agents personally to account in their domestic jurisdictions. In the rest of the discussion I leave aside the question of dealing with state officials' acts that are clearly outside the scope of their authority.

could meet the demands of agency—it could form beliefs (that the floor is not clean) and desires (to clean the floor), and it could act upon them (activate the cleaning brush)—but it is not yet a morally responsible agent. In order to be the appropriate subject of moral responsibilities, an agent must meet the requirements of *moral* agency. This means that it must have the capacity to bring into its decision-making process moral reasons, the capacity to make value-informed choices in light of these reasons, and the capacity to then act upon these moral choices. Group agents can obtain these further properties. They can have a decision-making process that incorporates moral reasons, and that—through appropriate deliberations between the members—settles on morally informed group beliefs and desires.[18] While these moral reasons will be brought into consideration by group members, the group's final decision remains distinct from those of its members, and its final value judgments can depart from those of most, or even all, of its members.

standards of state? [handwritten marginalia]

It is not hard to see that states comply with this further requirement. In democracies, mechanisms for the incorporation of moral reasons into the state's decision-making processes include parliamentary debates, constitutions, judicial reviews, and accountability structures.[19] In theocracies, to give one more example, they can include formal consultation and deference to religious leaders. Such mechanisms inform the state, and enable it to develop its (good or bad) moral attitude, both with regard to its own citizens and to people outside its borders. States that have such mechanisms in place are therefore—as List and Pettit suggest—corporate moral agents.[20]

---

[18] List and Pettit, *Group Agency*, 158. For other expressions of this idea, see French, *Collective and Corporate Responsibility*; May, *The Morality of Groups*; Kendy Hess, "If You Tickle Us . . . How Corporations Can Be Moral Agents without Being Persons," *Journal of Value Inquiry* 47, no. 3 (2013): 319–35.

[19] Lawford-Smith, *Not in Their Name*, 70–73.

[20] For endorsements of this conclusion, see Robert Goodin, *Utilitarianism as a Public Philosophy* (Cambridge: Cambridge University Press, 1995), chapter 2; Erskine, "Assigning Responsibilities"; Tanguay-Renaud, "Criminalizing the State"; Wendt, "The

As the corporate moral agents that have political authority over defined territories and their peoples, states incur many moral duties, to their own populations and to people outside their territory. The precise content of these duties, and how they balance against each other, is one of the most disputed questions in contemporary political theory. But this larger question need not be resolved here. My concern is not so much with the content of states' moral duties, but rather with what ought to happen when they fail to comply with these duties and commit wrongdoings. So, for the sake of argument only, let's assume that—at the least—states have the duty to promote the welfare and interests of their own citizens and to avoid violating the human rights of those who reside outside their borders. When states violate even these fairly minimal requirements, they incur moral responsibilities. Here, we typically distinguish between two meanings of this claim. The first is that wrongdoing states are *culpable* and the appropriate subjects of blame. Moral agents are culpable (or blameworthy) when the following conditions apply: they acted in a way that led to, or was causally related to, a wrongful outcome; they acted with a culpable state of mind (i.e., purposely, knowingly, recklessly, or negligently); and they had no excuse that diminished their control over their actions. When a moral agent acts in a blameworthy manner, we respond to it with reactive attitudes: anger, resentment, reproach, and even (where appropriate) punishment.

If states are corporate moral agents, they can be the appropriate subjects of blame. In other words, a state that acted in ways that led to a wrongful consequence (or, more precisely, directed its members to act in this way), that did so in a culpable "state of mind" (e.g., it acts recklessly or on morally reprehensible motives), and that could have acted otherwise (e.g., it could have cultivated a different set of values)—is blameworthy for its actions. We (i.e., its citizens, or

State as Person in International Theory"; Anna Stilz, "Collective Responsibility and the State," *Journal of Political Philosophy* 19, no. 2 (2011): 190–208.

the citizens of other states, or other states) ought to respond accordingly: perhaps resent it, perhaps feel angry at it, perhaps even punish it.[21] Crucially, these reactions will be directed at the state itself. That is not to deny—as we shall shortly see—that some members of the state might also be deserving of moral censure. But as proponents of the corporate moral agency thesis emphasize time and again, we should not conflate the culpability of group members for their contributions to state wrongdoings with that of the group itself for what it does. As an agent that is autonomous in regard to its members, and that has its own set of desires and beliefs, the state itself is morally responsible for its wrongdoings, and it can be the case that the state alone is to blame for the wrong.[22]

The second meaning of the idea of moral responsibility is being responsible in the sense of having a duty to remedy, to address, or to right the wrong in question.[23] At this level we are less concerned with our reactive response to the wrongdoer (as we are in the case of culpability) and more with the wrongdoer's task responsibilities—what they ought to do to rectify the harm they brought about. In the case of state wrongdoing, generally speaking, the state will typically need to do the following: First, offer *compensation* for economically assessable wrongful harms (e.g., loss of material assets and income, physical and mental harm). Second, provide *rehabilitation* (e.g., further medical and psychological care) to the victims of the harm. Third, engage in *reparative measures* that go beyond compensation to the victims (e.g., incurring punishment for the wrongdoings and

---

[21] William Wringe, *An Expressive Theory of Punishment* (London: Palgrave Macmillan, 2016), chapter 7. I return to the question of state punishment in chapter 6.

[22] List and Pettit, *Group Agency*, 163–69; Stilz, "Collective Responsibility," 193–94; French, *Collective and Corporate Responsibility*, 44–47; David E. Cooper, "Collective Responsibility (a Defense)," in *Collective Responsibility: Five Decades of Debate in Theoretical and Applied Ethics*, ed. Larry May and Stacey Hoffman, 35–46. (Lanham, MD: Rowman & Littlefield, 1991); Frank Hindriks, "The Freedom of Collective Agents," *Journal of Political Philosophy* 16, no. 1 (2008): 165–83; Isaacs, *Moral Responsibility*.

[23] For various conceptualizations of this term, see Robert Goodin, "Apportioning Responsibilities," *Law and Philosophy* 6, no. 2 (1987): 167–85; Miller, "Distributing Responsibilities"; Iris Marion Young, "Responsibility and Global Labor Justice," *Journal of Political Philosophy* 12, no. 4 (2004): 365–88.

investing in commemorative projects).[24] Finally, comply with the obligations of _nonrepetition_, including implementing legal and institutional reforms.[25]

Now, as we saw, advocates of the corporate moral agency thesis commonly agree that it is at least conceptually possible that a corporate agent is blameworthy, though none of its individual members share the blame. However, the separation between corporate and individual responsibility is far less straightforward when we turn to the state's remedial duties. Here, even though the state itself is remedially responsible for the wrong, it must turn to its members to discharge its remedial task responsibilities. As Joel Feinberg notes, "group liability is inevitably distributive: what harms the group as a whole necessarily harms its members."[26] In order for the group to meet its obligations, the group members will have to devote time and energy to initiate and support the required institutional policies and changes, and the monetary resources to pay for the compensation and reparation schemes. Paraphrasing John Coffee's memorable phrase—if the state catches a cold, its members end up sneezing.[27]

We see, then, that even if we accept the corporate state agency thesis, as I have, we face the core question I will be concerned

---

[24] On the duty of wrongdoers to incur punishment, see Victor Tadros, _The Ends of Harm: The Moral Foundations of Criminal Law_ (Oxford: Oxford University Press, 2011), chapter 13..

[25] This list corresponds to the legal duties of states as specified by UN Basic Principles on the Rights to Reparations of Victims. See discussion in Christine Evans, _The Right to Reparation in International Law for Victims of Armed Conflict_ (Cambridge: Cambridge University Press, 2012), 44–45.

[26] Joel Feinberg, "Collective Responsibility (Another Defense)," in _Collective Responsibility: Five Decades of Debate in Theoretical and Applied Ethics_, ed. Larry May and Stacey Hoffman (Lanham, MD: Rowman & Littlefield, 1991), 73.

[27] John C. Coffee Jr., "'No Soul to Damn: No Body to Kick": An Unscandalized Inquiry into the Problem of Corporate Punishment," _Michigan Law Review_ 79 (1981): 401; Stilz, "Collective Responsibility," 194. Elsewhere I have argued that conceptually, it need not necessarily be the case that a group distributes its task liabilities to its members. But this conceptual point does not bear much on the discussion at hand. See Avia Pasternak, "The Impact of Corporate Tasks Responsibilities: A Comparison of Two Models," _Midwest Studies in Philosophy_ 38, no. 1 (2014): 222–31.

with throughout the book: Given that the state is the moral agent that committed the wrongdoing, may it distribute the burden of addressing this wrong among its members? Before I turn to examine existing answers to this problem, it is first important to clarify what I mean by the term "state members." I will say more about state membership in chapter 3, but for now it's worth noting that it is not only the formal citizens of the state who end up sharing the burden of the state's policy. Permanent and temporary residents who pay taxes to the state and who enjoy its public services will also incur the burdens of their hosting state's remedial responsibilities—if their tax burden increases, for example. In the rest of the book I will often use the term "citizens" to refer to the group of individuals in question, mainly because citizens make up the bulk majority of this group, and because it is often harder to justify this burden on citizens, given their typically nonvoluntary participation in the state (where many permanent and temporary resident choose to migrate to their state of residence). That said, the group I refer to typically includes noncitizens, and the model I develop in the next chapters will apply to them as well.

I now turn to review the various ways in which the existing literature responds to the problem of the distributive effect. One early treatment of this problem appears in Peter French's influential work on the corporate responsibility of business corporations. Here French defends the practice of imposing punitive sanctions on corporations, although he acknowledges that such fines can ultimately harm "innocent employees" (especially if they lead to financial losses and job cuts). In response to that objection he writes:

> When a natural person commits a felony and is convicted and punished, his or her associates, often family members and dependents, are frequently cast into dire financial straits. The harm done to them, though they may be totally innocent of any complicity in the crime, may, in fact, outweigh that done to incarcerated felon. . . . In many jurisdictions, little or no official

interest is paid to these innocent sufferers. . . . by analogy . . . indirect harm to corporate associates should not defeat [corporate]
penalty.[28]

French presents the burdens that fall on employees and business
partners as collateral (or unintended) damage. But it is far from
clear that "little or no official interest" should be paid to this type
of harm. After all, as we have learned from the rich literature on the
ethics of self-defense, our response to an unjustified attacker must
account for the unintended yet foreseeable harm it will impose on
uninvolved parties. Punitive responses to criminal offenders—
whether they are individuals or corporate entities—should take
these considerations into account as well.[29]

A different approach is offered by Toni Erskine. She shares with
French the view that the costs that fall on citizens when their state is
held responsible are a form of collateral damage, and not dissimilar
to the costs that state punishment imposes on the family members
of a convicted criminal. However, unlike French, she gives a much
more prominent place to these costs in her overall assessment of
the practice of holding states responsible (her focus is on imposing
harm on states in the course of a just war). On her view these are
regrettable "overspills" that ought to be minimized wherever possible, and balanced against the overall benefit that holding the state
responsible may bring.[30]

Erskine's approach to the problem is clearly superior to French's.
However, there remains an important objection to her presentation

---

[28] French, *Collective and Corporate Responsibility*, 190; cf. Peter Cane, *Responsibility in Law and Morality* (Oxford: Hart, 2002), 171; Meir Dan-Cohen, "Sanctioning Corporations," *Journal of Law and Policy* 19, no. 1 (2010): 31; Nigel Walker, *Why Punish?* (Oxford: Oxford University Press, 1991), 106.
[29] Cf. Cécile Fabre, *Cosmopolitan Peace* (Oxford: Oxford University Press, 2016), 192–93; Tadros, *The Ends of Harm*, 357–59.
[30] Toni Erskine, "Kicking Bodies and Damning Souls: The Danger of Harming 'Innocent' Individuals While Punishing 'Delinquent' States," in *Accountability for Collective Wrongdoing*, ed. Tracy Isaacs and Richard Vernon (New York: Cambridge University Press, 2011), 284.

of the relationship between citizens and their state. I have in mind here, specifically, the parallel she (and French) draw between the state and its citizens, on the one hand, and the criminal and his family members or uninvolved business partners, on the other. These uninvolved family members and business partners are, by definition, "outsiders" to the criminal and to his illicit activities. But are citizens outsiders to their state? As a matter of fact, many citizens would not think the answer to this question is positive. Rather, they see themselves as part of their state, and as connected to its policies in some fundamental sense. For example, they take pride in its successes and shame in its moral failures.

The view that there is a special relationship between citizens and their state, which puts them in a different position to it than that of outsiders and third parties, is fairly common in the literature, and several authors have argued that we should model the distributive effect in light of this relationship. Here we can draw a broad distinction between two models that pursue this position. The first model argues that the burdens of the state's liability should fall on those citizens who are personally associated with its wrongdoing. The second model grounds a wider distribution of the burden across the population at large, in light of their membership in the state. I now turn to explore these two models in more detail.[31]

1.3 Proportional Distribution

According to the first model, which I shall call the "proportional distribution" model, the state should direct the burdens of compensation, rehabilitation, commemoration, and nonrepetition to the citizens who are personally associated with its wrongdoing, and in proportion to their level of association with it. A proportional

---

[31] In this section I draw on my analysis in Avia Pasternak, "Sharing the Costs of Political Injustice," *Politics, Philosophy, Economics* 10, no. 2 (2011): 188–201.

Sounds like Rectification

distribution model is advocated, for example, by Stephanie Collins, who presents the most detailed version of this model in recent debates. Collins's core suggestion is that the state's corporate liabilities should be distributed between its members in a way that will mirror the state's own relationship to the wrong. As Collins observes, there can be various sources for the state's remedial responsibilities to address a bad situation in the world, including the state's blameworthiness for causing this state of affairs, its benefit from the situation, or its special capacity to resolve it. On her "source tracking" model, we should first determine the source of the state's own remedial responsibilities, and then distribute its costs among the population "in proportion to members' individual instantiations of that source."[32]

As I already noted, my concern here is, specifically, with cases in which the state incurs remedial duties to victims given its own culpability for their plight. In these fairly simple scenarios, Collins's model suggests that the burden should be further distributed among the state citizens in light of, and in proportion to, their own blameworthy contributions to the state's wrongdoing. These will be determined on an individual basis, and in light of members' actions and omissions. For example, policymakers (e.g., the state cabinet ministers) might be wrongly contributing to the state's decision-making process—by feeding, or failing to feed, into it the appropriate normative reasons. Policy enactors (e.g., soldiers or members of the civil service) may be at fault for enacting the state's orders when they knew they were wrong, and when they could have avoided doing so, or by failing to do what it was in their power to do to prevent the implementation of the policy. Factors that will impact the extent and level of these actors' culpability is not just how much they did or failed to do (or their *actus reus*), but also their

---

[32] Stephanie Collins, "Distributing State Duties," *Journal of Political Philosophy* 24, no. 3 (2016): 351.

state of mind (the *mens rea*), and the extent to which they had valid excuses in contributing.[33]

Collins offers further refinements to her model, including how it should deal with scenarios where the state's remedial responsibilities are grounded in more than one source. But for the purposes of the discussion here I will put these further complexities aside, and turn to assess Collins's proposal as a model for the distribution of the state's remedial obligations in the fairly simple scenario where we only need to concentrate on culpable wrongdoing as the source of the state's remedial liabilities. Here there are various points that ought to be given consideration. The first is the normative soundness of the model: Does the model offer a pattern of distribution that is compatible with our core values and principles? The second is how feasible the model is: Does it generate a pattern of distribution that can feasibly enable the state to meet its remedial obligations? A third consideration is the implementation costs of the model, including those that are generated by existing institutional, cultural, and psychological factors. A costly implementation is a drawback for the model, *inter alia*, because it takes away resources from other valuable projects the state might want to invest in.[34] *Thesis of Supersession, Waldron*

So how does proportional distribution fare on these three levels? I'll examine first the normative soundness of the proportional distribution model. Here it seems that Collins's model succeeds in

---

[33] There are many ways of determining these factors in the context of complex collective wrongdoings. An excellent starting point for the debate around these issues is Chiara Lepora and Robert Goodin, *On Complicity and Compromise* (Oxford: Oxford University Press, 2013), chapter 4.

[34] Pablo Gilabert and Holly Lawford-Smith note that such factors can also become "soft feasibility constraints," in the sense that they render the implementation of a model less likely. In the case at hand, for example, if the costs of implementation are high, the population might resist its implementation. Whether or not the costliness of the model would also make it less likely to be implemented is a contingent question, which I leave open. I take it that a high cost of the procedure is problematic even if it does not diminish support in the model, as it takes away resources from other public services. See Pablo Gilabert and Holly Lawford-Smith, "Political Feasibility: A Conceptual Exploration," *Political Studies* 60 (2012): 809–25.

offering a response to the concern with which we started, namely that the distributive effect imposes unfair burdens on state citizens. The model accepts the individualist intuition that citizens should not be held liable for wrongs committed by others and beyond their control, and assigns the remedial burdens to fall only on those state members who wrongfully contributed to the wrongdoing. Not only does it exonerate the innocent parties, it also holds liable the guilty parties. In that sense as well, it is compatible with the common intuition that culpability is the clearest and strongest grounds for compensatory duties because, in making wrongdoers pay for their wrongdoings, we at least partially "restore the moral equality" between them and their victims.[35] As Holly Lawford-Smith points out, "[t]hose who are culpable in producing injustice are the 'ideal' bearers of obligations to repair the situation in order to create justice."[36] These are compelling reasons to adopt the proportional distribution model.

And yet this model faces serious challenges when we turn to the questions of feasibility and costs. Consider the feasibility of the model: Iris Marion Young's influential work on collective responsibility for "structural injustice" highlights some constraints in this context. As Young explains, structural injustices are injustices that are generated by the accumulative effect of the interactions of vast numbers of individuals, operating under shared practices and norms.[37] Unjust state policies can be quite close to this description, in the sense that while they are orchestrated by the state, often millions of citizens contribute to them in miniscule and indirect ways (e.g., through their tax contributions).[38] One argument Young

---

[35] Fabre, *Cosmopolitan Peace*, 152–53; Shelly Kagan, "Causation and Responsibility," *American Philosophical Quarterly* 25, no. 4 (1988): 294.

[36] Lawford-Smith, *Not in Their Name*, 14.

[37] Iris Marion Young, *Responsibility for Justice* (Oxford: Oxford University Press, 2011), 100.

[38] Notice that Young herself does not endorse the corporate moral agency of the state thesis. On her account there is no intentional state agent that orchestrates the unjust policies of the state. Rather, they are the product of the work of different policymakers

offers against "blame-tracking" distributions of responsibility for structural injustices is that she thinks it is practically impossible to trace their effects back to the specific contributions of individual participants, given the sheer complexity of the processes through which they are produced.[39] Furthermore, in her view participants in structural injustices are not blameworthy for their contributions, given that they do not intend to contribute to wrongdoing, or have valid excuses for their behavior (e.g., the costs they face for failure to comply).[40]

Eric Beerbohm presents a different view. He argues that ordinary democratic citizens who regularly contribute to their state's political decision-making can be blameworthy for these contributions, even if it is impossible to trace the precise causal links between their actions and the policy outcome. What matters for their moral responsibility, on his view, is that they helped to enable these policies by supporting them through voting, through their symbolic expression of support in opinion polls, or by failing to oppose them through available channels.[41] Beerbohm does not argue that all citizens share the blame for their state's policies in this way. Especially highly disadvantaged citizens have powerful excuses for their wrongful participation (if, for example, they support wrongful policies because of their excusable lack of political expertise).[42] But the core point of his book is that most ordinary citizens in democracies share some blame for their state's policies.

In my view, the positions offered by both Young and Beerbohm are too extreme. On the one hand, I am far less confident than

and citizens, who are not necessarily coordinated. See Young, *Responsibility for Justice*, 112.

[39] Young, *Responsibility for Justice*, 96; cf. David Miller, *National Responsibility and Global Justice* (Oxford: Oxford University Press, 2007), 116; Fabre, *Cosmopolitan Peace*, 156.

[40] See, e.g., Young, "Responsibility," 46.

[41] Eric Beerbohm, *In Our Name: The Ethics of Democracy* (Princeton: Princeton University Press, 2012), 67–72, 242–46.

[42] Beerbohm, *In Our Name*, 247.

Beerbohm that moral blame for political wrongdoing is that widespread among ordinary democratic citizens (and even less so among citizens in nondemocratic states, to whom I will return in chapter 4). As we will see in the next chapter, I agree with Beerbohm that we do not need to trace their causal contributions in order to hold the participants in collective wrongdoing responsible in a sense for the outcome. However, I doubt that for many democratic citizens this responsibility implies blame. When we blame someone, we assume they have done wrong, and that they should and could have acted differently. But, as Young suggests, it is not clear what wrong many democratic citizens commit when they contribute to their state policies in the usual channels, complying with the common norms of their society. For example, as Beerbohm himself notes, when citizens vote, they often have to choose between whole packages of party platforms. "Taking some bad with the good" can be an inevitable outcome that one simply cannot avoid.[43] Furthermore, I think that most ordinary citizens have valid excuses for their participation in their state: given that participation in one's state is part and parcel of our ordinary life, it is very hard to see how one could avoid participating in one's state without incurring unreasonable costs. Beerbohm is right to argue that citizens ought to attempt to resist the implementation of unjust policies. But here we should note that, firstly, in democratic states, many citizens do engage in various forms of resistance—via the normal channels of political participation (e.g., voting for opposition parties, or political protest) and less conventional channels. Furthermore, often citizens will face formidable collective action problems in this context. For example, a citizen may reasonably conclude that she does no wrong in not protesting further, given the political apathy of others. Thus, given that there are many state policies that citizens "cannot avoid helping or sustaining,"[44] or have

---

[43] Beerbohm, *In Our Name*, 230–31.
[44] Beerbohm, *In Our Name*, 230–31.

reasonable excuses for supporting, it is counterintuitive to argue that they should be blamed for their support when it is inevitable.

That said, I do not share the conclusion one might draw from Young's view, that *no* citizen is morally culpable for their state policies.[45] Surely it is usually the case that at least some state members will be acting (or failing to act) in ways that clearly promote, facilitate, and make more likely the implementation of bad policies, and in ways they could have avoided. I have in mind here, especially, highly politically influential citizens, key policy enactors, and high-level policymakers whose contributions are more essential or more proximate to the state wrongdoing, and who cannot excuse their actions. As Chiara Lepora and Robert Goodin suggest, such qualities help to determine how closely engaged an individual act is with a collective wrongdoing.[46]

Nevertheless, Young's observations about the difficulties in identifying blameworthy individuals do point to a different feasibility challenge for the proportional distribution model. If we accept the view that many ordinary citizens do not share the blame for their state failures, it follows that, in reality, we would be able to identify only a small number of individuals within the state who share the blame for the state's wrongdoing, and who ought to share the costs of remedying the harm it caused. But as the examples in the Introduction demonstrated, the task of remedying state wrongdoing can be on an enormous scale. Directing it solely to those who are blameworthy may lead to the outcome that those who are tasked with the job cannot complete it. Put differently, we end up with "responsibility shortfalls."[47]

---

[45] Notice that Young makes this observation with regard to structural injustices, rather than state injustices.

[46] For a concrete example, see Beerbohm's discussion of members of the segregationist South who acted to preserve Jim Crow legislation (Beerbohm, *In Our Name*, 242–43). I think Young herself acknowledges this fact at points. See, for example, Young, *Responsibility for Justice*, 95. For a related critique, see Andrea Sangiovanni, "Structural Injustice and Individual Responsibility," *Journal of Social Philosophy* 49, no. 3 (2018).

[47] Cf. Fabre, *Cosmopolitan Peace*, 157. Collins offers one solution to this problem: looking for alternative sources for the state's own responsibility to address the

According to Collins, we can, at least sometimes, overcome these challenges. For example, she argues that the state could devise tax schemes that target activities we consider to be wrongful contributions to state wrongdoing. Doing so would burden all those citizens who engage in them, and the state can then use the money to meet some of its remedial responsibilities.[48] However, I suspect that in many cases even such schemes can only offer fairly limited progress toward a full-blown proportional distribution in a fairly limited set of cases. Consider the case of climate change injustices. Collins is right to argue that the state can tax carbon-intensive activities (such as flying or oil drilling). But can it generate sufficient resources to tackle climate change only from the citizens who engage in these activities? The concern with the blame-tracking model, then, is that if the state adopts it, it may well be addressing the fairness claims of its own citizens, but it would fail the task of fully addressing the plight of the victims.

Young also points to other feasibility challenges that culpability-tracking models may face. One factor that Young mentions in this context is the negative psychological impact that a blame-tracking distribution has on the relations between group members. As she explains, this model can turn out to be counterproductive in the sense that it discourages group members' support in the overall reparation project. Rather than motivating the participants to engage together in the forward-looking task of addressing their group's wrong, the "rhetoric of blame in public discussion of social problems . . . usually produces defensiveness and unproductive blame-switching."[49] Group members will dedicate their energies

---

wrongdoing. For example, in the case of wrongdoings that target the state's own citizens, the state also has an associative duty to assist the victims who are its members. It follows that we can source the duty back to the citizens. But I am not convinced we can find alternative sources to culpability in all cases of state wrongdoing. I also return to discuss the alternative sources for citizens' responsibility that Collins points to in chapter 5. As I show there, they too have limitations and will not always help to resolve the shortfall problem.

[48] Collins, "Distributing State Duties," 352.
[49] Young, "Responsibility," 378–79.

to the task of exonerating themselves (and blaming others) rather than the task of addressing the plight of the victims.

Not everyone agrees with Young's empirical observations about the impact of blame on collective behaviors. Some highlight in response the constructive role of practices of blame (and of praise) in collective settings, in that they encourage actors to avoid bad outcomes and work toward good outcomes.[50] I suspect that in the real world there is no single pattern in which blame practices impact societies and organizations and render them more likely to comply with their duties. Young's concerns do seem to strike a chord, though, in some scenarios of state wrongdoing. I have in mind here postconflict societies, which often avoid the use of blame-based models when they apportion duties of redress for the crimes committed during a recent conflict, or by a recent regime. When adopting a forward-looking transitional justice model that avoids blame-tracking criminal prosecutions for past wrongs, such societies often cite concerns about the disastrous political effects that a blame-tracking model might bring, including the instigation of further conflict.[51] At least in these cases, then, the high costs that a blame-tracking model entails render it by far less attractive.

Finally, and continuing the discussion of the costliness of the model, even if Young exaggerates the negative psychological impact of the blame-tracking distribution on the state members, it is hard to deny that implementing it will require a lot of material resources from the state. After all, the state would need to determine its members' individual levels of blame, in light of the specific role they hold within the state (as policymakers, enactors, or ordinary

---

[50] E.g., Martha Nussbaum, "Introduction," in *Responsibility for Justice*, ed. Iris Marion Young (Oxford: Oxford University Press, 2013), ii. Cf. Crawford and Watkins, "International Responsibility," 290.

[51] See Robert I. Rotberg and Dennis Thompson, eds., *Truth v. Justice: The Morality of Truth Commissions* (Princeton: Princeton University Press, 2000); Priscilla B Hayner, *Unspeakable Truths: Facing the Challenge of Truth Commissions* (New York: Routledge 2002); Mark Freeman, *Necessary Evils: Amnesties and the Search for Justice* (Cambridge: Cambridge University Press, 2009).

citizens), their state of mind and their available excuses. Doing this on a national scale would be a very resource-intensive task, and would divert funds from the other important tasks that states have, especially in postconflict and postwar scenarios such as those that Germany, Iraq, Chile, and Argentina faced. Notice here that the task would be burdensome even if we adopt Beerbohm's more inclusive model of citizens' culpability. For while on Beerbohm's view the ordinary citizen is very likely to be blameworthy, he also thinks that disadvantaged citizens are off the hook, given their lack of political avenues of influence and/or lack of material resources and access to information. Furthermore, Beerbohm argues that democratic citizens can "reduce their 'complicity footprint,'" and exonerate themselves from moral blame if they resist the state's unjust policies (i.e., through political action).[52] It follows then that on his account, too, there will be many citizens who should not share the burden in a blame-tracking model, including the citizen who protests against the injustice or who was not yet alive when the injustice occurred. A fully justified blame-tracking model would have to account for such excuses, and on a national scale this can entail an incredibly taxing and prolonged process. Should the state take this path, despite these considerable costs, or is there an alternative model of distribution it could justifiably deploy?

1.4 Nonproportional Distribution

The alternative model for the distribution of the state's remedial duties is the one that states use, *de facto*, in the real world. On this "nonproportional distribution" the state does not "source track" the distribution, or aim to apportion it in light of the citizens' own blameworthy contributions to the wrong. Instead, the burden falls on the population at large. It is collected through general tax

---

[52] Beerbohm, *In Our Name*, chapter 10.

revenues, and all citizens are assumed to have a more or less equal share of the burden, adjusted to an extent to their level of resources and relative capacity to pay, as is usually done in most tax systems.

How well does this model fare in comparison to proportional distribution? As we saw in the previous section, the problem with the proportional distribution model is that it is unlikely to generate the amount of resources necessary for full compensation, and that it is likely to be very costly. A nonproportional distribution is likely to fare much better in both regards. First, because it falls on the population at large rather than on select individuals, it is able to generate more resources and thus meet the victims' demands. Second, because it falls on the population at large through the general tax system, its implementation does not require a very complex and costly process. Indeed, perhaps for these reasons, states like West Germany, Iraq, Argentina, Chile, and Canada turned to the general public funds pot to cover the expenditures of the compensation schemes they accepted upon themselves.

So the nonproportional distribution model is able to raise enough resources from the population, and allows the state to meet its obligations to its victims. But can it resolve the fairness concerns with which we started? This model has been advocated by some political theorists. Michael Walzer, for example, briefly notes, as part of his discussion of the distribution of war reparations that

> reparations can hardly be collected only from those members of the defeated state who were active supporters of the aggression. Instead, the costs are distributed through the tax system, and through the economic system generally. . . . In this sense, citizenship is a common destiny, and no one, not even its opponents, can escape the effects of a bad regime.[53]

---

[53] Michael Walzer, *Just and Unjust Wars: A Moral Argument with Historical Illustrations*, 2nd ed. (New York: Basic Books, 1992), 297; cf. Jaspers, *The Question*, 25.

In a similar vein, Debra Satz argues that "we can legitimately hold people accountable to redress wrongdoing that they did not them- selves commit by pointing to their responsibilities as members of a society that did commit wrongdoing."[54] Walzer and Satz allude then to the idea that, as members or citizens of their state, citizens may rightly be encumbered with the burden. But their brief remarks do not offer a full response to the objection by the citizen who had no option to resist state injustice, the citizen who protested against it, or the citizen who was not born yet when it was committed, who are also expected to share the burden.[55] These citizens might re- spond that membership in itself does not explain why they ought to incur such burdens. We need, then, a fresh exploration of the way in which states could justify the burden, even to those citizens.

It's time to take stock of what we have learned so far. I described in this chapter the way in which states, as corporate moral agents, are responsible for their wrongdoings, and—focusing on their re- medial responsibilities—I presented two models for the distribu- tion of state responsibility among its citizens. The proportional distribution model takes fairness to citizens as a primary concern, but, in doing so, it risks being unable to address the plight of their state's victims, or doing so at a high cost. The nonproportional dis- tribution model is better able to offer full remedy to the victims, but it does not offer a good reason why all the citizens, regardless of their personal association with the harm, should incur the burden. Perhaps, as Erskine suggests, in such scenarios we face a tragic choice. We might opt for nonproportional distribution, as states do in the real world, but only as a necessary evil, when the benefits that the reparation schemes bring to the victim significantly outweigh the costs that fall on the uninvolved citizens of the wrongdoing state. Quite possibly the implications of this conclusion would be

---

[54] Debra Satz, "What Do We Owe the Global Poor?," *Ethics and International Affairs* 19, no. 1 (2005): 50.

[55] In chapter 5 I discuss other attempts to justify a nonproportional distribution.

that, in the real world, states do often impose unjustified burdens on their citizens when they take this option.

But there is an alternative to this conclusion. Suppose that we could buttress Walzer's suggestion that members of a wrong-doing state *ought* to bear the burdens that result from their state's wrongdoings, given their membership in their state? If this can be shown, then it will follow that choosing the path of nonproportional distribution would not impose unfair burdens on the citizens of the wrongdoing state. If we can show this, we will find ourselves in a happier position, in which we can both meet the demands of the victims and also not be imposing unfair burdens on the wrong-doing state's citizens. In the next chapters I turn to this task, and develop a membership-based justification for a nonproportional distribution of the state's remedial duties.

2

Intentional Participation and Nonproportional Distribution

In the previous chapter I presented two models for the possible distribution of the state's remedial responsibilities among its citizens. The first model follows the commonly held normative intuition that those who committed a wrong should repair it. It suggests that the state should opt for a distribution of its remedial liabilities that tracks its citizens' blameworthy contributions to the state's wrongdoing. As we saw, this model faces serious challenges of implementation: First, typically relatively few members within the state will share the blame for their state's wrongful policies. A proportional distribution model is likely to lead to "responsibility shortfalls" where the state cannot raise enough resources to address its remedial obligations to the victims. Second, the model requires a complex and costly fact-finding process, which may inhibit the state's capacity to deliver on its other obligations.

Advocates of the proportional distribution model could argue in response that, although a blame-tracking process is costly, it is well worth the investment—given that it ensures that the distribution of state responsibility is fair to all the state's citizens. Furthermore, they can acknowledge that sometimes we will have to deviate from the blame-tracking model in order to raise additional resources, but when doing so we should recognize that we impose a serious harm on those citizens who are not to blame for their state's policies. Such harm could be justified as a "lesser evil," but only if the benefits it brings about are great in comparison to the harm they impose.

Responsible Citizens, Irresponsible States. Avia Pasternak, Oxford University Press. © Oxford University Press 2021. DOI: 10.1093/oso/9780197541036.003.0003

The second model leads to different conclusions. This model advocates a nonproportional distribution. It rests on the intuition that, as members of their state, citizens ought to accept a share of their state's remedial obligations even if they are not to blame for their state's policies. This model implies, then, that the state does not wrong its nonblameworthy citizens when it imposes remedial obligations on them. If a proportional distribution proves to be costly and time-consuming, then the state may opt for nonproportional distribution without moral compromise. An important pragmatic implication of this model is that—by and large— it defends the way in which states in the real world distribute their remedial liabilities. Is this defense viable?

I believe that it is, in some type of states. My goal in this chapter and the next is to present my justification for this model. As we saw in chapter 1, proponents of the nonproportional distribution point to the idea of state membership as grounding citizens' duties in this regard. But what precisely is it about state membership that renders citizens liable to share their state's obligations? Is it the fact that they are the primary beneficiaries of their state's wrongdoings? Or perhaps that they have a special capacity, given their citizenship status, to address their state's wrongdoings? Or perhaps they have special associative obligations, as members of their state, to ensure that it does not do wrong?

All these are important ways in which citizens could be connected to their state's wrongdoing, and they can ground at least some citizens' remedial obligations to their state's victims. But they too have their limitations. For now, I will put them aside and concentrate instead on the most straightforward link between the status of membership in a state and responsibility for state wrongdoing, which I think is the most promising route to ground nonproportional distribution. I will return to the factors of benefit, capacity, and associative obligations, and discuss their limitations, in chapter 5.

The most straightforward link between citizenship as membership and responsibility for the state's wrongdoing takes citizenship to be a form of collective action. On this view, which I develop in the rest of this chapter, citizens are acting together in their state, or participating in their state (I will use these terms interchangeably), and their state's policies can be attributed to them. Furthermore, I argue that—given this participation in their state—citizens can be expected to accept a nonproportional share of the burden of their state's responsibilities, if it turns out that a culpability-tracking distribution is infeasible or very costly. To illustrate these claims, consider the following example: On the 19th of March 2003, President George W. Bush gave a State of the Union Address in which he declared war on Iraq. Given that the president was speaking on behalf of the United States, and within the scope of his authority, his declaration clearly meant that the United States itself declared war on Iraq. But were ordinary American citizens also involved, in some sense, in the declaration of war? Could they sensibly say "*we* declared war on Iraq today?" I argue that the answer to this question is positive (with certain limitations I will present along the way). Not only that, I argue that, given their participation in the war on Iraq, American citizens may be expected to accept an equal share of the burden of their state's reparatory obligations to Iraq (assuming it has such obligations), one that does not track their personal blame for the war, if it turns out that a proportional distribution such as that which Collins endorses proves to be unfeasible or very costly.

My claim that citizenship involves collective action in the state rests on a specific theory of collective action, as developed by Christopher Kutz. I aim to show that once we accept this theory as a valid account of collective action, we are led to the conclusion that a very wide range of state policies are attributable to their citizens. In the current chapter I present Kutz's account of collective action and offer some modifications to it. In the next chapter I will demonstrate its applicability to citizens. In Section 2.1, I explain the core features of Kutz's account and address some objections that have been laid against it. In Section 2.2, I examine the moral obligations that flow from participation in a collective activity in the Kutzian sense. I argue that participation entails the duty to accept a nonproportional share of the burden, in circumstances where a proportional distribution is not feasible or is very costly.

In Section 2.3, I present an important qualification to the scope of my justification of nonproportional distribution. I argue that participation in collective action grounds liability for the group's wrongdoing only when group members are not forced, against their will, to participate in the group. This further condition will inform the discussion in the next chapter about the question of which citizens count as genuine participants in their state policies.

2.1 Participatory Intentions and Collective Action

As all accounts of collective action agree, collective action describes the acts of agents who are guided by shared intentions.[1] For example, the shared intention to take a stroll distinguishes two people who are walking together from two people who happen to walk side by side in the street. This very basic definition of collective action already points to two core challenges to the proposition that the state's policies are the product of its citizens' collective action. The first challenge concerns the nonvoluntary nature of membership in the state. Unlike the small-scale cooperative activities that typically appear in analyses of collective action (e.g., taking a walk, painting a house, doing a charity run), the vast majority of citizens

---

[1] For an introduction to the rich literature that surrounds the notion of shared intentions, see David Schweikard and Hans Bernhard, "Collective Intentionality," in *The Stanford Encyclopedia of Philosophy*, ed. Edward N. Zalta (Stanford, CA: Stanford University, 2013). Some authors in this literature use the term "shared intention," while others prefer the term "joint intention." Some suggest that "joint intention" denotes a more restrictive set of intentions (e.g., one that requires a commitment to acting together), but there is no agreement over the nature of distinction between these two terms. Given that I am opting for a minimalist definition of collective intentionality, I will use the term "shared intentions."

do not choose to become members of their state, nor do they have a viable opportunity to give up their membership. How can their state's policies be attributed to them if they have not chosen to be part of it?

The second challenge concerns the complex nature of the state, as a multilayered corporate agent. Here we can make use of Tracy Isaacs's distinction between "goal-oriented collectives" and organizations. In goal-oriented collectives, all participants "coalesce around action toward the achievement of a particular joint goal," and typically, it is fairly easy to define the activity around which all participants' intentions overlap (e.g., "painting the house," or "running for charity"). But the picture can become much more complex in organizational groups. As we already saw in chapter 1, in such groups there is usually a gap between the group's own representational and motivational states and those of at least some of its members. The group's decision-making process (and other mechanisms I mentioned in chapter 1) generates group-level beliefs and desires that are not necessarily supported by all group members. Some members may object to the group's goals, others might not even be aware of them, given their subordinate or marginal roles. Furthermore, when the group acts on its beliefs and desires, clearly not all its members will directly contribute to these specific executions.[2] Given all these gaps, can the group's acts be attributed to all its members?

In this and the next chapter, I will suggest that, despite these challenges, it is possible to show that citizens are acting together in their state. I do this by using Kutz's influential account of collective action.

Kutz's model rests on a <u>minimalist interpretation</u> of the notion of shared intentions. On his account, agents who act together should, <u>at the minimum, intend</u> to "do their part in a collective act." Doing one's part means doing "the task I ought to perform if we

---

[2] Isaacs, *Moral Responsibility*, 25.

are to be successful in realizing a shared goal."[3] Kutz refers to this formulation of the intentional stance as a "participatory intention." Agents who act with a participatory intention see themselves as contributing to the realization of a collective end or a shared goal. Importantly, when agents act with the intention to do their part in bringing about a collective end, they are part of the group that brings about the collective end. Put differently, they are the "inclusive authors" of that collective end (i.e., they can sensibly identify themselves as part of the "we" who did it).

I now turn to identify some core features of this account. These features will be particularly relevant in chapter 3, where I argue that citizens are acting together in their state. The first feature to notice is Kutz's usage of a "singular" rather than a "pluralist" notion of intention. A pluralist (or a group) intention is the intention that the group itself, or that *we*, act. A singular intention is the intention that *I* act, in the service of some common goal. Kutz suggests that a singular intention captures the way in which people typically act in hierarchical or complex groups. Those who lack a position of authority in such groups typically do not form the intention that "*we* act together." Consider, for example, the violinist in an orchestra or the trooper in a military unit. Unlike the conductor or the troop commander, these more marginal members do not necessarily intend for the group as a whole to act. And yet we commonly think that they act as part of the group. As Kutz suggests, this common intuition indicates that it is a sufficient condition for collective action that such participants have an individual-level intention to do their part.[4]

A second important feature of Kutz's account (which he shares with other accounts of collective action) is that it does not require that all participating members directly perform an act in order

---

[3] Kutz, *Complicity*, 81.
[4] Kutz, *Complicity*, 105. Cf. Scott Shapiro, "Massively Shared Agency," in *Rational and Social Agency: The Philosophy of Michael Bratman*, ed. Manuel Vargas and Gideon Yaffe (Oxford: Oxford University Press, 2014), 264–66.

to be its inclusive authors. For example, suppose that our group of friends collects money for a joint gift to our friend's new baby. We are all the inclusive authors of the purchase (we can all say "we bought the navy blue baby carrier"), even though it was Arthur who went to the shop and made the actual purchase.[5] As long as Arthur's choice is the execution of the decision we jointly made, or a "plausible refinement" of it,[6] we are all the inclusive authors of the purchase, even if some of us have reservations about Arthur's specific choice (e.g., the color he picked).

This example raises a thorny challenge: What counts as a "plausible refinement" of a collective goal, or—put differently—when does an agent's act count as an act of the group? The answer to this question depends, firstly, on how the group goal is defined. The more narrowly it is defined, the less freedom members have in interpreting what is a plausible refinement of it (though here it is worth bearing in mind that—as we saw in chapter 1—a group's "instructions" to its members need not necessarily be formal. An informal group ethos will also shape the expectations of the group and what they take they ought to be doing on its behalf). If our group explicitly stated that Arthur may only buy a baby carrier, but Arthur ended up buying a play mat, his choice is not the group's choice. If, however, the group gave only general instructions (e.g., "buy something cute"), then almost any purchase that complies with this open instruction will be attributable to the group. I say "almost any purchase" because even in the case of fairly open instructions there will be some minimal constraints on Arthur's choice, which flow from common conventions about what is an appropriate present for a new baby, and which set limits on what counts as a reasonable interpretation of the open instructions. Puppies are cute, but if Arthur bought a puppy as a present, the group could rightly point

---

[5] Kutz, *Complicity*, 105.
[6] Kutz, *Complicity*, 55, 106.

out that a puppy is just not the thing one buys for new parents, and that in this instance Arthur failed to act on behalf of the group.

The second dimension of the answer to the plausibility question concerns the question of who has the authority to define and revise the group's goal. In the example above, the shared goal was commonly defined by all the group members ("we want to buy a present for the baby"), and Arthur had no discretion to change this goal. If he decided to use the collection money for another purpose, he would be acting *ultra vires*. But sometimes a group will give a specific role-holder a wider discretion to define and to revise the group's shared goals. Think, for example, of the extensive authority the leader of a religious sect might have to define the group's religious purpose and to revise it in accordance with what she takes to be her daily communications with God. In the extremity of such cases, whatever the officeholder decides is a plausible interpretation of the group's goal is indeed the group's goal, because the officeholder role is to define these goals. At other times there will be more commonly acknowledged institutional restrictions in place on what goal-makers may declare as a reasonable interpretation of the group's common goals. In the next chapter we will see how these conditions relate to the case of states.

The third feature of Kutz's intentional participation account is that it does not require difference-making causation as a necessary condition for participation in the group act. Clearly, it is often the case that group members act in ways that do make an actual difference to the collective outcome (e.g., perhaps but for my contribution to the baby collection Arthur would not have bought the pricy baby carrier). But we commonly think that participants who act with an intention to do their part in bringing about a collective wrongdoing are part of the group, even if, as a matter of fact, their acts made no difference and even undermined the outcome. Consider the case of the lookout whose job is to alert the burglars if the police arrive at the scene, but who, as things turned out, never needed to act. Or consider the incompetent burglar who—despite his best intentions—actually makes it harder for the group to execute its plans.[7] As Kutz points out, these are not cases of actual causation, given that the agents in question have, in reality, not made a difference to the outcome. Instead, they are mere "potential" or "possible" contributions to the collective wrong. Nevertheless, both in criminal law and in common morality, we take agents who, when acting on participatory intentions, merely make possible contributions of this sort to be participants in the principal act. For an agent to be participating in a collective act it must be the case that her actions have some potential to affect the outcome (this is why mere fantasists are not participating in real-world events).[8] But, fundamentally, what ties the lookout or the incompetent burglar to the crime of burglary is not their actual causal contribution to this wrong, but rather their mental state—their intention to play a role in the plans of the group that orchestrated the wrong. In Kutz's words, what does the work here is not the actual causal link but the teleological link between the individual and the collective act, a link that is grounded in one's intention to do one's part in bringing about the collective outcome.[9]

[7] Cf. Robert Jubb, "Contribution to Collective Harms and Responsibility," *Ethical Perspectives* 19, no. 4 (2012): 733–64.

[8] See Christopher Kutz, "Causeless Complicity," *Criminal Law and Philosophy* 1, no. 3 (2007): 289–305. Another recent account that gives a central role to the idea of potential causal contributions in determining participation (or complicity) is developed in Lepora and Goodin, *On Complicity and Compromise.*

[9] Kutz, "Causeless Complicity." Cf. Kutz, *Complicity*, 84, 107, 38. Eric Beerbohm has rejected Kutz's view on the grounds that it offers an unclear account of "noncausal participation," which implausibly assumes an agent can "form an intention to noncausally participate in a larger structure" (Beerbohm, *In Our Name*, 234.). I think this is a misreading of Kutz. An intention to participate by definition includes a causal intent (to do one's role). Kutz's "noncausal" element applies to the act itself and its impact on the outcome, rather than to the mental state of the actor. Beerbohm himself also seeks to capture the idea of non-difference-making contributions. His account turns, albeit somewhat briefly, to the idea of "partial contribution, or of merely helping to bring about an event as an alternative to making an actual difference (Beerbohm, *In Our Name*, 68–70). But I think it remains unclear in what sense an act "influences" or "helps to bring about" an event if it plays no actual causal role, and if the event would have happened regardless of this act. As Kutz suggests, playing down the importance of actual causation, or of the actual impact of the act, and playing up the role of the actor's state of mind in intending her act to facilitate wrongdoing, better explains our common intuitions about complicity.

Finally, a fourth feature of Kutz's account that is relevant for the case of citizens is that it does not require that participants endorse the collective end, or be committed to its realization. Here, too, Kutz is motivated by the observation that people often intentionally do their part in furthering some common goal, and we commonly describe them as participating in that goal, even though they do not share and are even deeply alienated from the goal. Consider, for example, Primo Levi's memoir *Survival in Auschwitz*,[10] which describes his experience as a prisoner in the Auschwitz Concentration Camp. Throughout the memoir Levi suggests that a core feature of the horror of Auschwitz was that the prisoners themselves played an instrumental role in maintaining the camp and its murderous plans. These prisoners were participating in the activities of the camp—it made sense for them to utter statements such as "we unloaded the trains." Yet, clearly, they themselves were deeply alienated from these activities (and coerced to perform them). As we will see in Section 2.3, the attitude people have to their participation plays a crucial role in our assessment of the moral duties that flow from their taking part in a group act. But at a descriptive level, the endorsement of a collective outcome is not necessary for participation in the collective act to bring it about. As Kutz explains, "so long as [individuals] see themselves as part of a collective act, and whether or not they favor the collective goal . . . they are subject to the inclusive ascription of collective acts."[11]

This assertion opens up the following question: In what sense does an individual intend to do her part in a collective act, if she does not endorse the outcome of that act? To my mind, what is crucial here is that the agent in question performs her role with the knowledge that doing so will contribute to the collective end (or at least potentially contribute to it). Having that knowledge, or the "deliberative self-awareness of the instrumental relation of one's

---

[10] Published in the UK as *If This Is a Man*.
[11] Kutz, *Complicity*, 162.

part to the group act that is its end," is sufficient to count as intentional participation in a group act.[12] This is the reason why Miriam, a pacifist scientist who works in a lab funded by the Ministry of Defense, is an inclusive author of the military outcomes advanced by her work. She may disavow the outcome (and argue that she was merely pursuing her own research agenda), but she is well aware that she is playing a part in advancing them, and as such should recognize her inclusive authorship over them.[13]

I now turn to discuss two challenges to Kutz's notion of inclusive authorship over collective wrongdoing. The first challenge is that, perhaps, the idea of inclusive authorship is incompatible with the idea of corporate moral agency. Recall that in chapter 1 I discussed List and Pettit's theory of corporate agency, which many think explains the agency of states. We saw that on this theory the group's decision-making process creates a gap between the intentions of individual group members and those of the organization itself. Does this gap not imply that the group, and the group agent alone, is the author of its actions?[14] I think the answer to this question is negative. After all, a single act may have both an exclusive and an

---

[12] Kutz, *Complicity*, 84. Notice that this feature offers a response to Scott Shapiro's critique of Kutz's model. Shapiro argues that the model cannot capture large and complex groups (which Shapiro refers to as instances of "massively shared agency") because it requires that all participants would act with the intention to contribute to a collective outcome, which some alienated participants might not share. He gives the example of "alienated painters" who paint a house purely in order to get paid, and do not care if the job is finished (Shapiro, "Massively Shared Agency," 277). Shapiro suggests that rather than sharing a participatory intention to paint the house, the painters "accept a plan" to paint the house; that is, they are committed to doing their particular role, they do not prevent others from doing their role, and they are willing to peacefully and openly negotiate conflicts about their respective roles. However, I think here Shapiro mischaracterizes the notion of participatory intention: a participatory intention merely requires that one recognizes the role she plays in bringing about a collective outcome. Accordingly, the alienated painters are in fact intentional participants in the project of painting the house. Although they "could not care less whether the job is finished," they recognize their acts as contributing to its realization. Understood in this way, the gap between Kutz's account (which requires one to intend to contribute to the realization of an outcome) and Shapiro's (which requires that one is committed to do their particular role in the overall plan) dissolves.

[13] Kutz, *Complicity*, 163–64.

[14] Cf. Isaacs, *Moral Responsibility*, 118–19.

inclusive author. Consider again the baby present case. If Arthur bought the baby carrier on behalf of the group, then only Arthur can say "I bought the carrier." Arthur is the exclusive author of this act. But the other group members can also say "we bought the carrier." Arthur and the rest of the group are the inclusive authors of the purchase.[15] We can apply the same logic to the case of group agents. Suppose the College Art Committee chooses the various works of art that it plans to purchase in the coming year. We can sensibly say that "the CAC made the selection," but we cannot say for any member "she made the selection." In other words, the CAC is the exclusive author of the final decision. But we can *also* say that each member who contributed to the committee's decision is an inclusive author of the decision, together with the group agent (i.e., each can identify herself as part of the "we" who "decided this").

A second challenge to Kutz's account appears in Chiara Lepora and Robert Goodin's analysis of wrongful participation in collective wrongdoing. In contrast with Kutz, Lepora and Goodin argue that we ought to drive a wedge between the "co-principals" and "secondary agents" of a collective wrongdoing. Co-principals are acting on a shared plan (which they may have been party to designing),[16] and their actions are constitutive of, or "part and parcel of the principal wrongdoing."[17] Secondary agents "make potentially causal contributions to the principal wrongdoing of others," but "without their act in any way constituting part of that principal wrongdoing in themselves."[18] According to Lepora and Goodin, a secondary agent does not necessarily approve of the principal wrongdoing, but she contributes to it and "knows or should have known, that by [so acting] he or she will advance whatever intentions the principal has."[19] On Lepora and Goodin's account, only principal

---

[15] Kutz, *Complicity*, 105–106.
[16] Lepora and Goodin, *On Complicity and Compromise*, 36–40.
[17] Lepora and Goodin, *On Complicity and Compromise*, 33.
[18] Lepora and Goodin, *On Complicity and Compromise*, 41.
[19] Lepora and Goodin, *On Complicity and Compromise*, 42.

wrongdoers are the inclusive authors of the wrong—or part of the "we who did this." Secondary agents (which on their account are merely *complicit* in the principal wrongdoing) remain outside the scope of inclusive authorship—they contribute to the wrongdoing *of others*. Lepora and Goodin argue that Kutz elides this important distinction, which is "obvious as soon as it is stated."[20] His account of inclusive authorship, they think, is too expansive.

But is the distinction between insiders and outsiders as obvious as Lepora and Goodin claim? Can we indeed drive a clear wedge between acts that are constitutive of a wrongdoing and acts that are merely secondary and outside its scope? I am not persuaded that we can. Consider, for example, the case of a racist attack: Some attackers chase the victim, some catch and restrain him, some violently beat him. Some cheer from the side, while still others prevent the police from arriving at the scene. Which of these acts is constitutive of the crime of a racial attack, and which is merely secondary? Are only the people who physically assaulted the victim the principal wrongdoers, or should we include also those who caught and restrained him? And what about those who cheered from the side? Drawing a rigid line between "insiders" and "outsiders" is difficult and can seem quite arbitrary, given that all these participants intended the final outcome and did their bit to promote it. On the intentional participation account, rather than attempting to draw a line between constitutive and secondary acts, we should submit that all these people can sensibly say "we took part in the attack," in light of the fact that they intentionally played some role in bringing about this outcome. That is not to deny that some participants' roles are more central than others. However, rather than driving a wedge between the principal and secondary wrongdoers, it will be more useful to use a gradual "spatial metaphor" that locates at the core of

[20] Lepora and Goodin, *On Complicity and Compromise*, 79. For challenges to this claim in the sphere of criminal law, see James Stewart, "Complicity," in *The Oxford Handbook of Criminal Law*, edited by Markus D. Dubber and Tatjana Hörnle, 534–59. (Oxford: Oxford University Press 2014).

the activity those participants who intend the collective end and directly contribute to it, and at the periphery those participants who have more marginal roles.[21]

2.2 The Normative Implications of Participation

One of the core themes of Kutz's book is that participation in collective wrongdoing carries normative implications. In elaborating on these implications, Kutz rejects traditional, solipsistic models of moral accountability, which rely heavily on agents' causal, difference-making contributions to a wrongful outcome. As we already saw, he suggests that such models are inapplicable to the context of complex collective action, and incompatible with common-sense morality. Kutz captures the common intuitions about the implications of participation in collective action in his "complicity principle." According to this principle:

> I am accountable for what others do, when I intentionally participate in the wrong they do or harm they cause; I am accountable for the harm or wrong we do together, independently of the actual difference I make.[22]

This principle raises an immediate question. What does it mean for individuals to be *accountable* for the collective wrongs or harms they take part in bringing about? Kutz's own answer to this question is not as clear as it could be. At points, one might think that what he has in mind is moral accountability understood as culpability or blame.[23] Consider one of the running examples in Kutz's

---

[21] Kutz, *Complicity*, 159.
[22] Kutz, *Complicity*, 122.
[23] For such readings of his view, see Beerbohm, *In Our Name*, 234; Margaret Gilbert, "Collective Wrongdoing: Moral and Legal Responses," *Social Theory and Practice* 28,

book: the case of the British pilots who took part in the bombing of Dresden in February 1945 (an attack that targeted residential areas and resulted in an estimated 35,000 civilian deaths). Kutz argues that in the years that followed this event, the pilots were rightly seeking *atonement* for their actions. This idea suggests that they acted wrongly in taking part in the bombing raid.[24] Elsewhere, Kutz argues that our intentional participation in a group act "expresses what we desire, what we will tolerate, and what we believe," and that "the will of each is represented in what each other does qua group member, as well as what they do together."[25] Such statements might lead the reader to conclude that participation in a collective wrong amounts to wrongful contribution. For example, the victims of the Dresden bombing may rightfully resent each individual bomber for the suffering that he, together with other pilots, brought on them (irrespective of specific difference-making contributions of specific bombers), because in participating in the bombing raid, each pilot conveyed a wrongful and blameworthy attitude of disregard to their lives and well-being.[26]

The case of the Dresden bombers is one of a "goal-oriented collective": Each participant in the bombing directly contributed to the collective goal of a successful air raid. Perhaps, in such cases, each member's will is indeed represented in the outcome. And perhaps their feelings of guilt in the aftermath are justified. But, as we saw in chapter 1, it is much harder to draw such direct links between participants' beliefs and desires and the collective outcome in complex institutional agents. In such groups the group's goals can be far removed from the personal beliefs and desires of its members. Given their participation in the group, members are the inclusive authors of the group's acts, in the sense that they can sensibly say

no. 1 (2002): 181–82; Isaacs, "Collective Moral Responsibility and Collective Intention," 117–18.

[24] Kutz, *Complicity*, 143–44.
[25] Kutz, *Complicity*, 140–41.
[26] Kutz, *Complicity*, 141.

"*we* did this" (I will expand more on the scope of intentional participation in chapter 3, when I turn to the case of states). But that they participate in the group does not mean that all its acts reflect their own personal beliefs and desires, or what they would personally tolerate, and the more complex, compartmentalized, and hierarchical the group, the less likely this is to be the case. Furthermore, as we saw in chapter 1, in authoritative group agents like the state, it is likely that many ordinary participants will have powerful excuses for their participation in the group (e.g., because they were acting on good moral reasons, or they had no choice but to participate). As Young points out, it is counterintuitive to suggest that the majority of ordinary citizens should be blamed for their contributions to their state's wrongdoings.

But there is another interpretation of the notion of moral accountability in the complicity principle. This interpretation surfaces, for example, in Kutz's discussion of the accountability of the shareholders and employees of business corporations. Here Kutz points out that shareholders are not blameworthy—"they have done nothing wrong in purchasing a stock," but they are "accountable in the domain of repair for the company's accidents."[27] Here moral accountability cashes out as a forward-looking obligation "to help make good their company's debt to its victim."[28] Kutz refers to agents who have this duty as *complicit* agents. But, arguably, his deployment of this term is problematic, given that we commonly associate complicity with *wrongful* participation in collective wrongdoing (and perhaps this is what led Kutz's critics to associate his account with moral blame). To avoid such confusion, in what follows I will reserve the term "liability" to describe participants' forward-looking duty to bear the burdens of repair and compensation for the collective wrong they together brought about.[29]

---

[27] Kutz, *Complicity*, 245–46.
[28] Kutz, *Complicity*, 201.
[29] Lepora and Goodin's conceptual analysis of the term complicity suggests we should use it in a morally neutral sense, but given the common morally-laden usage of the term, I will not use it here.

What then is the moral basis for members' liability? We already saw that culpability does not necessarily ground their duty to accept a share of the burden. How does intentional participation ground this duty? Kutz does not give a detailed answer to this question, but I think we can find support for it in the notion of consequential or outcome responsibility. This familiar term was introduced and defended by Toni Honoré, as part of his defense of the legal practice of strict liability (i.e., legal liability for torts that is not conditional on fault).[30] The practice of holding people legally liable for the outcomes that their conduct brought about, Honoré tells us, is grounded in (and constrained by) the fundamental connection we assume between agents and their chosen actions. Our very notion of human agency suggests that as acting agents we receive some credit for the good outcomes of our actions, even if in acting so we have not done something praiseworthy; and that we receive some discredit, or bear the costs, when our actions lead to bad outcomes, even if we are not to blame.[31] This idea is particularly attractive, I think, when we face a choice between imposing the costs of a bad outcome on the agent who, through her choice, brought the outcome about, and imposing them on an entirely uninvolved victim. In such cases, it is only fair that the agent who brought the outcome about through her own choices will be liable for the remedial obligation to address the harm. Another way to explain this intuition is that we commonly accept that a voluntary action is a form of betting, where one is expected to take the benefit, or pay the price of one's choices.[32] Those who choose to perform an action accept the

---

[30] David Miller also makes use of this term, drawing on Honoré's work (Miller, *National Responsibility*, 84–85). Dworkin defends a similar idea in his notion of consequential responsibility—responsibility for consequences that "flow from our choices" (Ronald Dworkin, *Sovereign Virtue: The Theory and Practice of Equality* [Cambridge, MA: Harvard University Press, 2000], 286–88). Kutz briefly alludes to this idea; see Kutz, *Complicity*, 41.

[31] Tony Honoré, *Responsibility and Fault* (Oxford: Hart, 1999), 14. Cf. Miller, *National Responsibility*, chapter 4.

[32] As Honoré explains, this system should not be overly onerous to specific individuals—it should apply to everyone equally, and not include individuals who lack

bet, and it is only fair that it is they, rather than the victim who has not found herself in this position due to her own choices, address the harm.

This justification applies not just to cases of individual wrongdoing, but also to cases of *collective* wrongdoing. The idea here is that when we choose to act with others, or in the service of a collective goal, we consciously give up full control over what these others will do, and over the outcome of our shared endeavor. In doing this, we accept that we will be credited if our joint endeavor leads to beneficial outcomes, but we will also be burdened if it does not. Given that each participant makes the choice to act with others, it is only fair that the burdens of the group's remedial responsibility for the outcomes over which each is an inclusive author will be on the participants, *rather* than on the group's victims or on other agents in the world. Put differently, when taking part in a collective act we *ipso facto* commit ourselves to accepting a potential share of the consequences of the shared activity.

Now, as we have seen throughout the discussion so far, there are various ways to cash out the idea that participants should share in the burdens of compensation for their group's wrongdoing. In assessing how much each member should contribute, there are good reasons to attempt to apportion each member's share in light of their blameworthy contributions to the group, and sometimes in proportion to their role in the group.[33] But implementing a proportional distribution of the liability among group members—whether on the basis of culpability or the level of intentional participation

agential capacities and cannot choose to act in a way that renders them responsible for their actions.

[33] The distribution of liability in proportion to one's role in the group is another version of the proportional distribution model (but that tracks one's causal role and capacity to affect the group's policies rather than blame). Whether it should be adopted depends on the group in question. Larry May suggests that in the case of business corporations, the business leaders should pay the majority of corporate fines (May, *The Morality of Groups*, 98). In contrast, Kutz argues that shareholders should share the burden as well. As I will argue in chapter 3, this version of the proportional distribution model does not apply well to the case of states.

in the group—can at least sometimes face the challenges of implementation I discussed in chapter 1. When that is the case, the group may demand that all members—even those who played a marginal role—contribute to the collective effort of discharging the group's remedial obligations, irrespective of their personal level of blame or the role they played in the group. Though their role may be marginal, they act with the intention to contribute to the collective outcome. For that reason, they are better positioned than the group's victims to be burdened with the costs associated with the harm. Thus, to conclude the point, intentional participation in collective wrongdoing provides, under some circumstances, a membership-based justification for the nonproportional distribution of the group's remedial responsibilities. Put differently, to be liable for collective wrongdoing in this sense means to be in the position where the group might call upon you, if it is the case that more resources than those that the proportional distribution model can supply are needed, or a less costly distribution model is called for given the group's other tasks and obligations.

2.3 Coercion and Acceptance

I have argued so far that group members are liable for a share in their group's remedial responsibilities if they intentionally participate in their state. However, there is an immediate objection to this conclusion that applies specifically to nonvoluntary groups. As we saw earlier, a core objection to the idea that citizens share liability for their state policies is the nonvoluntary nature of the state: citizens do not choose to become members of their own state, nor do they have a viable opportunity to leave it. This fact does not affect their participation in the state in the conceptual sense, but it could affect their moral duties. After all, we commonly think that agents who are forced to perform a task against their will (such as the prisoners in Auschwitz) are neither culpable nor liable for the outcomes. Perhaps it follows that if citizens had no choice but to be members of their state, they are the inclusive authors of its actions but not liable for the outcomes of their inclusive authorship. Kutz seems to resist this conclusion when he briefly notes that even coerced agents fall under his account of complicity. But his passing remarks neither justify nor qualify this assertion.[34] In my view, such a fuller justification is required. My final task in this chapter is to address this problem and to investigate how nonvoluntariness affects group members' liabilities for collective outcomes.

Recall that earlier I suggested that members' liability (namely, their duty to accept a nonproportional share of the burden when necessary) is grounded in the idea that people are responsible, in some sense, for the consequences that flow from their choices. This idea suggests that when we examine nonvoluntary groups, we should pay attention to participating agents' own assessment of their situation, or to their own attitude to their membership status. I have in mind here, in particular, Harry Frankfurt's influential account of the relation between "coercion" and moral responsibility. As Frankfurt explains, we should draw a distinction between people who *are forced against their will* to perform an action, and people who—although lacking alternate options—are also acting on their own will (Frankfurt thinks the term "coercion" applies only to the former group).[35] To illustrate this distinction, specifically in the context of group membership and collective action, consider the following case:[36] Tony is a low-ranking mobster. He is a member of a Mafia syndicate in the descriptive sense: he has passed the Mafia's initiation ceremony and is therefore a "formal" member, playing the various roles allocated to him by the syndicate, not always understanding or knowing the details of the criminal activity

[34] Kutz, *Complicity*, 102. Cf. 60–64.
[35] Harry G. Frankfurt, "Alternate Possibilities and Moral Responsibility," *Journal of Philosophy* 66, no. 23 (1969): 829–39.
[36] I draw here on a passage from Avia Pasternak, "Limiting States' Corporate Responsibility," *Journal of Political Philosophy* 21, no. 4 (2013): 371 .

he is contributing to, but recognizing he is playing a role in the success of his syndicate as a criminal organization. Tony cannot quit his Mafia syndicate without incurring highly unreasonable costs (e.g., his life or the life of his family). But does the lack of alternate options imply that Tony is not liable for the wrongdoings he takes part in? The answer, I suggest, depends on Tony's own perception of his membership. If he himself rejects his membership status— that is, if he perceives it as forced on him against his own will and resents taking part in activities he cannot reasonably opt out of— then his participation in the descriptive sense does not ground his liability for the syndicate's crimes. If anything, Tony himself is a victim of the syndicate, as he is forced to take parts in actions he himself recognizes as morally wrong.

But let's assume that Tony accepts his membership status. Agents who *accept* their membership status choose not to leave their group even though leaving the group is not unreasonably costly. Or, if leaving the group is impossible or unreasonably costly, that fact is not what motivates them to stay. Instead, they are motivated by their own reasons. Tony accepts his mobster status if he would have incurred only trivial costs were he to leave the Mafia (e.g., free lunches at his favorite restaurant), or even if leaving the mafia is unreasonably costly for Tony, that is not, or not only, the reason why he stays. Instead he is motivated by, say, the luxurious lifestyle he enjoys.[37] In other words, Tony accepts his role if he would have remained a mobster even if he could have left the Mafia without incurring unreasonable costs. When Tony has this disposition, there is not much to distinguish him, at a normative level, from the mobster who could have left the syndicate but chose not to do so. That Tony accepts his membership status means that his will is not alienated from his own actions. Rather than a victim who is forced

[37] Tony may be motivated by both the cost of leaving and the luxurious lifestyle, but it must be the case that the luxurious lifestyle is sufficient to keep him in the Mafia even without the threat.

to take part in crime, he is a genuine participant in the activity. For that reason, it is fair to hold him liable, in the sense I described before, for the syndicate's criminal activities.[38] As we saw, my argument is not that Tony should necessarily bear the same burden as, say, the Mafia Boss. But if it were the case that the only feasible way of extracting sufficient resources from the group members is on a nonproportional basis, Tony does not have a valid complaint against this distribution.

Let's conclude. I have provided in this chapter an explanation for a nonproportional distribution of a group's remedial obligations among its members. As we saw, this justification is grounded in the idea that group members intentionally participate in a collective endeavor. They make the choice to be part of it, and—assuming that choice is genuine—it is fair to demand of them that they accept a share of the costs of remedying the harms the groups caused, when a proportional distribution is infeasible or too costly. In the next chapter I show that this account applies to the states and their citizens.

---

[38] Cf. Harry G. Frankfurt, "Freedom of the Will and the Concept of a Person," *Journal of Philosophy* 68, no. 1 (1971): 20. Larry May also refers to intentional stances of participants in collective wrongdoings, but he argues these can ground participants' moral taint; see Larry May, *Sharing Responsibility* (Chicago: University of Chicago Press, 1992), chapter 5. Moral taint may well be appropriate in the case of Tony, who is probably blameworthy in light of his decision to accept his status, given the evil nature of the Mafia's activities. But the state is not an evil organization, and citizens are likely to be accepting their citizenship status for legitimate and worthy reasons. The notion of taint, with its morally censuring implications, is therefore not fitting in this case.

3

Intentional Participation in the State

In chapter 2, I developed a conditional justification for the nonproportional distribution of a group's remedial responsibilities among its members. I argued that a deviation from proportional distribution can be justified to group members if two conditions are met. First, the members are intentional participants in their group in the sense that they intend to do their part toward the realization of a collective outcome, or at the least they recognize the instrumental role they play toward the realization of that outcome. Second, their participation in the group is genuine (i.e., it is not forced on them against their will). When people are genuine participants in a collective wrongdoing in this sense, it is not unfair to impose on them a portion of the burdens of compensation, reparation, rehabilitation, and nonrepetition that is not proportional to their level of personal blame, if a proportional distribution is infeasible or very costly.

In this chapter, I apply this justification of nonproportional distribution to the case of states. First, I argue that to be a citizen can involve acting together in the state, and that citizens who act together in this sense are the inclusive authors of a very wide range of their state's policies. Second, I argue that it can be the case that participation in the state is genuine and grounds moral obligations. My argument at this stage remains largely theoretical. I will examine its application to states as we know them in chapter 4.

As we saw in chapter 2, I ground my justification of nonproportional distribution in a modified version of Christopher Kutz's model of collective action. My core proposal, then, is that this account applies to citizens in the state, with relation to a wide

Responsible Citizens, Irresponsible States. Avia Pasternak, Oxford University Press. © Oxford University Press 2021. DOI: 10.1093/oso/9780197541036.003.0004

range of their state's policies.[1] Here it is worth noting that there are other accounts in the literature that argue that citizenship involves collective action, but they utilize more restrictive models of collective action for this purpose.[2] Margaret Gilbert, for example, grounds her observation that citizens are acting together in their state in a theory of collective action that revolves around the idea of a "plural subject." The plural subject, Gilbert tells us, is formed when individuals "intend as a body to pursue a joint goal."[3] On her account, individual citizens form a plural subject in the state in the sense that they are committed to accept as a body the authority of the officeholders of their state.[4] Anna Stilz also argues that citizens in democracies are engaging in collective action, using Michael Bratman's model of collective action. According to Bratman, people act together when they form interdependent we-intentions (e.g., the intention that we paint the house).[5]

While Gilbert and Stilz do not reflect directly on the question of the distribution of remedial responsibilities in the state, it is

---

[1] I began to develop these claims in Pasternak, "Limiting States' Corporate Responsibility." Kutz himself does not apply this model directly to the case of states, but he discusses its application to other institutional agents, such as business corporations. There he argues that shareholders, by virtue of their participation in the company, are inclusive authors of its policies (Kutz, *Complicity*, 238–53. In other work Kutz argues that citizens are acting together when they, for example, vote. But he does not consider the implications in terms of their inclusive authorship over their state's policies, which I think follow from the account. See Christopher Kutz, "The Collective Work of Citizenship," *Legal Theory* 8, no. 4 (2002), 486.

[2] Cecile Fabre also suggests that Kutz's participatory framework could in principle explain why some citizens and soldiers are liable for reparations for war crimes; see Cécile Fabre, *Cosmopolitan War* (Oxford: Oxford University Press, 2012), 187. But she is skeptical that, in practice, this basis would have a sufficiently wide application. In her view many citizens would not be participating in the war in the morally relevant sense (Fabre, *Cosmopolitan War*, 158.) As we will see in chapter 4, I think the participatory framework can actually capture the majority of populations at least in some states.

[3] Margaret Gilbert, "Walking Together: A Paradigmatic Social Phenomenon," *Midwest Studies in Philosophy* 15, no. 1 (1990): 1–14.

[4] Margaret Gilbert, *A Theory of Political Obligation: Membership, Commitment, and the Bonds of Society* (Oxford: Clarendon Press, 2006).

[5] Anna Stilz, *Liberal Loyalty: Freedom, Obligation, and the State* (Princeton: Princeton University Press, 2009), 181–204. Bratman's model on which she relies is developed in Michael Bratman, *Faces of Intention: Selected Essays on Intention and Agency* (Cambridge: Cambridge University Press, 1999).

plausible to think that their accounts, too, show that citizens who participate in their state ought to accept a nonproportional share of the burden.[6] But a common critique of their accounts is that they do not apply to most citizens in most real-world states. Most citizens, so the objection goes, do not intend to act as a body in accepting the authority of the state,[7] nor do they intend that "we act together in the state," per Bratman's model.[8] This is an empirical objection, which perhaps could be proven wrong. But rather than attempting to test its strength, I opt to use Kutz's model, which, as we saw in chapter 2, is more minimal than either Gilbert's or Bratman's proposals.[9] As I argued in chapter 2, it is sufficient for a group member to merely have a participatory intention (albeit a genuine one) to generate liability for group wrongdoing. In this chapter I suggest that this model captures the intentions of ordinary citizens (although, as we shall see in chapter 4, it too leaves some citizens outside the scope). This is not to deny that some (perhaps even many) citizens are acting together in their state in Bratman's or Gilbert's sense. But we do not have to rely on these more restrictive accounts in order to ground citizens' liability for their state's policies.

In chapter 2, I mentioned two objections to the claim that citizens are the inclusive authors of their state's policies. The first concerned the nonvoluntary nature of the state: If citizens do not choose to be part of their state, and can hardly renounce their citizenship in it, how are they genuinely participating in the state? The second

---

[6] Stilz does address this question in a different work, but there she does not use the collective action account. I examine her justification for nonproportional distribution in chapter 5.

[7] For this critique, see David Miller, "Review: A Theory of Political Obligation by Margaret Gilbert," *Philosophical Quarterly* 58, no. 233 (2008): 755–57; Stilz, *Liberal Loyalty*, 177–79.

[8] For this critique, see Shapiro, "Massively Shared Agency."

[9] See discussion and comparison with other accounts in Christopher Kutz, "Acting Together," *Philosophy and Phenomenological Research* 61, no. 1 (2000): 1–31. This is not to suggest that Kutz's account captures all types of collective action. As Michael Bratman notes, collective action can manifest itself in different forms. See Michael Bratman, *Shared Agency* (Oxford: Oxford University Press, 2014), 36–37.

challenge concerns the gap between state policies and citizens' personal beliefs and desires. Most citizens play a very marginal role in the state's decision-making process, and many of them are unaware or even oppose policies it enacts. How can they be participating in a meaningful sense in these policies?

In this chapter, I address these objections. I begin, in Section 3.1, with my account of participatory intentions in the state. As we will see, these intentions revolve around the maintenance of the state's political and legal authority. In Section 3.2, I tie the account of genuine acceptance I developed in chapter 2 to the case of citizens and argue that—despite not choosing to be part of their state—citizens may nevertheless accept their citizenship status. In Section 3.3, I address the problem of the gap between the state and its citizens, and defend the claim that citizens are the inclusive authors even of policies they object to or are unaware of. In Section 3.4, I conclude the analysis by going back to the issue of citizens' liability. I examine the circumstances under which the state may plausibly argue that a nonproportional distribution is preferable to proportional distribution.

3.1 Participatory Intentions in the State

Before I apply the account of participatory intentions to citizens, I first need to clarify who is included in this group. On one definition a citizen is simply a person who is defined as such by the state's nationality laws (as long as these comply with the standard restrictions of public international law).[10] But this formalistic

---

[10] Public international law permits states to set their own nationality laws, but not in a way that undermines the nationality laws of other states, or their citizens' basic human rights. For example, a state cannot declare the citizens of another state as its own, and it may not deprive its own citizens of their nationality on the basis of their gender, religion, or race. See Peter Spiro, "A New International Law of Citizenship," *American Journal of International Law* 105, no. 4 (2011): 694–746.

definition says nothing about citizens' own recognition of their citizenship status or their agency. It is not only that cases where people are citizens of a state only in this formal sense are quite rare, but I am also not convinced that being a citizen in just this formal sense, devoid of one's own recognition, could confer any meaningful moral duties. So instead my focus here will be on the much more familiar cases where citizenship involves not just the formal inclusion by one's state (and the familiar set of legal rights and duties that come with it), but also the recognition of that status by the citizen herself. The citizens I am concerned with recognize themselves as members of their state, and that fact informs and structures a relevant set of their actions: they obey their state laws, they pay their taxes, they vote in general elections, and so on.

Furthermore, as we already saw in chapter 1, it is not only state citizens that incur the costs of the state's liabilities. There are other people who reside in the state, obey its laws, pay taxes, and contribute to its decision-making process. This would include, for example, permanent residents and temporary migrants. I take it that, by and large, these people, too, typically count as intentional participants in the state in which they live (subject to the restriction that they are not forced to participate against their will). But for simplicity's sake I will continue to use the term "citizens," given that they constitute the vast majority of members in the state.

In what sense, then, are citizens acting together in their state? Recall that, as we saw in chapter 1, the state is not a mere "goal-oriented collective." Rather, it is an institutional entity—a complex, integrated, and hierarchical system. As we saw in chapter 1, in order for complex organizational entities to be able to act consistently and rationally over time, they must "collectivize their reason," *inter alia*, by endorsing decision-making procedures that create a gap between their own goals and those of some and even most, if not all, of their individual members.

It follows then that individuals who are members in institutional entities are different from members in goal-oriented collectives in at least one important sense. In goal-oriented collectives (such as, say, a charity run[11]), each individual participatory intention is directly related to the collective goal (e.g., all those who take part in the run intend to take part in the run). In institutional groups— given the gap between the representational and motivational states of the members and those of the group—members intend to perform their roles in the maintenance of the corporate agency of the group, meaning its ability to generate independent goals and to execute them.[12] This "basic level" intention, to contribute to the maintenance of the corporate agency of the group, knowing that it will generate policies that one will not necessarily agree with, renders one the inclusive author of what the group does. For in performing one's tasks in such a group, one recognizes the instrumental (or potentially intestumental) role one plays in executing the group's own decisions.

This general account applies to states and their citizens. The state requires group-level agency in order to exercise its role as the holder of legal and political authority—and the various tasks that come with this role. As an authoritative legal and political agent, the state sets its vision, goals, and objectives (which may or may not be democratic). It then assigns its citizens different roles, in line with its subsidiary plans. The content of these roles changes from state to state. In some states they amount to little more than obeying the laws of the state. In others, citizens are expected to take a more active part in the support of their state institutions: vote, perform compulsory military service, attend political rallies, or report on their neighbors' political behavior. In performing such roles, citizens see themselves as contributing to the maintenance of their state as a corporate agent with the ultimate legal and political authority over the territory they live in. They are intentional

---

[11] Isaacs, *Moral Responsibility*, 25.
[12] Philip Pettit and David Schweikard, "Joint Actions and Group Agents," *Philosophy of the Social Sciences* 36, no. 1 (2006): 18–39. Isaacs, *Moral Responsibility*, 29–32.

participants in their state as long as they recognize that these acts contribute (or potentially contribute) to the general maintenance of the corporate agency of their state and to the execution of its subsidiary plans, as defined by the state. Thus, going back to the example from chapter 2, when President Bush declared war on Iraq, it did make sense for all American citizens to say "we declared war on Iraq," because each citizen performs certain roles with the intention to contribute to the project of maintaining the state as a corporate agent with the authority to make foreign policy decisions.

Not everyone agrees that citizens are participating in their state. In a recent book, Holly Lawford-Smith argues that we should treat citizens as outsiders to the state. She advocates what she calls a "citizens-exclusive model" of the state, according to which the state is constituted only by the apparatus of governance. Lawford-Smith agrees with me that Kutz's model of collective action does apply to most citizens in most states (conditional on some empirical observations, to which I return in chapter 4).[13] However, she identifies a different problem for this model, which is that it provides an account of a collective agent that cannot comply with the conditions of corporate moral agency. As we saw in chapter 1, to be a moral agent, a group should be able, as a group, to incorporate into its decision-making process normative reasons so that it can make normative judgments. However, Lawford-Smith argues, it is not the case that the collection of citizens who intentionally participate in the state have these capacities as a group. Individual citizens may well have access to normative reasons as individuals, but as a group they do not have a collective deliberative mechanism that incorporates all these judgments and generates a decision that is constituted of them. Even in democracies, where citizens do get to occasionally participate in the decision-making process, their contributions remain extremely minimal (voting in

[13] Lawford-Smith, *Not in Their Name*, 47.

national elections and some contributions to the public debate).[14] Lawford-Smith suggests that, given this problem, if we want to maintain the idea that the state is a corporate moral agent, we must opt for a citizens-exclusive model, which includes only those individuals who are part of the formal state apparatus, and are direct participants in its decision-making process or the implementation of its decisions.[15]

Lawford-Smith offers a serious challenge to citizen-inclusive models. But notice that this critique relies on the controversial assumption that in a corporate agent *all* the group members are tied to the group's intentional stance. To be a member is to be part of the individuals who form the group's intentions. A group whose members are participating in it only in the Kutzian sense can form only few, if any, intentions based on its members' collective input, and as such cannot meet the demands of corporate agency over time. But why should we accept that in a group agent all group members should be related to its intentional stance in the same way? On an alternative view, the state (like most sophisticated group agents) is constituted of a core and a periphery. At the core we find members who take part in the decision-making process in a way that allows for group-level autonomy and rationality. The periphery is made up of citizens who relate to the state by virtue of their more loosely defined participatory intentions. These people are members of the state, in the sense that they see themselves as contributing to its maintenance, even though they do not form part of the state's locus of intentional action in a deep sense.

To see this, consider the following example, taken from Lawford-Smith: A small group of students is standing outside the university offices. Ten of those students have gathered in order to protest against the university fees, while the remaining thirty are just hanging around the building (unaware of, or indifferent to,

[14] Lawford-Smith, *Not in Their Name*, 51.
[15] Lawford-Smith, *Not in Their Name*, 60.

the protest). Assume that the ten protesting students are related to each other in a way that renders them a corporate moral agent (e.g., they have set the appropriate decision-making procedure). I agree with Lawford-Smith's assessment that under these circumstances, it would not make sense to argue that the group of forty students is the "agent of the protest."[16]

Consider now a tweak of this example. The ten students who form a corporate agent decide to turn their protest into a disruptive event (e.g., they start spraying the walls of the administration building, throwing bricks at it, blocking its entrance, etc.). As before, there are another thirty students who find themselves in the area of the protest, but this time, excited by the commotion, each of them decides to stay put and contribute to the disruption (some assist in blocking the entrance, others in the spraying, etc.). Are these thirty students now part of the "agent of the protest"? On the one hand, they did not take part in the group's original decision-making process. Furthermore, as Lawford-Smith would point out, the group that includes them seems incapable of normative reasoning that incorporates the arguments of all forty students (or let's assume so for the sake of the argument). But, on the other hand, they are intentionally contributing to the implementation of the smaller group's decision-making process, enabling its will to be executed. Given their contributions, I think it would be strange to argue that they are not part of the protest group, even if their membership is not as central as that of the original ten: They are not full participants in its decision-making process, nor do they constitute that part of it that is able to make decisions as a corporate moral agent. But they are the inclusive authors of its activities and part of the group that can say "we took part in the protest." On my reading of group membership then, a group member need not be a constitutive part of the smaller subset that has the necessary features to be the moral agent itself. To count as a member

---

[16] Lawford-Smith, *Not in Their Name*, 24–25.

in a group all that one needs is to be intending to contribute to the group's goals, and that is sufficient to render one a participant in the group agent's actions, and liable to its actions in the sense I described in chapter 2.

Going back to the case of the state, I think then that Lawford-Smith is right to argue that only the subset of a state's citizens—namely government employees (and perhaps even only a subset of those)—constitute together an agent that is able to make normative decisions and to follow them. But it also remains the case that the citizens of the state intentionally participate in maintaining this corporate agent and in executing its decisions, in light of the roles it allocates to them. As such, they are "members" of that group—i.e., intentional participants in its activities. As I argued in chapter 2, membership even in this sense can have important normative implications.

3.2 Voluntariness and Acceptance in the State

I described in the previous section, the sense in which citizens fulfill the first requirement of intentional citizenship: they intend to do their part toward the realization of a collective outcome. I now turn to the second requirement, that their participation in the group is genuine.

As we saw in chapter 2, genuine participation requires that group members choose not to leave their group even though leaving the group is not unreasonably costly. Or, if leaving the group is impossible or unreasonably costly, that fact is not what motivates them to stay. Instead, they are motivated by their own reasons. Going back to the case of citizens, this framework suggests that citizens are genuine participants in their state if they could leave their state without incurring unreasonable costs but choose not to; or if, even if the costs are unreasonable, that fact is not what motivates them to stay. Instead, they participate in the state for their own reasons. The reasons for participating in one's state can be varied. Some might see their citizenship as constitutive of their self-understanding and self-worth, others will be motivated by a sense of obligation to their fellow citizens, and others will have a merely instrumental approach to their citizenship. What matters for genuine participation in the state is that citizens do not view it as forced on them against their own will. On the other hand, citizens who genuinely reject their citizenship status—who would like to give it up had they the real opportunity to do so—are participants in their state in a thin sense. They see themselves as contributing to its goals. But—like the group of coerced prisoners mentioned in chapter 2—their participation in the state does not imply that they are liable for what it does.

My model of intentional citizenship thus gives a central role to citizens' subjective attitudes with regard to their participation in the state. As such it raises two immediate objections. The first objection is empirical. Earlier on I argued that the model of intentional citizenship potentially applies to many ordinary citizens in real-world states. But how common are such subjective attitudes? And how can we test for their presence? I will return to this question in chapter 4.

The second objection is normative, and concerns the source of citizens' acceptance of their membership status. Here one can argue that our disposition to accept our citizenship status is itself shaped by external factors, including—prominently—the state itself. After all, states typically endeavor to instill in their citizens a sense of civic duty and loyalty, and to achieve that they use public education, social incentives, and legal sanctions. Are citizens then genuinely accepting their citizenship status? And what if the state uses very intrusive measures to indoctrinate their citizens, including radical manipulation and very serious sanctions for those who refuse to comply? Can we draw the line between "authentic" or "genuine" acceptance, which does generate normative implications, and "non-authentic" acceptance, which is forced on citizens from the outside and does not render them liable for their state's policies?

These questions bring to the fore a more foundational problem in moral and political philosophy, which concerns the conditions under which people can be said to be truly autonomous, or the authors of their own characters, values, beliefs, and dispositions. As a starting point for answering these challenges, we should note that the idea that normal human beings, in their normal lives, are standardly the authors of their character, their dispositions, and their values is foundational to the human experience. It is something most of us believe in, even though we also recognize that the process of self-development through which we have come to have our character, personality, and dispositions includes a variety of external influences (family, school, culture, etc.). I take it that any plausible account of autonomy must be able to accommodate this common belief, which is probably integral to all human societies, and must be able to explain how competent adult individuals who are not subjected to serious mental manipulation and coercion are indeed the authors of their own mental dispositions, even though they do not have full control over their formation.[17]

One influential account of autonomy that attempts to show this has been offered by Harry Frankfurt. He argues that an agent is an author of her own personality, desires, and attitudes if she does not resist these internal states: she accepts them without reservations and does not have "an acting interest in bringing about a change" in them.[18] John Christman agrees; on his view, the autonomous person should not feel deeply alienated from the characteristic in question, in the sense that, upon reflection, she does not see herself as "constrained by it" and "wanting decidedly to repudiate it."[19]

---

[17] Cf. John Christman, *The Politics of Persons* (Cambridge: Cambridge University Press, 2009), chapter 7; Dworkin, *Sovereign Virtue*, 287–96.

[18] Harry Frankfurt, "The Faintest Passion," in *Necessity, Volition and Love* (Cambridge: Cambridge University Press, 1998), 109.

[19] Christman, *The Politics of Persons*, 144.

But Christman adds a further condition to Frankfurt's account. He argues that the reflection on one's personality traits must be "historic"; that is, it must consider the conditions that brought about this characteristic (e.g., one's education, social environment, and so on). The autonomous agent should not, upon reflection, resent the process by which she has come to be the person she is. Finally, Christman notes that the autonomous person must have the basic competency for adequate self-reflection, which itself has not been distorted by external manipulation, and which allows for "minimal self-understanding."[20] So people who are under the influence of drugs, those who have been manipulated so that they are misinformed or lack the information to understand what they are doing, or those who have been "brainwashed" so that they are unable to recognize or understand other options, are not the authentic authors of their personality.

I think this account of autonomy can help us to see when acceptance of one's membership status is genuine or authentic. Consider again Tony, the Mafia member, whom I described in chapter 2. Let's assume that Tony's loyalty to his criminal organization was shaped by the way in which he was brought up and the norms of his social circle. As long as Tony is not alienated from his disposition, and from the way it was instilled in him—as long as he sees it as constitutive of who he is—we (and Tony) would commonly see this disposition as *his*, and we would hold him liable for the consequences of the actions that flow from it.

The same principle applies to citizens. Citizens' political participatory intentions are indeed shaped and influenced by external factors. Yet they are still their authors as long as they have not been subjected to extreme forms of coercion and manipulation, and as long as they, when they reflect on their participation in light of the processes that led to the creation of their attitudes to it, do not experience a sense of deep alienation and resistance. When they do

[20] Christman, *The Politics of Persons*, 146.

experience such a sense then, in participating in their state, they are not acting on their own reasons, and hence are not genuine inclusive authors of its policies. In chapter 4 I will apply this general principle to real-world states, in order to gauge the extent of intentional citizenship in them.

3.3 The Scope of Participation in the State

I argued in Section 3.1 that citizens who intend to play their role in their state are the inclusive authors of its policies. But how wide is their inclusive authorship? Does it make sense to argue that citizens are participating in policies they disagree with, or with policies they are not aware of?

I believe the answer to these questions is affirmative, and that citizens can be the inclusive authors of a very wide range of their state's policies. Put differently, I argue that—within certain restrictions I outline below—specific state policies count as "plausible refinements" of the collective project citizens take part in, even if some citizens disagree with them. Recall that in chapter 2 I suggested that the question of whether a group member's act counts as a plausible refinement of a group's shared goals depends on who has the authority to define the group's goals and on how precisely they are defined. In the case of states, all states share the vaguely defined purpose of serving the interests of their citizens, but it is the state itself that has the authority to interrupt what this basic purpose entails, and to make and revise the laws of the land and to conduct the political community's affairs with other states in the world in accordance with this interpretation. Citizens who participate in the state perform their role toward the maintenance of the corporate agency of the state to generate independent goals and to execute them. This is not to deny that most states impose restrictions on the scope of their policies, both at the level of the procedures that generate these policies and at the level of the content of the laws they may make. For example, some states commit themselves to a democratic policy formation process, and to written (or unwritten) constitutions, or basic laws. As we saw in chapter 1, these restrictions can help to ensure the state's collective rationality over time. Nevertheless, it remains the case that the limitations which such mechanisms set remain vague and open to interpretation, and, furthermore, that the state itself, rather than its individual citizens, sets the authoritative interpretation of these core commitments.

To see this, consider the following example:[21] During the Cold War the United States adopted the Domino Theory as the guiding principle of its foreign policy in Southeast Asia and South America. According to the Domino Theory, the rise of a Communist government in one country will lead to Communist takeovers in its neighboring states, and should therefore be preempted, even by the use of force. This theory led to a highly aggressive foreign policy, including American military interventions in Korea and Vietnam. Many American citizens disagreed with the rationale for these military interventions and protested against them. Indeed, many of them believed that these interventions were not a plausible interpretation of the US's basic commitment to, say, the protection of human rights and democratic governance worldwide. And yet it remains the case that it was in the US state apparatus's authority to decide how to interpret core US values and commitments. Of course, the US, like many other states, has procedures in place that aspire to ensure its decision-making process will yield only reasonable interpretations of its core values, and its legislative and judiciary branches have important roles to play in that regard. But it remains the case that the answer to the question of how the US should conduct its foreign affairs was settled by the state itself, and not by its citizens.

---

[21] I thank Christian Barry for the example and for pressing me to explore this point.

Not only that, the fact that the state has the authority to set its own goals, and to revise them, is common knowledge among its citizenry. Indeed, notice that the claim that states execute policies its citizens may deeply disagree with is integral to the very idea of political authority. As Leslie Green and others have pointed out, to have authority is to generate content-independent commands, namely commands that are obeyed not because their subject agrees with their content, but because they were issued by an authoritative agent.[22] Citizens who participate in the state are contributing to the maintenance of a group agent that—by its very definition—has the power to issue commands they may disagree with. Being part of a corporate body that has this power is just what being a citizen is. The protesting citizen sees herself as contributing to the maintenance of the state as an authoritative agent who may execute policies that she might disagree with. She therefore remains the inclusive author of her state's policies, as long as she does not reject her participation in the state, despite her knowledge of its character as an authoritative agent.

A similar conclusion applies to many policies that citizens are unaware of. After all, it is common knowledge in complex corporate group agents that, given the division of labor within them, not all group members need to be aware of all group-level decisions in order to take part in them. An employee in an investment bank can sensibly ask her colleagues, "Did we invest in those shares?" The employee is assuming her participation in a specific investment decision, even though she was unaware of it at the time it was made. Her inclusive authorship of that decision flows from her sense of herself as a participant in the business corporation at a more basic level—playing her role in contributing to its capacity to make such decisions, while being aware that the terms of her membership do

---

[22] Thomas Christiano, *The Constitution of Equality: Democratic Authority and Its Limits* (Oxford: Oxford University Press, 2008); Leslie Green, *The Authority of the State* (Oxford: Oxford University Press, 1990), 37–42. Cf. Joseph Raz, *The Authority of Law: Essays on Law and Morality* (Oxford: Clarendon Press, 1979), chapter 12.

not require her knowledge of all decisions made by the organization at any point in time. The same logic applies to citizens who
learn about policies of which they are unaware. Like the bank employee, it would make sense for such a citizen to utter statements
such as "I had no idea we declared war on Iraq!"

At this point I am in partial disagreement with Robert Jubb's
analysis of the scope of citizens' responsibility for state wrongdoing. Jubb, whose account of citizens' responsibility for their
state's actions is also grounded in Kutz's model of collective action, discusses the case of Dame Shirley Porter, whose notorious
gerrymandering policies in Westminster Council in the 1980s were
deemed by the British court as willful misconduct. He argues that
in this case, "citizens as such have no involvement at all in the wrong
in question *because of its secrecy*."[23] But I disagree. In my view, secret
state policies do not necessarily fall outside the scope of inclusive
authorship. After all, it is common knowledge—even in democratic
states—that some state policies are kept hidden from the public.
Indeed, while, generally speaking, most political theorists point to
a tension between secrecy and democratic accountability, it is also
commonly acknowledged that secrecy can be necessary in order
for the democratic state to be able to execute many of its roles.[24] In
fact, some level of secrecy can be an effective tool of collectivizing
the state's reason. As Dorota Mokrosinska points out, secrecy can
allow for more consistent reason formation at the state level by
"cutting it off from the external environment—lobby groups, the
media, and citizens at large—and thereby minimize the risk of

---

[23] Robert Jubb, "Participation in and Responsibility for the State," *Social Theory and
Practice* 40, no. 1 (2014): 15 (emphasis added).
[24] Dennis F. Thompson, "Democratic Secrecy," *Political Science Quarterly* 114, no. 2
(1999): 182. On the positive link between secrecy and effective policymaking, see David
E. Pozen, "Deep Secrecy," *Stanford Law Review* 62 (2009): 257–339; Amy Gutmann and
Dennis F. Thompson, *Democracy and Disagreement* (Cambridge, MA: Belknap Press of
Harvard University Press, 1996), chapter 3. As these authors note, the positive correlation is restricted in important ways. Too much secrecy can lead to ineffective and cor-
rupt policymaking.

external manipulation and interference."[25] As she continues to argue, the very idea of authority as generating content-independent commands implies that, in the same way that the state's authority does not depend on its citizens agreeing with the content of command, it does not require that citizens to be aware of the content of the state's policies.[26] Put differently, it is part of the very nature of the state as an authoritative corporate agent that it generates policies that citizens will not necessarily be aware of.

So does this account suggest that British citizens were involved in the secret policies of Dame Porter? I agree with Jubb that the answer to this question is negative, but I don't think the reason for this is that Porter acted in secrecy. Rather, the problem in Porter's case was that she acted *ultra vires*. As the British court ruled, she violated her role obligations as a city councilor and enacted policies that were illegal. She was a rogue official. For that reason, her actions were not the actions of the British state, and also not attributable to its citizenry.

However, while in the Porter case it is not the secrecy of her actions that rendered them outside the scope of British citizens' inclusive authorship, I accept that secrecy can undermine inclusive authorship. I have in mind here, specifically, the problem of "deep secrets." Deep secrets are commonly defined as state policies or processes, "the very existence of which is hidden from the public."[27] Deep secrets are different in this regard from "shallow

---

[25] Dorota Mokrosinska, "Why States Have No Right to Privacy, but May Be Entitled to Secrecy: A Non-consequentialist Defense of State Secrecy," *Critical Review of International Social and Political Philosophy* 23, no. 4 (2020): 415–444. Note that Mokrosinska refers here to *privacy* rather than secrecy. She rejects the idea that the state has the right to privacy, and instead defends the claim that it may be entitled to secrecy. But she accepts that as part of the substantive justification for secrecy, the state may argue that it requires it in order to maintain its collective rationality and ability to act. I thank Dorota Mokrosinska for several illuminating conversations on this point.

[26] Mokrosinska, "Why States Have No Right to Privacy"; Dorota Mokrosinska, "The People's Right to Know and State Secrecy," *Canadian Journal of Law & Jurisprudence* 31, no. 1 (2018): 87–106. Of course, in order for the command to be action-guiding, its subject needs to be aware of its content, but as Mokrosinska points out, not all state policies are action-guiding for their citizens in this sense.

[27] Gutmann and Thompson, *Democracy and Disagreement*, 121.

state secrets." In the case of shallow secrets, citizens "know that they don't know"—they know that there is a secret policy, but they do not know what the content of that policy is. Shallow secrets, then, have a "second order publicity": The fact that they are a secret, and the process by which they are designated as secret, is known to the public.[28] Deep secrets have neither first- nor second-order publicity.

While, as I argued above, the presence of shallow secrets is common knowledge and, indeed, part and parcel of the state's functioning as a corporate moral agent, deep secrets present a serious challenge to the idea of inclusive authorship in the state. Two problems arise here. The first is that the deeper its secrecy is, the less clear it is that the policy is indeed enacted on behalf of the state rather than *ultra vires*. After all, states (and especially the democratic state) have formal processes in place for setting out their policies, and state officials are required to follow these processes. When some state official enacts a policy that is not authorized or scrutinized through the usual channels, and that very few officials know about, one may wonder whether this policy is indeed attributable to the state itself. Consider again the case of Porter. On one presentation, her actions were a very deep secret. On another presentation (and the one favored by the British court), the secret was so deep it was no longer a state policy as such.[29]

The second problem with deep secrets is that, as David Pozen observes, they very quickly shade into misinformation and deception.[30] After all, in order to protect a deep secret, the state may need to deny its existence and/or its contents to the citizenry, and to misrepresent or misinform those officials whose role it is to scrutinize

---

[28] Thompson, "Democratic Secrecy," 185.

[29] As we saw in chapter 2, it is not the case that if a state official acts outside the formal requirements of her role she is not acting on behalf of the state. Informal culture and ethos and implicit instructions play an important role in filling the information gaps about how officials should execute their roles. But the deeper the secret is, the more likely it is that an official will have crossed the line and is no longer acting on behalf of the state.

[30] Pozen, "Deep Secrecy," 270.

state policies about what is actually going on. State deception and misinformation are different from shallow secrets: Rather than acknowledging in the open that citizens are barred from information about a specific policy, the state presents to them a false picture of itself. It publicly defines its goals in one way (e.g., it ratifies the Geneva Convention), giving them reason to believe that they are participating in a collective project that is committed to those goals, but then acts in direct violation of these goals, without the citizens being aware of that fact (e.g., torturing terror suspects).

Deep secrets that turn to deception and misinformation render the idea of *genuine* participation in the state unintelligible. In the case of shallow secrets, citizens are aware that the details of a policy are held from them, and are aware of the procedures by which the decision to exclude the information from them has been reached. Their genuine participation is conducted in light of this information. In the case of deep secrets, deception, and misinformation, citizens are not aware of the gap between what the state says it does and what it actually does. As Kutz notes in his analysis of the problem of deep secrets, this level of secrecy undermines each citizen's capacity to assess their state: "I cannot thereby understand myself either as in harmony or in dissonance with my polity. . . . [P]olitically speaking [a deep secret] severs me from membership in my state."[31]

To conclude, I have argued in this section that, ordinarily, when citizens orient their participatory intentions around the idea of the state itself as an authoritative agent with legal and political authority, they are the inclusive authors of a wide range of its policies, including policies they disagree with or an unaware of. However, if the state misinforms or misrepresents the true nature of its activities, citizens' genuine participation in their state is undermined, and we can no longer assume they accept their role in the state as it

---

[31] Christopher Kutz, "Secret Law and the Value of Publicity," *Ratio Juris* 22, no. 2 (2009): 214.

is, rather than as they perceive it. In chapter 4 I will examine how these general observations apply to different states in the real world, in light of their regime type.

3.4 Nonproportional Distribution in the State

We can now go back to the question of the distribution of liability in the state. My analysis so far leads to the conclusion that if a state's citizens are its intentional participants, then the state can be justified in resorting to a nonproportional distribution of its remedial liabilities with regard to a very wide range of its policies. Recall that, as I argued in chapter 2, when people act together they *ipso facto* accept that what they do together will no longer be under their exclusive control, that the consequences of their collective action may not be compatible with what they personally hoped or planned would happen, and that they may be called upon to remedy the bad outcomes of their joint venture. This idea also applies to the citizens who intend to contribute to the maintenance of their state as a corporate agent, and who may be required to accept a share of the burdens that result from their state's policies that they too are the inclusive authors of, including policies they protested against or were unaware of.

At this point it is worth emphasizing again that my claim is not that the state should necessarily deploy a nonproportional distribution of its remedial responsibilities among the citizenry. As we saw in chapter 1, there are strong considerations in favor of a distribution that does track group members' blameworthy contributions. In light of these considerations, the state may well be justified in imposing a higher burden on those individuals who made clear and tangible blameworthy contributions to the wrongdoing (such as, perhaps, some policymakers).[32] But I argued that in real-world

---

[32] Assuming, as we saw in chapter 1, that such distribution will not have side effects with detrimental consequences.

scenarios a fuller proportional distribution is likely to face formidable challenges. In the first instance, it faces feasibility challenges, in the sense that it is likely to lead to responsibility shortfalls, which—if not met—will leave the burden with the victims of the state wrongdoing. In such fairly common scenarios, it is permissible to demand that all those citizens who intentionally participate in the state contribute to the collective effort, regardless of their personal level of blame. This demand is reasonably justified, given that these citizens have formed the intention to participate in the state, which entailed the possibility of incurring some level of unexpected burdens if things go badly wrong.

Furthermore, the other challenge that a proportional distribution faces is that of the direct and indirect costs of its implementation. Imagine that the state could generate sufficient compensation to the victims through proportional distribution, but that the process of doing so will be very costly, and will divert resources needed for other important public tasks. In such scenarios, too, the state may permissibly refuse to implement a blame-tracking process of distribution. In justifying its refusal, the state can plausibly argue that the moral price of deserting proportional distribution is not very high—given that its citizens have intentionally participated in it and are the inclusive authors of its wrongdoings. When balanced against the costs of diverting resources from its other task responsibilities, it becomes apparent that the goal of achieving proportional distribution may simply not be worth the price, if those who will benefit from it are intentional citizens.

That said, although the state may refuse to engage in a fully proportional distribution in light of these considerations, it does not follow that it may revert to any pattern of nonproportional distribution. Rather, the pattern of distribution it opts for ought to be a reasonably equitable one. For example, it would be unreasonable for the state to target a specific group within the state on an arbitrary basis (say, a racial minority), even if the citizens who belong to this group are intentional participants in their state.[33] Distributing the burden unequally and on some arbitrary basis would be an unnecessary violation of distributive fairness within the political community, and should be rejected for that reason.[34]

I have argued so far that intentional citizenship is sufficient to justify a shift to a nonproportional distribution of the state's remedial responsibilities, even if citizens disagreed with or were unaware of their state's wrongdoings. At this point one might raise the following objection: As we saw in chapter 2, typically the participants in any collective endeavor will take part in it to varying degrees. In the specific case of states, for example, some group members—e.g., some office holders—will be more centrally located in terms of their contributions to the state apparatus, their knowledge of its policies, and the extent to which they endorse them. Put differently, while all citizens are the inclusive authors of their state's policies, some have a greater degree of authorship over these policies than others. If what grounds citizens' liability for their state's policies is their inclusive authorship, shouldn't the distribution of liability in the state track their degrees of participation in the state?[35]

In considering this challenge, we might wonder what the distribution that merely tracks degrees of participation in the state may look like, in pragmatic terms. One model that seems to follow this idea, and that has been proposed elsewhere, suggests that the state should impose a higher proportion of the burdens on government officials, given the more central role they play in the state. On this model the portion of the burden that each government official can be expected to share will be adjusted in light of her position within

[33] As we will see in the next chapter, as a matter of practice it is unlikely that oppressed minorities will be intentional participants in their state.

[34] In principle, if the state can show that there is no other feasible way for collecting the necessary resources than imposing the costs on a specific group within the state, then members of that group, who are intentional participants in their state, ought to accept that share of the burden. But as a matter of practice it is hard to see how this will ever be the case.

[35] I thank Christian Barry for raising this objection.

the administration—which tracks her level of participation in it. Those with more central roles have more control over the group's decision-making process and its execution of its policies, and therefore are more central participants in its policies and ought to bear a greater share of the burden.[36]

One advantage of this participation-tracking model is that it is not vulnerable to the feasibility objection I mentioned earlier. For here it is not the case that ordinary citizens will be "off the hook," as they are likely to be in the blame-tracking model. Ordinary citizens will still be required to contribute to the compensation pot, given that they too are intentionally participating in the state in some sense. But the more marginal one's role is, the less one should contribute.

However, I think there are reasons to reject a model that places higher burdens on government officials in light of their role in the state. First, I am not persuaded that being a government official implies that one has greater a degree of authorship over the state's policies. Some government officials play as marginal a role in the state apparatus as that of the ordinary citizen. For example, in what sense is a post office clerk more of an inclusive author of the state's foreign policy decisions than the ordinary citizen? Second, some citizens do not have an official role in the state and yet play a highly influential role in its central decision-making. These citizens have a higher degree of inclusive authorship over the state's policies, and a participation-tracking distribution should track that fact. These complications suggest that the process of determining levels of inclusive authorship in the state is likely to be as complex and as costly as a blame-tracking distribution.

Furthermore, there is also a more principled objection to the idea that government officials in particular should bear a higher

---

[36] A proposal along these lines is offered by Holly Lawford-Smith, though she focuses on the distribution of state punishment rather than compensatory duties (Lawford-Smith, *Not in Their Name*, 151–58). I will address the question of the distribution of punishment in chapter 6.

share of the burden of the state's remedial liability. I have in mind here specifically those government officials who are not *culpable* for their contributions to the wrongful policies, but who are expected, on the participation-based model, to bear a larger share of the burden given their mere participation in the state apparatus.[37] These government officials' contributions to the state's decision-making processes and to the execution of its policies may be quite central, but they are not blameworthy for them. For example, they may have done all in their power to prevent the state wrongdoing. Such government officials, I believe, fall within the scope of Daniel Viehoff's defense of government officials' "right to err," and for that reason should not be expected to take a higher share of the state's remedial obligations.[38] As Viehoff explains, government officials (e.g., judges, legislators, policymakers, police officers) sometimes commit wrongful violations of others' rights due to errors in judgment. A judge might deliver the wrong verdict. A legislator may support a law that leads to an unfair distribution of burdens on the population. Viehoff argues that government officials have a right to commit such mistakes if they are acting in good faith. By that he means that the official is acting in the interests of the citizens, and is guided only by reasons that pertain to the citizens' interests. Consider, for example, a police officer who arrests citizen A because she has good grounds to believe that A committed a crime. As a matter of fact, A did not commit the crime, so the arrest is wrongful. And yet, Viehoff argues, the police officer has acted legitimately, or within her rights, if she arrested A in good faith: she followed the right procedures and acted reasonably in light of the information she had, and she was guided only by considerations that pertain to the citizens' interest (including A's) in the maintenance of law and order in the state. When this is the case, Viehoff

---

[37] As I have already suggested, there is a good case to be made for imposing higher burdens on blameworthy members.

[38] Daniel Viehoff, "Legitimacy as a Right to Err," in *Political Legitimacy*, ed. Jack Knight and Melissa Schwartzberg, 174–200. (New York: New York University Press, 2019).

argues, the officer is insulated from compensatory demands from A for having unjustly arrested her. This is not to deny that citizens like A may be entitled to compensation from the state as a whole for the good faith mistakes its officials make. But if compensation is due, it should not be taken from the officials who committed the mistake in particular. Rather, it should be distributed among the population at large. Given that a state official acts blamelessly and on behalf of all citizens, it is unfair that she should be particularly burdened when a reasonable mistake was made in good faith.[39]

Viehoff's defense of officials who committed a wrongdoing in good faith can be extended to government officials who blamelessly contribute to state wrongdoings. As we saw, these officials contribute to the maintenance of the state, and are the inclusive authors of all its policies, but they do so in "good faith." They follow the right procedures, are guided by the interests of the population on whose behalf they act, and act reasonably in light of the set of considerations that is relevant to these interests. Yet despite all this, it turns out that their actions have contributed to state wrongdoing. As in the case of the wrongdoing police officer, here too their contribution to the wrongdoing is more direct and central than that of many ordinary citizens. But nevertheless, given that they acted on behalf of the citizenry, they are insulated from the demand that they accept a larger share of the burden. Like all citizens, they intentionally participate in the state, and in doing so they take a risk that they will be encumbered with remedial obligations when the state ends up doing wrong, but that they have an official role in the state should not be held against them when that burden is distributed.

---

[39] Notice that Viehoff seems to adopt a stronger position. He argues at points that a victim of good-faith mistakes has no straightforward claims of compensation against the officer or against the political community on behalf of which the officer acts (Viehoff, "Legitimacy as the Right to Err," 179.) But this strikes me as implausible. Consider again the case of A's unjust arrest. The officer who arrested A acted on behalf of the political community as a whole. All citizens, and not just A, benefit from the officer's maintenance of law and order in the state. It is therefore unreasonable to expect A alone to bear the burdens of the officer's mistake. The burden should be distributed among all those who benefit from law and order, and on whose behalf the officer acts.

Let's conclude. I have developed in this chapter the idea, present in Michael Walzer's words, that "citizenship is a common destiny," and that membership in the state entails liability for its actions. In cashing out this idea we must be careful not to stray too far from the guiding intuitions of normative individualism, which suggest that people ought not be made to suffer due to ascriptive characteristics, such as their place of birth or the groups into which they were born. My account of the distribution of liability shares with Walzer the core intuition that people are liable for the outcomes that flow from what they do together, and that citizenship is a thing that we do together. In that sense, indeed, citizenship is a common destiny. But I have also set important limits on the scope of this claim. In the first instance, I have argued that the distribution of liability for state wrongdoing ought not to desert the idea of blame-tracking and of imposing higher burdens on those state members who are at fault. Where such distribution is feasible and not overly costly, it ought to be pursued. Put differently, my claim is that intentional participation in the state entails being part of the group that may be "called upon" when necessary if resources other than those that the proportional distribution model can supply are needed. Second, I argued that all those who are in the group that may be called upon in this sense are genuine participants in the activities of the state, rather than forced ones.

This last observation raises an important objection. My model aims to offer guidance to states in the real world, but how common is genuine intentional participation in those states? Is it not the case that the typical citizen—given her nonvoluntary participation in the state—is not genuinely taking part in state activities? In the next chapter I turn to examine this challenge, and gauge the extent of intentional participation in the real world.

4

Intentional Citizenship and Regime Types

In the previous chapters I developed the theoretical model of intentional citizenship. I defined intentional citizens as individuals who intentionally contribute to the maintenance of their state as a corporate agent, and who accept their citizenship status: they can leave their state without incurring unreasonable costs, or they would have stayed in their state even if the costs of leaving were not unreasonable. As we saw in the previous chapters, being a member of the state in this sense carries with it an important normative implication: intentional citizens may be expected to accept a nonproportional distribution of their state's remedial obligations for its wrongdoings.

So far, my discussion of intentional citizenship was theoretical. I suggested that the state is the type of corporate agent in which genuine intentional participation is possible, but I have not demonstrated this claim for states as we know them. Are citizens of real-world states their intentional citizens?

In answering this question, one might point out that the vast majority of people in the world do indeed live their whole lives in the countries in which they were born and in which they have been citizens from birth. Does it follow that they accept their citizenship status? Not necessarily. After all, as we all know, the option of emigration is not readily available to many people, given that most states are very reluctant to open their borders to new members.

But some countries do open their borders for outsiders to settle. Some welcome migrants from a certain socioeconomic or cultural

Responsible Citizens, Irresponsible States. Avia Pasternak, Oxford University Press. © Oxford University Press 2021. DOI: 10.1093/oso/9780197541036.003.0005

background (e.g., the Canadian Comprehensive Ranking system, which gives priority to skilled workers, or the Israeli Law of Return, which grants the right of citizenship to all Jews). Others have relaxed immigration restrictions for people of certain countries of origin (e.g., the right to free movement within the European Union). Indeed, in all likelihood, we all know at least one person who has relocated to a new country. Does it follow from this observation that all those citizens could in principle find another country to live in, but who choose not to emigrate, are intentional participants in their current state? This question points to a thorny challenge: even if the option of relocating to a new country may be formally open to some people in the world, it typically involves leaving behind one's family, friends, language, culture, and familiar landscapes. Given these costs, is the option of emigration viable in any meaningful sense?

This is a difficult question. it is commonly agreed that if emigration involves unreasonable costs it is not a viable option, but the literature on coercion in general, and on the ethics of migration in particular, does not provide a clear standard for what counts as an unreasonable cost in this context.[1] A related discussion within the literature on migration concerns the circumstances under which people have a *right* to migrate. David Miller, for example, has suggested that people have the right to migrate only if they do not have a chance to live a "minimally decent life" in their home country.[2] Perhaps we could argue, in a similar way, that if a person faces a situation where, were she to move to a new country, her chances of being able to live even a minimally decent life would be

---

[1] See, e.g., Laura Valentini, "Correction and (Global) Justice," *American Political Science Review* 105, no. 1 (2011): 205–20; Alan Wertheimer, *Coercion* (Princeton: Princeton University Press, 1987), 35.

[2] What a "minimally decent life" precisely means is open to interpretation. Miller suggests it means access to basic social and goods so that one "would not feel degraded, socially excluded, worthless, etc." (Miller, *National Responsibility*, 181).

threatened or undermined, that person is barred from leaving her country of birth.

But I believe that this account of a freely made choice to stay leads in one's country is counterintuitive.[3] Consider a scenario where a citizen can emigrate to a new country, but she will have to give up her current flourishing life, which involves, say, a fulfilling and rewarding job, a rich network of family and friends, and a familiar public culture, and replace it with a minimally decent life in a new country, which only gives her some job security and access to basic social goods. Most of us would agree that the price of emigration for this person is unreasonable. People have legitimate expectations to be able to access more than just the bare necessities, and when one has already created a flourishing life for herself, giving it up will be a very high price to pay. A more palatable standard for the reasonable costs of emigration, then, which is in line with common intuitions, is that the emigration will not involve a serious decline in one's level of well-being. Accordingly, when one emigrates, one must be reasonably confident that the new country will provide the opportunity to secure a level of well-being that is more or less equivalent to the one she leaves behind. Anything less than that is an unacceptable cost, which people cannot be reasonably expected to incur.

While this standard is fairly restrictive, it remains the case that some people in the world comply with it. After all, in all countries there are people who could choose to live in another country without a serious threat to their overall level of well-being (perhaps this applies in particular to the wealthier individuals in most societies). But for most people in most states, emigration is not a viable option, because there is no other country that would welcome

---

[3] Many think it is too strict as an account of the right to migrate as well. See, for example, Sarah Fine, "Refugees, Safety and a Decent Human Life" *Proceedings of the Aristotelian Society* 119, no. 1 (2019): 25–52; Kieran Oberman "Immigration as a Human Right" in S. Fine and L. Ypi (eds) *Migration in Political Theory: The Ethics of Movement and Membership*, (Oxford, Oxford University Press), 41.

them, or because emigration poses a serious compromise to their well-being, including their access to employment, to a familiar culture, to family, and to friendships.

It follows from all this that most people in the world cannot be characterized as intentional citizens in the sense that they could leave their country if they wanted to. But what about the second sense of "acceptance"? A person can be an intentional member of a group even if she cannot *de facto* leave it, as long as she is not deeply alienated from her membership and views it as forced on her against her will. Is it the case that the citizens who cannot *de facto* leave their country view their membership in it as forced on them against their will?

This is an empirical question, which pertains to people's internal and subjective attitudes with regard to their country and their citizenship status. In order to answer it, then, we need to turn to empirical data about people's attitudes. In Section 4.1 of this chapter I turn to this task. I examine existing cross-national attitude surveys, which ask participants about their levels of attachment to their country. I first argue that such surveys can be used to gauge citizens' acceptance of their citizenship status and to indicate how prevalent intentional citizenship is in real-world states. I then analyze specific questions from these surveys. This analysis produces encouraging results suggesting that most people in many countries do seem to be intentional citizens in their states.

But there are two important limitations to this conclusion, which I discuss in the rest of the chapter. First, the attitude surveys suggest that in many countries there are some parts of the population whose level of identification with their country is low. In Section 4.2, I will identify two such groups and suggest that they cannot plausibly be categorized as intentional citizens. To recall, the implication is that the justification of nonproportional distribution I developed in chapter 3 does not apply to these citizens. In chapter 5,

I will examine whether there are alternative reasons to hold these citizens liable on a nonproportional basis.

The second limitation concerns the attitudes of citizens in nondemocratic states, whose political and civil liberties are restricted. Here, the answers people give in attitude surveys are less reliable, and even if they express very positive attitudes about their state and their membership in it, we have good reasons to question their authenticity. Section 4.3 turns to deal with this problem. Drawing on literature from comparative studies of regime types, I distinguish between different types of nondemocratic states, and then develop criteria for gauging the extent of intentional citizenship in them. I conclude that intentional citizenship is possible, but unlikely to be widespread, in nondemocratic states.

4.1 Testing for Intentional Citizenship

Intentional citizens are marked by certain internal attitudes they have toward their citizenship status. So just how prevalent are such attitudes? In order to answer this question, I turn to data on people's reported attitudes, as it is regularly collected in cross-national attitude surveys. These surveys do not directly track the internal dispositions that characterize intentional citizenship. However, they do contain related questions on people's attitudes to their national identity and state membership. In what follows I will first suggest that the factors that these questions aim to track have a close enough conceptual affinity with the constituent elements of intentional citizenship, and that we can therefore use these questions to gauge the prevalence of attitudes of acceptance in real-world states. I will then proceed to analyze the survey questions I find most relevant to the question at hand.

Social Identity and Intentional Citizenship

Cross-national surveys commonly try to gauge people's sense of national identity, using a variety of fairly standard questions. One useful framework for analyzing these questions and how they decipher the idea of national identity revolves around the notion of social identity.[4] As Henry Tajfel's influential model suggests, our social (or group) identities are made of three interdependent components.[5] First, a *cognitive* component, which concerns a person's awareness of the group she belongs to. Second, an *emotional* component, which concerns a person's sense and level of attachment to her group. Finally, an *evaluative* component, which concerns how good or bad a person perceives her group to be. The survey questions we typically find in attitude surveys about people's sense of national identity track these three components.[6]

The social identity model is not identical to intentional participation in a group. However, as I now turn to show, there are important parallels between these two models. Given these parallels, those survey questions that track the various components of national identity can also be used to get a grasp of the extent of intentional citizenship in real-world states.

The first component of social identity is cognitive, and requires awareness of one's group. This component corresponds to the requirement that intentional citizens recognize themselves as group members who contribute to their state's goals and policies.

[4] Elizabeth Theiss-Morse, *Who Counts as an American?: The Boundaries of National Identity* (Cambridge: Cambridge University Press, 2009), 8.

[5] Henri Tajfel, *Differentiation between Social Groups: Studies in the Social Psychology of Intergroup Relations* (London: Academic Press, 1978). For a general review of Tajfel's model, influence, and more recent developments, see Stephen Reicher, Russell Spears, and S. Alexander Haslam, "The Social Identity Approach in Social Psychology," in *The SAGE Handbook of Identities*, ed. Mararet Wetherell and Chandra Talpade Mohanty (London: SAGE, 2010): 45–62.

[6] Cf. Theiss-Morse, *Who Counts as an American?* For a critical evaluation of national identity surveys that challenges their conceptual framework, see Sundas Ali and Anthony Heath, *Future Identities: Changing Identities in the UK—The Next 10 Years* (London: Government Office for Science, 2013).

Cognitive awareness is not identical to participatory intentions. One can recognize oneself as a member of a group in a way that does not involve an intention to take part in a group act. For example, a person can self-identify as a woman without intending to act with other women in the service of some common goal. But the conceptual affinity between cognitive awareness and participatory intentions is closer when one is part of a group agent (rather than part of an unstructured group like womankind).As we saw in the previous chapters, group agents are by definition sites of collective action that revolve around the group's decision-making procedure and internal authority structure: the former defines the group's goals and the latter allocates different roles in the service of these goals, some more central than others. It follows that in identifying oneself as a member of a group agent, one, *ipso facto*, recognizes that one has a role to play in one's group. This sense of recognition is equivalent to Kutz's definition of participatory intentions, which involves at the minimum a deliberative awareness of the instrumental role one plays in bringing about a collective end.

A possible objection at this point is that the typical citizen does not go about obeying the laws of her country, or paying her taxes, while being conscious of the fact that these routines contribute to the operation of the state. However, it is not the case that continuous awareness is required in order to be intentionally participating in the state. Michael Billig's observations about "the banality of nationalism" are useful here. As Billig points out, citizens' sense of belonging to their nation-state is typically "manifested in the banality of everyday life"—in the flag at the corner of the post office, in the printed images on money bills, in the way newspapers report the news. And yet the "banality" of these manifestations does not undermine the importance of nationalism as a powerful social factor.[7] Participation in the state has a similar quality to it. Rather than being present in their active consciousness, citizens' sense

---

[7] Michael Billig, *Banal Nationalism* (London: SAGE, 1995), 42–46.

of belonging to and acting in the state plays a background role in directing a relevant set of their routine actions, as these actions are performed out of habit rather than reflective awareness. None of this implies, however, that their membership in the state does not offer an explanatory role for their behavior. Were they asked to explain their actions, they would refer to it (e.g., "I pay my income tax because this is the law of my state").

Most cross-national attitude surveys that examine people's national identities typically contain questions that could be interpreted as capturing respondents' bare recognition of membership in their state (e.g., "Are you a citizen of country X"?). Unsurprisingly, the vast majority of people report they are aware of their citizenship status. I think we can assume that when people recognize their citizenship status they are also aware of its implications, in terms of the roles and obligations they have as citizens. In what follows, I'll put these aside, and simply assume that most of us are aware of which state(s) we belong to and participate in.[8]

The second component of social identity is *affinitive* and refers to people's sense of attachment to their group—how closely they feel related to it, or to what extent they feel being part of the group is constitutive of their personal identity. The affinitive dimension lies "at the heart of social identity," and several typical cross-national survey questions attempt to gauge it.[9] This affinitive dimension is also closely related to *acceptance*. When a person feels closely *attached* to a group she also *accepts* her membership in it. After all, if her membership is important to her and constitutive of her identity, it follows that she does not perceive it as external to her, as forced upon her, or as something she would like to give up if she had the option to. This does not mean that acceptance and attachment amount

---

[8] This assumption is supported by empirical studies that show that people generally tend to obey the laws of their state. See discussion and analysis in Tom R. Tyler, *Why People Obey the Law* (Princeton: Princeton University Press, 2006), chapter 3. The study focuses on citizens in democratic states.

[9] Theiss-Morse, *Who Counts as an American?*, 3.

to the same thing. In fact, people can accept their membership in a group without being attached to it. Consider, for example, the typical shareholder who invests money in various business enterprises. This person is an intentional participant in the businesses she has invested in—she intentionally contributes resources to the business with the hope of making a profit.[10] But, typically, investors' attitude to their financial investments are entirely instrumental and do not involve even a weak sense of attachment. That being so, it is also the case that if people do report a high sense of attachment to their national membership, we can assume that they, *ipso facto*, also accept it. Typically, survey questions that capture this sense in existing attitude surveys include questions such as: "How attached do you feel to Germany?" (Eurobarometer, 2014); "How strongly do you agree with the statement 'I see myself as part of the United States'?" (World Values Survey, Wave 5); or "How close do you feel to Britain?" (International Social Survey Programme, 1995).

Finally, Tajfel's original model contained a third dimension, which concerns people's *normative* evaluation of their group. Attitude surveys on national identity capture this dimension with questions such as "How strongly do you agree with the statement 'There are some things about Britain today that make me feel ashamed of Britain'?" (International Social Survey Programme, 1995) or "How proud are you to be a French Citizen?" (European Value Study 2010). However, this dimension is less relevant for my conception of intentional citizenship, which does not include an evaluative assessment of one's membership in the group. This is not to deny that there can be a dependency between the affinitive and evaluative components of social identity. After all, people naturally seek to develop a positive evaluation of their group, and when they perceive their group in negative terms, their attachment to it, as well as their acceptance of it, will likely diminish over time.

---

[10] For discussion, see Ian B. Lee, "Corporate Criminal Responsiblity as Team Member Responsibility," *Oxford Journal of Legal Studies* 31, no. 4 (2011): 755–81.

However, as David Miller and Sundas Ali point out in their analysis of national identity attitude surveys, we should not draw too strong a link between a positive evaluation of a group and an attachment to the group. For it is precisely those people who feel more attached to their country who might also express a higher sense of shame and disapproval when it acts wrongly in their view. This stronger sense of shame is generated from their stronger sense of belonging to their group and their identification with it.[11] Furthermore, as I argued in chapter 3, membership in the state involves the recognition that one is part of a group agent, which may well make policy decisions one disagrees with. Citizens who recognize this fact will pass criticism of their state's decision while at the same time continuing to accept their role in maintaining the corporate authority of the state. What matters for intentional citizenship is not how proud citizens are of their state, but whether they continue to see themselves as attached to it (even if they disagree with it). In what follows I will therefore focus on survey questions that track affinitive rather than evaluative attitudes.

Intentional Citizenship in Attitude Surveys

I now turn to examine some of the existing data on people's affinitive attitudes to their national identity. Here I use various cross-national surveys that are conducted on a regular basis (sampling random years or waves from each one).

I'll start with the Eurobarometer, which surveys attitudes in European countries each year. The relevant question from this survey, appearing in questionnaires across several years, concerns participants' degree of attachment to their country, ranging from

---

[11] David Miller and Sundas Ali, "Testing the National Identity Argument," *European Political Science Review* 6, no. 2 (2014): 245. Cf. Theiss-Morse, *Who Counts as an American?*, 25.

"very attached" to "fairly attached," "not very attached," and "not at all attached." In the data collected in 2005, for example, in 27 countries over 90% of respondents said they are very attached or fairly attached to their country. In the remaining 2 countries the number averaged 80%. In 2014, in 24 countries over 90% of respondents said they are very attached or fairly attached to their country. In the remaining 9 countries the numbers average around 84%.[12] If we also include respondents who say they are "not very attached" (which means some level of attachment, albeit a weak one), and exclude only those who say "not attached at all," the average is 98% for all 33 countries (the lowest being Spain, with 93%) (for the data, see Appendix).

The World Values Survey also includes a question about participants' attachments. Here respondents are asked how strongly they agree with statements such as: "I see myself as a citizen of Canada as a whole," "I see myself as part of the United States," or "I see myself part of the French nation."[13] Combining the answers to this question for Waves 5 (2005–9) and 6 (2010–12) gives a wide selection of countries around the world. In 59 out of 75 countries surveyed in both waves, over 90% of respondents "strongly agreed" or "agreed" with the statement. In the remaining 14 the average is 86.5%, with the lowest being 77% in Bahrain (Wave 6). If we look only at democratic countries defined as "free" by Freedom House, in 26 out of 33 countries, 90% strongly agree/agree with the statement, and in the rest the average is 86.6% (see Appendix for the results).

The International Social Survey Programme (ISSP) National Identity Survey also included a question on how "close" people feel to their country. In surveys conducted in 1995, in 20 out of the 24 democratic countries more than 80% of respondents reported

---

[12] I present here the numbers for two years chosen at random.
[13] Here the same question appears in slightly different variations in different countries. I will comment on this variation later in the chapter.

themselves to be "very close" or "close" to their country, and in all countries extremely low percentages report themselves as being "not close at all." In the 2003 questionnaire, in 31 out of 35 countries, more than 80% described themselves as "very close" or "close" to their country, and in all countries extremely low percentages reported themselves as being "not close at all."[14]

Finally, the Afrobarometer also includes a question about national identity, this time contrasted with ethnic identity. Respondents are asked to agree with the following statements: "I feel only [R's Country]"; "I feel more [R's country] than [R's ethnic group]"; "I feel equally [R's country] and [R's ethnic group]"; "I feel more [R's ethnic group] than [R's country]"; "I feel only [R's ethnic group]." In 22 out of 28 countries, more than 85% of respondents stated that they are either more or equally attached to their country and to their ethnic group. In the remaining 6 countries, the average was 84% (the lowest being Nigeria with 81%). In the 10 democratic countries defined as "free" by Freedom House, an average of 89% showed some attachment to their country (the lowest being Cape Verde with 83%). (See Appendix for the results).

In conclusion, the data collected in these various surveys suggests that in most countries, and certainly in most democratic countries, large majorities of the population report that they have a fairly strong attachment to their country. As I argued earlier, people who have a strong sense of attachment to their country also accept their membership in it. They are not alienated from their citizenship, nor do they resist their *de facto* participation in their state. Being a citizen is part of their own identity and of how they define themselves.[15] Such people, I argue, are intentional citizens of their

---

[14] See Appendix for the data. An interesting exception is Israel, where the data distinguishes between Israeli Arabs and Israeli Jews. The positive identification responses among Israeli Arabs are much lower than among Israeli Jews. I return to this issue in the next section.

[15] Tom Tyler's qualitative research supports these conclusions. He shows that at least in democracies, people obey the law not because of fear of deterrence but in light of their sense of personal duty and the legitimacy of their state in their eyes. See Tyler, *Why People Obey the Law*, chapter 4.

state not just in a descriptive but also in a normative sense. As we saw in the previous chapters, being a member in this sense has important normative implications.

Objections

I have suggested so far that attitude surveys can be used to generate assessments of the prevalence of intentional citizenship in real-world states. I now turn to discuss two important objections to the conclusions I drew from the data.

The first objection questions the validity of my conclusions, given the reported strength of people's sense of attachment to their country. The concern here is that the data shows that in all countries only a minority of respondents report that they have a *strong* sense of attachment. For example, in the World Value Survey, on average, only 49% of respondents across democratic countries reported that they feel *strongly* attached to their country.[16] In the ISSP 2013 National Identity Survey, only an average of 31% in 34 countries reported that they feel *very* close to their country. In the Afrobarometer 2004 survey, on average, only 35% in the 8 democratic states surveyed said they identify only with their nationality. If intentional citizenship requires strong levels of identification, it follows that most citizens are not intentional participants in their state.

However, I don't believe a strong level of identification with a group is necessary for intentional participation. Recall that acceptance of one's membership has a fairly low threshold, and excludes only people who view their membership as forced on them against their own will. It is implausible to suggest that a person who describes herself as quite attached to her country, though not very strongly, sees her membership in her state as

---

[16] As before this data relates to Waves 5 and 6 combined.

forced on her. People who are deeply alienated from their citizenship status are far more likely to report no or hardly any sense of attachment to their national identity. As we saw earlier, the numbers for these groups remain quite low across many countries in the world.

The second objection to my conclusions concerns the content of citizens' sense of attachment, and the group to which the respondents refer to when they report about their national attachment. Consider for example the question from Waves 5 and 6 of the World Value Survey, which starts with the word "I see myself as a . . ." In some countries this question reads "I see myself as a [country] citizen"; in others, "I see myself as part of [country]"; and in still others, "I see myself as part of the [country] nation." Are citizens then reporting their attachment to their state or to their nation? This problem arises in other surveys as well. The ISSP survey asks people to report their level of attachment to their "country" (e.g., to "Britain," "Denmark," "France," etc.). The Afrobarometer asks them to respond to statements such as "I see myself as a South African" or "as a Nigerian." These terms can be interpreted in various ways. They can be thought to refer to seeing oneself as a citizen of the said state, or they could refer to seeing oneself as a member of a nation, understood as a cultural or ethnic community, rather than a politically institutionalized entity. Given this ambiguity there is a concern that when people say they identify themselves as a French citizen, or as part of Taiwan, or as Nigerians, they might not mean that they are attached to their citizenship status per se, but rather to a specific cultural or ethnic group.

This is an important concern, but I believe it is not detrimental to my conclusions. Here I am guided by the thought that for most ordinary people, the terms "country," "state," "nation," and "people" are deeply connected and interdependent, and it is hard for them to draw meaningful distinctions between them, especially given that—in the examples above—the "nation" to which one belongs also, by and large, shares the same name as the country or state one is part of.[17] This close affinity between the nation and the state is recognized in most existing theories of nationalism. According to these theories, the "nation" or "the people" is a cultural pre-political entity that is separate from the state. And yet, typically, one of the distinctive characteristics of this entity is that it aspires to political self-determination, and often achieves it through the institutions of a state. On this view then, the "Nigerian people" or the "Canadian people" may be a cultural-ethnic group, but in the world as we know it, this group is *also* organized politically, and is acting through the institutions of the state.[18] As Bernard Yuck pointed out, this close affinity between the nation and the state is part and parcel of the experience of the modern citizen: she might perceive her political community as a cultural community that is distinct from the state, but she will also recognize it as a community that "makes use of the state for purposes of self-government."[19] For our purposes the implication is that even if one reports that she sees herself as part of a "nation," *de facto* this means she also sees herself as a member of the state that is acting on behalf of that nation.

Thus, my response to the content objection is that, typically, when respondents state that they identify themselves as, say, "a member of the Australian nation," they may well be describing themselves as attached to an ethnic or cultural community. Yet it is also a group with a clear political identity, which acts through the institutions of the Australian state. Therefore, the respondent is also expressing an affinitive relationship to their identity as a member of the Australian state (acting on behalf of the Australian nation). Given this deep connection between the nation (or the people) and

[17] Mikael Hjerm, "National Identities, National Pride and Xenophobia: A Comparison of Four Western Countries," *Acta Sociologica* 41, no. 4 (1998): 338. I will discuss some exceptions in the next section.

[18] This is acknowledged, for example, by David Miller, who has a cultural view of national identity but who suggests that nations, and especially those governed by democratic states, are active through the institutions of the state (Miller, *National Responsibility*, 126).

[19] Bernard Yack, "The Myth of the Civic Nation," *Critical Review* 10, no. 2 (1996): 201.

the state that acts in its name, we can assume with relative confidence that citizens who express affinity to their country, their people, or their nation as a whole are also expressing their recognition of and sense of attachment to the political institutions through which that nation acts.[20]

A third objection to my conclusions concerns the normative implications of intentional citizenship. As we saw in chapters 2 and 3, intentional citizenship can serve to justify a nonproportional distribution of the state's remedial responsibilities for its wrongdoings. A concern here is that, if it is the case that intentional citizenship is measured by citizens' responses in attitude surveys, then all it takes for a citizen to be released from the duty to accept a nonproportional share of the burden is that she verbally reports a lack of attachment to her state. Deploying attitude surveys for this purpose may well create perverse incentives for citizens to misreport their attitudes in such surveys.

But notice in response that, in citing the empirical findings from attitude surveys, I am not suggesting that such surveys should be used on a regular and formal basis to test intentional citizenship. I use current attitude surveys only to gauge the scope of intentional citizenship in the real world and to suggest that it is quite prevalent. A more reliable test for intentional citizenship will not rely on attitude surveys alone, and will also examine citizens' observed behavior. In democratic states (and in some nondemocratic states, as we will shortly see), citizens are able to engage in political activities that would signal their lack of intentional participation in the state, and it is not unreasonable to expect that, in order to make a persuasive claim about their lack of intentional participation, citizens who are not oppressed by their state should signal this fact in a public, clear,

---

[20] Cf. Billig, *Banal Nationalism*, 77–78. This claim is compatible with the idea of a single state presiding over several nations (e.g., Scots and English), or that a citizen can have more than one national identity. According to the surveys I cited, vast majorities in most countries see themselves as members of the nation that is most closely associated with the institutions of their state (e.g., the Brazilian nation, the Australian nation, etc.).

and consistent manner. Put differently, citizens' lack of support in their state should be expressed not just in the occasional survey, but also through their actions on a routine basis. If citizens fail to act in ways that reliably communicate their alienation (and especially if they are informed that in the absence of engagement in such activities, they will be presumed to be its intentional participants), then it makes sense to assume that they are intentional members of their state.

To conclude, I have so far suggested that attitude surveys suggest that intentional citizenship is quite prevalent in real-world states. If my argument is correct, it follows that in many states, the justification I offered in the previous chapter for a nonproportional distribution of the state's corporate burdens applies to vast majorities of their populations.

4.2 Who Is Not an Intentional Citizen?

Although the survey attitudes I cited indicate fairly high levels of intentional citizenship in many states, they also suggest that in all states there are some people who have low levels of identification with their citizenship status. At an individual level people can be alienated from their state for a variety of reasons, some of which may well be idiosyncratic. Nevertheless, it is useful to identify the groups that typically fall outside the scope of intentional citizenship. Doing so will allow us to better understand in what type of states intentional citizenship is less likely to be prevalent, and can also help us to try and close nonintentional participation gaps. Drawing on qualitative studies of people's national identities, I suggest there are two main groups in which intentional citizenship is likely to be low: first, secessionist minorities, and second, oppressed citizens who are marginalized by their state and fellow citizens.

I'll start with secessionist minorities. Not all national minorities seek to secede from their state. Some states give room to the political

110   RESPONSIBLE CITIZENS, IRRESPONSIBLE STATES

aspirations of more than one nation, and—as we saw in the data from earlier on—their citizens can identify with both their state and their ethnic or national group. For example, a Flemish Belgian can express strong levels of identification with Belgium, and at the same time maintain she is also part of the Flemish nation. However, some members of some national minorities are alienated from their state membership, and aspire to depart from it. For example, in a survey conducted in 2006, 35% of respondents in Scotland defined themselves as having only "Scottish" identity. In surveys in Catalonia (2010) and in Quebec (2007) 19% of respondents defined themselves as having only a minority identity.[21] I take it that individuals who express such strong secessionist sentiments, and who lack any sense of identification with their state, are unlikely to be accepting their citizenship status in the sense I have developed here. While they are participating in the state, they are not, *de facto*, accepting their participation, and would have given it up if they could.[22]

A second salient group comprises citizens who are marginalized within their state, and—given their lack of substantive equal citizenship status—do not develop strong attachments to their political community. Consider, for example, the case of African American national identity. As is commonly acknowledged, many African Americans experience serious and pervasive social, political, and racial marginalization and discrimination at the hands of

[21] This data appears in David McCrone and Frank Bechhofer, *Understanding National Identity* (Cambridge: Cambridge University Press, 2015), 180.

[22] The same applies for religious minorities who are disassociated from their state on religious grounds. It's worth noting that theorists of secession differ on the question of the circumstances under which a national minority has the moral *right* to secede from a state. Several accounts suggest that if the state is sufficiently just, democratic, and respects the cultural rights of the group in question, it has no right of secession (see, for example, Allen Buchanan, "Theories of Secession," *Philosophy & Public Affairs* 26, no. 1 (1997): 31–61; Alan Patten, "Democratic Secession from a Multinational State," *Ethics* 112, no. 3 (2002): 558–86. But, as far as intentional citizenship is concerned, whether a group has a right to secede is beside the point. The model of intentional citizenship has a strong subjective element, rendering citizens liable in light of their intentional participation and acceptance of it. Even if one ought to participate in a state, this does not render one an intentional participant in it. In chapter 5 I discuss attempts to justify the distributive effect by appealing to the state's justness and its citizens' duty to support it.

their society and their state.[23] In her analysis of American national identity, Elizabeth Theiss-Morse shows that such racial marginalization is expressed in white Americans' sense of national identity. Many American whites, she suggests, associate the idea of "being American" with that of "being white," and classify the stereotypes of "being black" as "deviant" from the American normative identity model. As a result, American whites are also less likely to show solidarity with nonwhite Americans (e.g., support economic policies that would benefit African American citizens).[24]

These perverse yet prevalent attitudes affect some African Americans' attachment of their national identity. Given their ongoing marginalization, and their exclusion from the national identity "ideal type," some African Americans report themselves as not being attached at all to their "American identity." Instead, they withdraw from the national group and express feelings of anger with and alienation from it.[25] Similar results occur elsewhere. In the UK, for example, surveys conducted among disadvantaged black communities also show low levels of identification with the state. In a survey taken in 2005, about 40% of respondents who were of British Black Caribbean/Black Other young people (aged 16–24) reported they had no sense of "belonging to Britain."[26]

As with the case of secessionist groups, marginalized and socially oppressed citizens are participating in their state in the sense that they too recognize their membership in the state and act in ways that contribute to its maintenance. However, given their high levels of alienation from the political community, it is far from evident that they accept their role. As the data suggests, at least some of them perceive

---

[23] For analysis from a political theory perspective, see Charles W. Mills, *The Racial Contract* (Ithaca, NY: Cornell University Press, 2014); Tommie Shelby, *Dark Ghettos: Injustice, Dissent, and Reform* (Cambridge, MA: Harvard University Press, 2016).

[24] Theiss-Morse, *Who Counts as an American?*, 76–83.

[25] Theiss-Morse, *Who Counts as an American?*, 129.

[26] Ali and Heath, "Future Identities." The survey found out that, generally speaking, young people have a lower sense of belonging to Britain than older generations.

their state as an oppressive force in their lives, and their citizenship status as forced on them against their will. Citizens who harbor these attitudes are "nonintentional citizens" of their state. The claim that citizens ought to share in the burden of their state's wrongdoings in light of their participation in the state does not apply to them. I'll return to the implications of this important qualification in the next chapters.

4.3 Intentional Participation
in Authoritarian Regimes

Much of the existing literature on citizens' responsibility for their states' policies concentrates on democratic states. Consider, for example, Anna Stilz's influential discussion of the problem of the distributive effect. Stilz's justification for a nonproportional distribution of the burden revolves around the idea of authorization: Citizens of democratic states authorize their state to act in their name and are therefore liable for its actions (I will return to this account in chapter 5). But clearly the problem of the distributive effect also arises in nondemocratic states. Around a quarter of the states in our world today are not democratic, and about a third of the world's population lives in nondemocratic states. These states too are at least sometimes held accountable for their wrongdoings by the international community, and the burden of their liability falls on their populations. Indeed, consider the four examples that open Stilz's discussion: France's payment of reparations in 1871, Germany's reparations after World Wars I and II, and the Iraqi reparations to Kuwait after the First Gulf War. These are all examples of nondemocratic states, to which the idea of democratic authorization does not apply.[27] But is intentional citizenship prevalent in such states, and could it offer an alternative justification?

---

[27] France was under the authoritarian rule of Napoleon III, in which the male suffrage was heavily restricted; Germany under Bismarck denied the vote to female voters

To answer this question, let's look first at attitude surveys conducted in nondemocratic states. Here the data seems to suggest that intentional citizenship is very prevalent in authoritarian states, even more so than in the typical democratic state. Recall the question from the World Value Survey about how strongly respondents see themselves as part of their country. In Wave Six of the survey (2005–9), 88% of Chinese respondents strongly agreed or agreed with this statement. In Russia, 92% of respondents strongly agreed or agreed, and in Iran, 97%. Or consider the question about national identity versus ethnic identity from the Afrobarometer: in Wave 5 of the survey (2012–13), 96.4% of the respondents in Cameroon and 95.3% of respondents in Uganda showed some level of attachment to their country (both countries are defined as Unfree in the Freedom House Democracy Index). However, there are two reasons to be cautious here. First, as is commonly acknowledged, it is harder to collect reliable data on people's attitudes in at least some nondemocratic states, especially when people are asked about their attitudes toward and affinity with their state. When citizens face intense political repression, they will be inclined not to report dissenting views, even if they hold them.[28] Second, even when the citizens of authoritarian states do acquire positive attitudes toward their country, we might be concerned about the way in which they have come to adopt these positions. After all, as I argued in chapter 3, genuine acceptance of one's citizenship in the state should not be the result of extreme coercion and manipulation.

These cautionary comments suggest that, rather than taking the data collected in attitude surveys at face value, we should examine it in light of the relation between citizens and their governments in nondemocratic states. As the burgeoning literature in

and imposed serious restrictions on freedom of speech and expression; during WWII, Germany was under the rule of the totalitarian Nazi regime; and during the Gulf War, Iraq was under the highly autocratic rule of Saddam Hussein.

[28] Johannes Gerschewski, "The Three Pillars of Stability: Legitimation, Repression, and Co-optation in Autocratic Regimes," *Democratization* 20, no. 1 (2013): 20.

comparative politics on the dynamics of nondemocratic, or authoritarian, states shows, all authoritarian states share in common some core negative characteristics: they do not hold universal, free, fair, and open elections, and they do not provide a *de facto* protection of a fairly wide range of political, civil, and personal rights, including freedom of expression, freedom of association, freedom of religion, and personal liberties.[29] But at the same time there is a great deal of divergence between them—in the way in which political power in them is obtained and lost,[30] the levels and modes of repression they deploy,[31] the levels and types of rights they respect, the modes of political legitimation they use,[32] and their domestic and international performances.[33] Given this considerable variety, we should not expect a uniform answer to the question of the extent of intentional participation in nondemocracies. Instead, we should isolate the factors that are most likely to influence it: the extent to which citizens actually participate in the state, the extent to which citizens are subjected to state repression, and the type of information about their state policies that they have access to.

[29] For a review of this literature, see Patrick Köllner and Steffen Kailitz, "Comparing Autocracies: Theoretical Issues and Empirical Analyses," *Democratization* 20, no. 1 (2013): 1–12.

[30] See José Antonio Cheibub, Jennifer Gandhi, and James Raymond Vreeland, "Democracy and Dictatorship Revisited," *Public Choice* 143, no. 1–2 (2010): 67–101; Erica Frantz and Natasha M. Ezrow, *The Politics of Dictatorship: Institutions and Outcomes in Authoritarian Regimes* (Boulder, CO: Lynne Rienner, 2011).

[31] Christian Davenport, "State Repression and Political Order," *Annual Review of Political Science* 10 (2007): 1–23; Juan J. Linz, *Totalitarian and Authoritarian Regimes* (Boulder, CO: Addison-Wesley, 1985); Mikael Wigell, "Mapping 'Hybrid Regimes': Regime Types and Concepts in Comparative Politics," *Democratization* 15, no. 2 (2008): 230–50;

[32] Gerschewski, "The Three Pillars of Stability"; Steffen Kailitz, "Classifying Political Regimes Revisited: Legitimation and Durability," *Democratization* 20, no. 1 (2013): 39–60.

[33] Ronald Wintrobe, "The Tinpot and the Totalitarian: An Economic Theory of Dictatorship," *American Political Science Review* 84, no. 3 (1990): 849–72; Natasha M. Ezrow and Erica Frantz, *Dictators and Dictatorships: Understanding Authoritarian Regimes and Their Leaders* (New York: Continuum International, 2011).

Participation

As we saw in chapter 3, intentional citizens are members of their state not just in a thin, formal sense. Their state assigns them various roles that give active content to their citizenship status. In democracies, citizens typically participate in their state by obeying the law and contributing to the effort of the state to impose a legal order; by paying taxes and contributing to the provision of various public goods and services; and by taking part in the democratic decision-making process, whether directly, by voting, or indirectly, by contributing to discussions in the public sphere about governmental policies. The channels of civic participation in democratic states are clearly defined and part of these state's common and public culture.[34]

But the picture becomes more muddled when we turn to nondemocratic states. As I noted earlier, studies in comparative politics offer different typologies of nondemocracies. Some suggest that a key factor that distinguishes between types of nondemocracies is the pattern of civic participation in the state. Juan Linz's influential typology, for example, takes this factor into account. Linz distinguished between two ideal types of nondemocratic states, which he refers to as the "totalitarian state" and the "authoritarian state." Totalitarian states are run by a single mass party, which is guided by a comprehensive and systematic ideology, and they also deploy high levels of repression. Furthermore, they encourage and even demand very high levels of civic participation in both formal and semi-formal state organizations, from membership in the leading political party and in state-sponsored labor and youth organizations, to employment in state-owned industries and service in the military. Citizens are also required to serve as the "eyes of the state"

---

[34] For discussion of patterns of participation in democracies see Beerbohm, *In Our Name*; Stilz, *Liberal Loyalty*, chapter 7. Holly Lawford-Smith argues that citizens are not members of their state. I discussed her critique in chapter 3.

by contributing to its internal police and monitoring systems, and they are expected to express their loyalty to the state both in the public sphere and in the privacy of their homes.[35] As Linz points out, as far as civic participation is concerned totalitarian states are equivalent and even surpass democratic states—their citizens play an active role in maintaining and supporting the state and its ideological apparatus. Going back to my model of intentional citizenship, it follows then that in totalitarian states, the vast majority of the population are active participants in their state's activities, as this model requires.

While mass political participation is typical of totalitarian states, it is by far less prevalent in what Linz calls "authoritarian states." Unlike totalitarian states, authoritarian states allow for some degree of political pluralism, and their overall political organization does not revolve around an elaborate comprehensive ideology. Furthermore, authoritarian states often discourage their citizens' political participation, preferring low levels of political mobilization and political apathy. Not only that, such states often have a limited presence in their ordinary citizens' lives, as they are not considered to be a relevant "domestic audience" to whose interests' the leaders ought to cater in order to survive. Levels of corruption in authoritarian states tend to be higher than in totalitarian regimes, and they also tend to provide fewer public goods and services to the population.[36]

Given this separation between the state and its citizens in what Linz refers to as "authoritarian states," it is less likely that many of their citizens will comply with the first condition of intentional citizenship, which requires that citizens see themselves as contributing to the maintenance of their state. After all, if the state discourages its citizens' contributions to its apparatus, and also fails to provide

[35] Linz, *Totalitarian and Authoritarian Regimes*, 70–73.
[36] Linz, *Totalitarian and Authoritarian Regimes*, 16–67. Cf. Wintrobe, "The Tinpot and the Totalitarian," chapter 3; Eric Chang and Miriam A. Golden, "Sources of Corruption in Authoritarian Regimes," *Social Science Quarterly* 91, no. 1 (2010): 1–20.

them with public services, the claim that they are participating in its activities becomes by far less tangible. In the extreme examples of Linz's authoritarian states, many citizens will probably be members of their state only in a formal sense, and for that reason alone will not fall within the scope of intentional citizenship.

Not only is actual participation in "authoritarian states" likely to be low, we also have reasons to be especially wary about expressions of high levels of attachments in attitude surveys conducted in such states. Recall that, as we saw earlier, these surveys often do not draw a clear distinction between the "nation," or the political community and "the state" as the object of the respondents' attachment. I suggested earlier that in democracies these concepts are closely related in people's minds, but when the state behaves like an authoritarian state, this is far less likely to be the case. If the state itself is present in people's lives only rarely, or only as an oppressive force, it becomes far more likely that—if respondents say they feel strongly attached to their "country"—what they have in mind is not the state itself, but their political or cultural community (whose interests may well stand in tension with the state itself). In other words, attitude surveys on national identity become far less reliable when the state separates itself from the people, and we have more reasons to assume that people are in fact less inclined to accept its rule over them.

Repression

The second factor that may well affect intentional citizenship in nondemocracies is political repression. All states deploy some level of repression, but autocracies use it more regularly and at higher levels than democracies. Higher levels of repression undermine the idea that citizens *accept* their participation in the state (if they indeed participate in it). In the first instance, it is likely that citizens will feel alienated from a state that denies their political and personal liberties. This claim is supported with empirical findings from democratic states, which, as we saw in Section 4.2, suggests that citizens who feel that they are treated unjustly by their state are less likely to feel attached to it. Drawing on that data we can infer that the more intense the state repression is (i.e., restricting a wider set of rights), the more inclusive it is (i.e., targeting larger portions of the population), and the more indiscriminate it is, the less likely it is that large sections of the population would view their participation as not forced on them against their will.[37]

Repression undermines intentional citizenship in another sense. Recall that in chapter 3, I argued, following Christman, that the acceptance of one's membership must be "historic": a person who genuinely accepts her membership in her state should also be able to reflect on the process by which her attachment to her state has come about and not resent it. It follows that, even if citizens in highly authoritarian states do develop high levels of attachments to their state, we should not treat those attachments as genuine in a full sense, if they have been shaped in light of extreme forms of "brainwashing", coercion, and manipulation, because their citizens would clearly resent this type of treatment by the state and how it shapes their attitudes to it (we will see one concrete example of the use of such extreme methods in chapter 6). In states where extreme repression is prevalent, intentional citizenship on a wide scale is unlikely (despite what attitude surveys taken in these countries might tell us).

That said, it is not the case that wide-scale intentional citizenship is necessarily ruled out in all nondemocracies. As many studies of authoritarian regime types suggest, they vary in the level and type of repression they deploy.[38] As we already saw, according to Linz,

[37] Jørgen Møller and Svend-Erik Skaaning, "Autocracies, Democracies, and the Violation of Civil Liberties," *Democratization* 20, no. 1 (2013): 82–83; Lisa Blaydes, *State of Repression: Iraq under Saddam Hussein* (Princeton: Princeton University Press, 2018), 45–48.

[38] See Davenport, "State Repression and Political Order"; Møller and Skaaning, "Autocracies, Democracies, and the Violation of Civil Liberties."

authoritarian states use much less repression than totalitarian states (although both use more political repression than democracies). More recent typologies of regimes concur with Linz to a degree, pointing to certain types of nondemocratic states that are fairly respectful of some political rights (such as freedom of association and expression, the right to alternative information, and freedom from discrimination), while at the same time denying their citizens' electoral rights.[39] Furthermore, it is commonly agreed in that literature that repression is never the only tool on which nondemocracies rely in order to generate popular loyalty and overall stability. Other important ways to increase their legitimacy in the eyes of the population are (1) the reliance on a popular comprehensive doctrine to justify their authority structures (e.g., a popular religious doctrine), and (2) strong output performance (e.g., the provision of public goods such as the rule of law, or good economic performance).[40] Some nondemocracies deploy these latter means to a greater extent and are able to use lower levels of state repression (although, admittedly, low-level repression is very much the exception rather than the rule). In such states it can be the case that citizens do form a genuine attachment to their state and accept their membership in it for their own reasons—for example, because it is compatible with their religious outlook, or because they are satisfied with the benefits it provides them. Here intentional citizenship can be much more widely spread. Moreover, given the lower levels of state

---

[39] See, for example, Christian Davenport, "State Repression and the Tyrannical Peace," *Journal of Peace Research* 44, no. 4 (2007): 485–504; Wigell, "Mapping 'Hybrid Regimes.'" Møller and Skaaning are more skeptical about variations in repression of civil liberties across types of nondemocracies. They measure four civil liberties: freedom of opinion and expression, freedom of association, freedom of religion, and freedom of movement. Although their data suggests that on average there is not much difference between types of nondemocracies (excluding "hybrid regimes"), it also shows that there are more isolated cases of nondemocracies that have imposed more modest restrictions on these freedoms (e.g., Bhutan and Brazil in the 1990s, and Mexico in the 1980s). See Møller and Skaaning, "Autocracies, Democracies, and the Violation of Civil Liberties."

[40] David Beetham, *The Legitimation of Power* (Basingstoke, UK: Palgrave Macmillan, 2013), 179–204; Gerschewski, "The Three Pillars of Stability," 20; cf. Kailitz, "Classifying Political Regimes."

repression in such nondemocracies, and the fact that their citizens are relatively free to express their political opinions, we can be less wary of treating their observed behavior—such as their expressions of political support and their answers in attitude surveys—as expressions of their real preferences.

As for more oppressive regimes, I do not deny that people can be genuinely and authentically accepting of their participation in such states. As I noted above, nondemocratic regimes may well tap into people's preexisting ideologies, and citizens could in principle welcome state repression because it fits with their own ideological preferences or serve their own interests. Consider, for example, the case of Nazi Germany. Recent historical scholarship suggests that the Nazi regime enjoyed widespread popular support among German citizens well into the war years. According to these studies, most ordinary German citizens welcomed the regime's anti-democratic and, later on, its genocidal platforms. Not only that, they also had ample information about its plans and their execution, and their support was not conditional on state repression and manipulation. In fact, it has been argued that for the greater part of its rule, the Nazi state did not need to use much repression against ordinary Germans (provided, of course, they were not members of persecuted minorities).[41] It follows then than in order to understand the scope of intentional citizenship, we must investigate the conditions that pertain in a specific state, including how the regime came into power.

---

[41] For recent studies that offer an in-depth examination of ordinary Germans' political attitudes under the Third Reich, and which reach these conclusions, see Robert Gellately, *Backing Hitler: Consent and Coercion in Nazi Germany* (Oxford: Oxford University Press, 2002); Ian Kershaw, *The Nazi Dictatorship: Problems and Perspectives of Interpretation* (London: Bloomsbury, 2015), chapters 7, 8; Nicholas Stargardt, *The German War: A Nation under Arms, 1939–1945* (London: Hachette UK, 2015). For a more skeptical view, see Geoff Eley, "Hitler's Silent Majority? Conformity and Resistance under the Third Reich (Part Two)," *Michigan Quarterly Review* 42, no. 3 (2003).

Information

The third factor that affects levels of intentional citizenship in authoritarian regimes is their awareness and knowledge of their state policies. As we saw in chapter 3, intentional citizens are the inclusive authors of a very wide range of their state's policies, but only when they have sufficient access to information about what their state does. All states deploy some level of secrecy, especially with regard to specific policy areas such as national security and defense. Such secrets do not undermine citizens' inclusive authorship when they are shallow secrets—citizens are aware of their existence and of the processes by which they are excluded from public knowledge. However, inclusive authorship is undermined when the state resorts to deep secrets, misinformation, and deception. When the state uses these methods, its citizens will not even be aware of the gap between what it says it does and what it actually does, and their capacity to assess its actions and their participation in them will be seriously hampered.

As many authors have noted, deep secrets stand in contrast to the very idea of democratic governance, and we can hope that, although all democracies deploy them, they do so to a limited extent. The picture is different in the case of nondemocratic regimes, which often resort to public lies and deception, and which use political repression in order to hide information from their publics. Here too there is some variation among different types of authoritarian regimes. Some nondemocracies deploy high levels of repression of citizens' political rights, including the right to information about government policies. Others are more lenient in that regard. Consider, for example, the case of the "competitive authoritarian regime," a type of hybrid nondemocratic regime.[42] Such regimes

---

[42] Steven Levitsky and Lucan Way, "The Rise of Competitive Authoritarianism," *Journal of Democracy* 13, no. 2 (2002): 51–65.

(which are becoming the more prevalent type of authoritarianism today, overtaking the more traditional "totalitarian" and "authoritarian" states from Linz's typology) fail to meet basic democratic standards, and yet they contain some democratic elements. Importantly, while they do not offer meaningful arrays of democratic participation, they often allow for a relatively free media, and their citizens have high levels of access to alternative sources of information about state policies.[43]

In contrast, more totalitarian political systems do commonly impose strict limits on their subjects' access to information about their policies, and also are more likely to engage in distortion of information and deception on a mass scale. Consider, for example, China's online censorship policies. As recent studies suggest, the Chinese government encourages the general public's use of the Internet and even creates online platforms for citizens to voice concerns about government policies. Such measures give citizens a sense of freedom and involvement in policymaking. But, at the same time, the government is deploying a highly sophisticated system of censorship and monitoring, which many citizens remain unaware of. Furthermore, the government uses various methods to manipulate and distort the online information that is available to citizens about its policies, and it also permits very little access to alternative sources of information.[44] The government's regular deployment of deep secrets, disinformation, and deception leads to a situation where citizens do view themselves as taking part in their state and do not view their participation as forced on them. And

[43] Similarly, what Mikael Wigell calls "constitutional oligarchies" respect the right to freedom of expression and the right to alternative information (Wigell, "Mapping 'Hybrid Regimes'"). Wigell suggests that states such as Malaysia and Hong Kong (At the time of his writing) bear similarities to this ideal regime type. The freedom to access alternative information is also less likely to be restricted in weak nondemocratic states that do not have an extensive state apparatus and lack the resources to enforce such restrictions.

[44] For analysis, see Rebecca MacKinnon, "Liberation Technology: China's 'Networked Authoritarianism,'" *Journal of Democracy* 22, no. 2 (2011): 32–46.

yet their perception of what it is that they do together in their state is distorted without them even being aware of that distortion. It is implausible to suggest that these citizens are the inclusive authors of state policies about which they are lied to and about which they have no real option to obtain information.[45]

Let's conclude. I assessed in this chapter the applicability of my intentional citizenship model to states in the real world. I suggested that, by and large, in democratic states large sections of the population harbor the type of attitudes that would render them intentional participants in their state, and inclusive authors of its policies, regardless of whether they can actually leave it. Nevertheless, even in democracies there are citizens who remain outside the boundaries of intentional citizenship. In nondemocracies the picture is even more complex. I argued that in order to gauge the level of intentional citizenship in such states, we need to examine various aspects of the relationship between the state and its citizens on a case-by-case basis: the avenues of participation the state offers for its citizens, the level of repression it deploys, and the extent to which citizens are aware of their state's activities. Assessing real-world nondemocratic states in light of these factors is likely to lead to the conclusion that in many nondemocracies, intentional citizenship is not prevalent, regardless of what the attitude surveys conducted in them say. However, there are some nondemocratic states where many of their citizens may well be intentionally participating in them, because, for example, they deploy relatively low levels of repression of political and civil liberties, are supported by a comprehensive doctrine that is widely shared among the population, and

---

[45] Notice that it is not always the case that totalitarian states hide their policies from their citizens. Robert Gellately, in *Backing Hitler*, suggests that the Nazi state provided ample information to its citizens about its genocidal plans, and routinely conducted opinion polls to gauge citizens' support of its policies. David Pozen notes that totalitarian states often resort to what he calls "open secrets"—policies "about which the entire community knows a tremendous amount but has no official confirmation." For example, in the Soviet Union under Stalin it was an open secret which type of "dissident acts" would lead to arrest though there was no official codification of these offences (see Pozen, "Deep Secrecy," fn. 45).

offer sufficient access to information about their policies. In these cases, we have fewer reasons to doubt their citizens' reported and observed attitudes.

What follows from all this is that the justification I developed in the previous chapters for the nonproportional distribution of state responsibility applies to many citizens in the real world, but certainly not to all of them. Does this mean that nonproportional distribution cannot be justified in such states? And what are the pragmatic implications for the way in which we currently hold states responsible for their wrongdoings? The next chapter turns to discuss these questions and—based on the empirical findings from the current chapter—offers a comprehensive framework for the distribution of the state's remedial obligations in both democratic and nondemocratic states.

5

Distributing State Responsibility

In chapter 4, I demonstrated that intentional citizenship is prevalent in many states of the world. But I also identified groups of citizens who are unlikely to be genuine participants in their state. In democratic states, nonintentional citizens are likely to be, mainly, secessionist and oppressed minorities. In many (though not all) nondemocratic states, the majority of citizens, in all likelihood, will not be genuinely participating in their state.

Given that nonintentional citizens are unwilling participants in their state, it seems unfair to demand that they accept a nonproportional share of their state's obligations of compensation, rehabilitation, commemoration, and nonrepetition. This will be so especially for nonintentional citizens who are themselves the victims of state oppression, and who are forced to support it against their will. If the state, or agents outside the state such as the international community, holds them equally liable for its wrongdoings, it will be appearing to communicate that there is no difference between them and those who genuinely supported the state's policies. Doing so constitutes then a further mistreatment of oppressed citizens. After all, a core dimension of the wrongness of oppression is that their agency is involved, against their wishes, in their own mistreatment.[1] The victims of state oppression will therefore have an especially strong claim against a distribution that associates them with the agency of the state and with its policies.

These concerns might lead us to conclude that nonintentional citizens cannot be expected to accept an equal portion of the

---

[1] Ann Cudd, *Analyzing Oppression* (Oxford: Oxford University Press, 2006), chapter 6.

Responsible Citizens, Irresponsible States. Avia Pasternak, Oxford University Press. © Oxford University Press 2021. DOI: 10.1093/oso/9780197541036.003.0006

burdens of their state's remedial responsibilities. This conclusion poses a problem for the intentional citizenship account. I argued in chapter 1 that the key advantage of nonproportional distribution is that—unlike the proportional blame-tracking distribution—it does not require a complex and costly fact-finding process. But if a distribution that is grounded in intentional citizenship does require, as a matter of fact, that we first distinguish between intentional and nonintentional citizens, it loses this advantage. For clearly, finding out who is and who is not an intentional participant in the state is going to be very difficult in practical terms.

My task in this chapter is to address this concern, and to offer a viable model for the distribution of the state's responsibility within the state, despite the pragmatic limitations faced even by the intentional citizenship argument. I do this in two stages. First, in Section 5.1, I examine alternative justifications for a nonproportional distribution, which do not revolve around intentional participation. Could these alternatives capture nonintentional citizens as well and, in that sense, overcome the problem of distinguishing between them and intentional citizens? To answer this question, I first look at two recent accounts that directly aim to justify a nonproportional distribution of the state's remedial obligations: David Miller's national responsibility model, and Anna Stilz's democratic authorization model. I then look at three other factors that are used more generally to explain how people become remedially responsible for a wrongdoing irrespective of their intentional participation in it: *benefiting* from a wrongdoing, having a special *capacity* to address it, and having special *associative obligations* to the victims of the wrongdoing.[2] As I show, each of these alternatives has its own

---

[2] This list follows Miller, *National Responsibility*, chapter 4; and Miller, "Distributing Responsibilities." Miller's full set of sources of remedial obligations also includes moral responsibility, outcome responsibility, and pure causal responsibility. Moral responsibility is captured by the proportional distribution model. As we saw in chapter 2, I agree with Miller that outcome responsibility can justify distribution of responsibility to citizens, but only if they accept their membership in the state. As for pure causal responsibility, Miller argues that even agents who have contributed to a bad outcome but in a way

limitations, and none of them offers a more comprehensive alternative to intentional participation under all circumstances of state injustice. At the same time, there are scenarios where these factors do play a role in explaining both intentional and nonintentional citizens' obligations with respect to their state wrongdoings.

Based on these observations, in Section 5.2, I turn to outline the process by which we should determine how a state's responsibility is to be distributed between its citizens. Here I argue that there is no single model of distribution that can fit all cases of state wrongdoing, across all types of states. Rather, several factors need to be examined in each scenario, and they will determine the shape of the distribution, given the specific circumstances at hand. These factors include the extent to which we can determine the level of blame of key actors within the state, our assessment of the scope of intentional citizenship in the state, and the nature of the regime that perpetrates the wrongdoing. I also suggest that, by and large, in democratic states it is likely to be the case that nonproportional distribution will be overall justified, while in many authoritarian states it will not. Finally, I examine how the burden should be distributed when a nonproportional distribution cannot be overall justified.

5.1 Alternative Bases for Nonproportional Distribution

what defines a democratic state?

The problem of the distributive effect of the state's remedial obligations has received some attention in recent literature. While, as we saw in previous chapters, some contributors to this debate advocate a proportional distribution of the burden, there have also been attempts to justify the common real-world practice of

that does not involve their agency incur some remedial responsibilities (for example, if A caused damage to B by falling on her due to a gust of wind). But I don't think these obligations are weightier than what may be expected of an uninvolved agent at the scene. At most A should explain what happened and offer some immediate assistance.

nonproportional distribution, but which do not rely on citizens' intentional participation. In this section, I first look at two such attempts. I then examine three other factors that could be used to justify citizens' liability for their state's wrongdoings.

Like-Mindedness

The first alternative I examine here is developed by David Miller, as part of his defense of the idea of national responsibility.[3] Miller describes two types of groups in which collective responsibility may be distributed to members on a nonproportional basis, so that "every participant bears an equal share."[4] He then argues that nations, and especially nations governed by democratic institutions, typically exhibit characteristics from both group models. It follows then that a nonproportional distribution of a nation's collective responsibility can be justified.

In what follows I focus on the first part of Miller's argument, where he describes the two types of groups in which nonproportional distribution can be justified. For brevity's sake I will examine only the first of these groups, which Miller refers to as "like-minded."[5] In my view, Miller is right to argue that in like-minded groups, nonproportional distribution can be justified. But, *pace* Miller, I argue that what grounds this distribution is intentional participation rather than mere like-mindedness. It follows

---

[3] Miller, *National Responsibility*, 111. In this section I partly draw on my paper Avia Pasternak, "Mobs, Firms and Nations—a Critique of David Miller's Account of Collective Responsibility," in *Political Philosophy, Here and Now: Essays in Honour of David Miller*, ed. Daniel Butt, Sarah Fine, and Zofia Stemplowska (Oxford: Oxford University Press, forthcoming).

[4] Miller, *National Responsibility*, 116.

[5] The other model is that of "cooperative practices." As Miller explains, in cooperative groups members receive a nonexploitative share of the *benefits* of the group's activities and have a *democratic* right to participate in its decision-making procedure. I return to the factors of benefit and democratic authorization later in the chapter, so I leave this model aside for now. I discuss it more extensively in Pasternak, "Mobs, Firms and Nations."

that—to the extent that nations do indeed share the properties of "like-minded" groups—their members can indeed be expected to accept a nonproportional share of the burdens that are created by the nation's wrongdoings. But the justification for this distribution is that co-nationals are intentionally participating in their nation.[6]

As Miller explains, members of like-minded groups "share aims and outlooks in common, and . . . recognize their like-mindedness, so that when individuals act they do so in light of the support they are receiving from other members of the group."[7] The examples Miller gives for like-minded groups are a rioting mob and a racist local community. In both cases, some group members, acting in light of the group's shared goal, ethos, or way of life, impose wrongful harm on others. The burden of undoing this harm and of compensating the victims may be distributed among all group members on an equal basis, given their shared outlooks and aims, which have brought about the harm in the first place.[8]

Does this model offer a viable alternative to the intentional participation framework? I think the answer to this question is negative. Notice, first, that Miller cannot argue that shared outlooks and aims are *sufficient* to ground a duty to share in the costs of a group's wrongdoing. To see this, consider someone who merely shares the outlooks and aims of a group, but remains an outsider to it. Imagine, for example, a present-day Nazi sympathizer and admirer of Adolf Hitler. This person may well share the aims of the historic German Nazi Party, but we do not commonly think that

---

[6] I am less confident than Miller that we should focus on the liability of co-*nationals* for what they do together as a nation, rather than on that of citizens for what they do together in the state. Miller suggests that the collective responsibility of the nation is "more basic" than that of the state (Miller, *National Responsibility*, 111). In contrast, I believe that given the unstructured nature of the nation as a pre-political entity, it is much harder to define what it is, precisely, that nations do together, including what their culture is, and which specific actions count as plausible interpretations of that culture. My account instead focuses on citizens who are members of the state as a corporate agent, with clear procedures for defining its goals. I return to one of Miller's critiques of state responsibility in chapter 7.

[7] Miller, *National Responsibility*, 117.

[8] Miller, *National Responsibility*, 117–18.

just by virtue of his odious views he shares equal liability for the crimes of the Nazis and ought to contribute to German reparations to surviving Holocaust victims.[9] Miller seems to acknowledge this when he suggests that the distribution of liability in like-minded groups is justified given that all their members *contribute* to the foreseeable harms other group members commit, by sharing the ethos or outlook that motivated the wrongdoers. Thus, for example, in the case of the rioting mob, he writes, the equal liability of individual participants is justified because "they *contributed* to a collective activity that was certain to inflict damage on other people, whether they specifically intended the overall outcome that actually occurred."[10]

Grounding group members' duty to accept a nonproportional share of the burden in their contributions to the group's wrongdoing rules out the counterintuitive conclusion that the present-day Nazi sympathizer shares equal liability for the historical crimes of the Nazi party. However, it opens two other difficulties for Miller's account. First, as Kasper Lippert-Rasmussen has noted, the shift to contribution seems to render superfluous the "like-minded" element of the model, which Miller argues is central.[11] What matters

---

[9] Cf. Richard Child, "Should We Hold Nations Responsible? David Miller, National Responsibility and Global Justice," *Res Publica* 15, no. 3 (2009): 200–201; Kasper Lippert-Rasmussen, "Responsible Nations: Miller on National Responsibility," *Ethics and Global Politics* 2, no. 2 (2009): 120. Farid Abdel-Nour argues that mere identification with the past deeds of the nation could ground current members' responsibility; see Farid Abdel-Nour, "National Responsibility," *Political Theory* 31, no. 5 (2003): 693–716. However, his account does not seek to ground remedial duties. He argues that identification grounds collective responsibility only in the sense that it grounds the moral requirement to feel ashamed for past wrongs committed by one's nation. Elsewhere Abdel-Nour argues that citizens' obedience to the state can render them responsible for its actions, even in authoritarian regimes. But there too he only seeks to establish the "bare bones" responsibility of subjects for their authoritarian state's policies. "Bare bones" responsibility is the mere recognition that one's agency is somehow involved in the state's acts. It does not translate into remedial duties. See Farid Abdel-Nour, "Responsible for the State: The Case of Obedient Subjects," *European Journal of Political Theory* 15, no. 3 (2016): 259–75.

[10] Miller, *National Responsibility*, 116 (emphasis added). Cf. David Miller, "A Response," *Critical Review of International Social and Political Philosophy* 11, no. 4 (2008): 558.

[11] Lippert-Rasmussen, "Responsible Nations," 120.

for the purpose of justifying nonproportional liability is that one has contributed to a foreseeable wrongdoing, and not that one did so in light of one's shared outlooks and aims with other members of the group. Indeed, as we saw in the previous chapters, people can contribute to foreseeable wrongful outcomes while being deeply alienated from the wrongdoers' outlooks and aims. The second difficulty runs deeper: Miller develops the like-minded group model in order to justify the distribution of liability in massive groups like the nation-state. However, as Miller himself emphasizes time and again, in such massive groups it can be very hard to "disentangle individual contributions"[12] and to draw a clear causal link between ordinary citizens' specific actions and the harmful outcomes.

In chapter 2, I argued, following Kutz, that the way to resolve this difficulty is to focus on group members' intentional participation in their group. As we saw, when individuals intentionally take part in a group action, they may become liable for the consequences even if we cannot point to the difference that their specific contribution made to the harm. As long as a person sees herself as contributing to the group, and her actions have some potential to affect the outcome, she is participating in the group. This argument can help Miller identify why members of like-minded groups are liable for their group's wrongdoings. Consider first the rioting mob. Here all the rioters are participating in the attack on an ethnic minority (in Miller's words, they all intend to "teach them a lesson").[13] As intentional participants, their attitude to this collective project amounts to much more than mere identification. They don't just share an outlook with other rioters, but act *in light* of this outlook, and perform various roles to promote it. Different rioters are doing different things ("some actively attack persons or property; others shout abuse or issue threats; yet others play a more passive role"),[14]

---

[12] Miller, *National Responsibility*, 131.
[13] Miller, *National Responsibility*, 131.
[14] Miller, *National Responsibility*, 131.

but regardless of the specific role each plays, they are all the inclusive authors of the outcome (i.e., part of the "we" who rioted).[15]

Similar conclusions apply to racist communities, whose general ethos inspires racist crimes. As with the case of the rioting mob, it is not mere identification with the community's way of life that grounds their liability for the crimes. Rather, their liability for a nonproportional share of what is owed to the victims is grounded in their intentional participation in the community and their continual support of it, despite the racist crimes it inspires (assuming that these racist crimes fall within the remit of what counts as a plausible interpretation of the group's shared goals).

It's worth noting that Miller himself is reluctant to use collective intentionality to ground the equal liability of co-nationals, because, he suggests, this framework does not capture group members who do not endorse the group's wrongdoing. Here he mentions, as an example, the Mafioso who "very much wishes [the Mafia] would abandon its criminal activities and become legitimate." This Mafioso occasionally acts against the Mafia's code, but most of the time he "goes about his duties with a heavy heart."[16] Given that this Mafioso resents the Mafia's criminal activities, argues Miller, he is not intending to take part in them. The collective intentionality framework leads, then, to the implausible conclusion that the

---

[15] Miller suggests that the rioters are liable even for outcomes that they did not specifically intend. But this conclusion is harder to support in the case of unstructured groups like mobs, where the group's shared goals are not necessarily clearly defined. In contrast with the state, in such groups it is far harder to draw a line at what counts as a plausible refinement of the group's goals. Consider a peaceful demonstration, where some radical members turn violent. Given that most demonstrators did not intend this outcome, are they liable for it? (This example is from Roland Pierik's critique of Miller's account. See Roland Pierik, "Collective Responsibility and National Responsibility," *Critical Review of International Social and Political Philosophy* 11, no. 4 [2008]: 476.) As I suggested in chapter 2, whether a specific group member's action counts as a group act or not depends on the authority structure within the group and the nature of instructions it gives its members. As a corporate agent the state has procedures in place to resolve these questions.

[16] David Miller, "Collective Responsibility and Global Poverty," *Ethical Perspectives* 19, no. 4 (2012): 636.

reluctant Mafioso should be let off the hook for the Mafia's crimes, given his mere reluctant participation. But this objection does not apply to my intentional participation account. For on this account, all that is required of group members to count as the inclusive authors of the group's actions is that they accept their membership in the group.[17] Assuming the Mafioso in Miller's example could leave the Mafia but chooses to remain part of it despite his moral qualms, he is a genuine member of the Syndicate.[18] As such he is an inclusive author of the Mafia's activities, and could be expected to accept a nonproportional share of the burden, if such a distribution is necessary in order to compensate the victims.

To conclude the point, in Miller's "like-minded" groups, a nonproportional distribution can indeed by justified, but not merely because of their members' like-mindedness, but rather in light of their intentional participation in the group. It follows then that in like-minded groups, members who are not intentional participants will not fall within the remit of Miller's defense of equal liability. Miller's defense cannot then ground the duty of nonintentional citizens to accept a nonproportional share of the burden.

I now turn to examine whether democratic authorization can ground nonproportional distribution. As I already noted, Miller describes a second model, that of cooperative practices, which in his view justify the liability of group members who do not share the group's core values, but who benefit from the group's actions and who participate in its decision-making process. I will return to the benefit argument at a later point in the discussion.

---

[17] Notice that in arguing this I am not endorsing the legal practice of accomplice liability, which in some jurisdictions pays no attention to the participating agent's degrees of participation and awareness of the crime. For critical discussion see Kutz, *Complicity*, 206–35.

[18] As we saw in chapter 2, if the Mafioso is not accepting his membership status and is forced to perform his role, then he is not an inclusive author of the Mafia activities. But I don't think this conclusion is counterintuitive.

Democratic Authorization

A second justification for a nonproportional distribution in the state is offered by Anna Stilz. Stilz's account is grounded in Immanuel Kant's justification of political authority.[19] Kant's starting point is the observation that all persons have a right against interference and a duty to respect the freedom of all others. These rights and duties can only be realized under a joint political authority, which coordinates individuals' actions and subjects them to a common set of laws. It follows, then, that a state that performs these functions has the right to be obeyed, and, adds Stilz, it is also authorized by its subjects, in the sense that they grant it the right to act in their name. According to Stilz, if the state "credibly interprets my basic right then I necessarily authorize it—whether I agree to join it or not—since I require its system of laws to secure me against others' interference." It follows that a legitimate state can justifiably dis-tribute its liabilities for wrongdoing among the citizens, regardless of their personal level of blame.[20] For, as Stilz explains, "a *member's will* is implicated in his state when that state counts as 'authorized,' and therefore . . . he has a reason to 'own up' to what an authorized state does."[21]

The key difference between the democratic authorization and the participatory intentions accounts is that the latter is grounded in an attitudinal component, which requires citizens' own inten-tion to act in their state and acceptance of their participation in it. In contrast, according to Stilz, citizens authorize their state, and share equal liability for its actions, whether or not they intend to

---

[19] Stilz, "Collective Responsibility." In other works, Stilz's conception of citizenship does make use of the idea of participatory intentions. I focus here on her earlier work, where there are starker differences between our accounts. See, for example, Anna Stilz, "The Value of Self-Determination," *Oxford Studies in Political Philosophy* 2 (2016).

[20] Stilz, "Collective Responsibility," 200.

[21] Stilz, "Collective Responsibility," 198. Cf. John Parrish, "Collective Responsibility and the State," *International Theory* 1, no. 1 (2009): 130.

be part of it and whether or not they accept their membership.[22]
This feature seems to suggest that the democratic authorization
argument has a wider scope than the intentional participation account, because it applies to nonintentional citizens as well. After
all, they too authorize their legitimate state to act in their name,
even if they reject their membership in it. But notice that in arguing
this, Stilz stretches the notion of authorization beyond its common
usage. We typically understand the relationship of authorization as
one in which the authorizing party is an autonomous agent who is
aware of and accepts the role of the agent that acts in her name.[23]
The core reason to limit authorization in this way is the concern
that, without it, the authorizing principal has too little control over
what is done on her behalf and—following from that—on the scope
of her own liabilities.

But Stilz has a ready response to this concern. For while her justification of nonproportional distribution is not conditional on
citizens' accepting their membership in the state, it is restricted
to states whose policies are "reasonable public interpretations" of
their citizens' rights. A reasonable public interpretation of the citizens' basic rights needs not necessarily be the correct or best interpretation. Rather, as Stilz explains:

> [As long as] some minimal threshold is passed, we are bound
> to act in accordance with the authority's judgment, since by
> accepting such a procedure we "do better" overall in securing
> our rights than by substituting our private judgment for the
> authority's.[24]

---

[22] At some points in her argument, Stilz does refer to citizens' attitudes to their membership status. For example, she writes that the authorized state "is not simply forcibly
imposed on us, but an institution we can understand and endorse, in a moment of calm
reflection" (Stilz, "Collective Responsibility," 200). But she does not suggest that this *de
facto* acceptance attitude is a necessary condition for her justification of the distributive
effect.

[23] See, e.g., Hanna Pitkin's classic *The Concept of Representation* (Berkeley: University
of California Press, 1972), esp. pp. 209–40.

[24] Stilz, "Collective Responsibility," 200.

When the state complies with this minimal threshold, it is a legitimate state, and is acting in the name of the citizens. This threshold then provides an alternative constraint to acceptance on the type of policies citizens are liable for.

In the quote above, Stilz seems to offer a rather low threshold for state legitimacy and authorization, according to which the state should "overall" secure a better bundle of rights for its citizens than they would have had in the absence of political authority. But given that Stilz's starting point is Kant rather than Thomas Hobbes, it is clear that the correct interpretation of the bar she offers for political legitimacy is higher. As she explains elsewhere in the paper, the state should not only secure its citizens' rights better than a state of nature, but must also comply with three further conditions. First, it must "grant a sphere of private freedom to its citizens," which includes a familiar range of basic liberal freedoms. Second, it should guarantee all its citizens' equality before the law, formal equality of opportunity, and at the least comply with requirements of basic economic justice. Third, it should be democratic—giving all citizens equal rights to take part in the interpretation of justice through the making of public policy.[25] Only when a state complies with these conditions are its policies "plausible interpretations" of what it is authorized to do in the name of its citizens. Notice that, somewhat surprisingly, these conditions say nothing about the state's treatment of nonmembers: the legitimate state must respect its own citizens' freedoms, equality, and democratic rights. But a state could be respecting its own citizens' rights while at the same time be committing serious rights violations against nonmembers. However, given the Kantian roots of Stilz's account, it should recognize that an egregious abuse of outsiders—even if it is agreed upon democratically and even if it has no bearing on the state's citizens themselves—could not pass as a plausible interpretation of these citizens' rights. It follows then that Stilz's threshold for democratic

[25] Stilz, "Collective Responsibility," 202–3.

authorization should include not only the requirement that the state respects its own citizens, but also at least a minimal set of nonmembers' rights.

So how does this revised version of Stilz's democratic authorization fare as a justification for a nonproportional distribution, in comparison to the intentional participation account? I noted earlier that Stilz's justification appears to have the advantage of applying to all the citizens of democratic states, even to nonintentional citizens. In that sense it seems to offer a more inclusive model, which does not require difficult-to-draw distinctions between types of citizens within the state. But notice, first, that this will not be true for many real-world states. As we saw, Stilz's account is restricted to states that are committed to certain standards. Many states in the real world, even democratic states, violate these standards with regard to some portions of their populations (e.g., racial minorities).[26] These oppressed citizens, denied *de facto* political equality, cannot be expected to own the policies of their state on Stilz's own account. The democratic authorization argument applies, then, only to nonintentional citizens who wish to secede from the state, or who object to it for their own idiosyncratic reasons.

Furthermore, the democratic authorization argument faces another problem, which concerns the type of policies it applies to. Consider again Stilz's definition of legitimate state policies. To what level of policymaking does it apply? One answer to this question is that it applies to the general structure of the state rather than to the specific policies it pursues. The definition describes the general features that "the state has to have if its laws are to qualify as interpretations of our rights, rather than some other kind of judgment."[27] The thought here is that as long as the state as a whole complies with the demands of freedom, equality, democracy, and

---

[26] With regard to the American context, see discussion in Tommie Shelby, "Justice, Deviance, and the Dark Ghetto," *Philosophy & Public Affairs* 35, no. 2 (2007).

[27] Stilz, "Collective Responsibility."

respect of human rights, all its policies are authorized by its citizens and they bear remedial responsibility for them.

However, this interpretation strikes me as too broad.[28] After all, all theories of political obligations and legitimacy—including those that, like Stilz's, rest on the Kantian notion of a natural duty of justice—acknowledge that even in reasonably just states, citizens have the right (and maybe even the duty) to resist seriously unjust laws or policies, which their state may not pursue in their name.[29] In resisting a seriously unjust law or policy, citizens justifiably deny the state's assertion that the law in question is a plausible interpretation of their rights. In such cases, then, it is no longer the case that—on Stilz's account—they are equally liable for the policy. To see this, consider one of Stilz's running examples: the United States before the civil rights era. At that time many African American citizens did not have even their formal equality of opportunity protected, and their voting rights were effectively denied. Stilz suggests that, despite these specific violations of the three conditions, the American state was *overall* complying with the requirements of freedom, equality, and independence, and that therefore all white American citizens were authorizing the state's treatment of their fellow African American citizens, and equally liable for the harm.[30] But why should this be the case? An American citizen could plausibly argue that the serious racial discrimination of her fellow citizens cannot be a plausible interpretation of her rights on any reasonable account, regardless of whether the state promotes justice in other policy areas. The racially discriminatory laws and policies advocated by the state were sufficiently wrong to

comply or not comply

[28] Cf. Robert Munro "Should Citizens Pay for the Costs of Their State's Unjust Actions? Defending an Individualist Moral Responsibility-Based Account of Liability" (PhD diss., Manchester University, 2015), chapter 5.

[29] Assuming that disobedience would not undermine the system as a whole. For a comprehensive exploration of the duty to resist from various theories of political obligations, see Candice Delmas, *A Duty to Resist: When Disobedience Should Be Uncivil* (Oxford: Oxford University Press, 2018).

[30] Stilz, "Collective Responsibility," 204.

relieve her of her obligation to obey them (e.g., to comply with the legal demands of segregation) and to ground her duty to resist them (e.g., by taking part in civil disobedience campaigns), and they were also not policies for which she should be held liable, at least not on an account that grounds her liability in what her state is entitled to do in her name.

The upshot of this objection, then, is that, on the democratic authorization account, it is not sufficient that the state, at some general level, complies with the conditions of equality, freedom, democracy, and basic respect to nonmembers. Rather, the specific policies for which the state citizens are held remedially responsible on a nonproportional basis should also comply with these conditions. I agree with Stilz that in scenarios where a state policy complies with these conditions, the democratic authorization argument could ground even nonintentional citizens' nonproportional liability. In reality, however, the problem of the distributive effect usually arises precisely when states' policies do not comply with these requirements, as was certainly the case in the US before the civil rights decade. This was also the case in Stilz's other running example—the 2003 US and UK invasion of Iraq, which led to devastating humanitarian consequences.[31] Assume that the US and the UK at the time of the invasion have overall complied with the conditions of freedom, equality, democracy, and basic respect to nonmembers. It is still hard to see how an aggressive and illegal invasion of Iraq was a plausible interpretation of their citizens' rights. This is not to deny that, in principle, a state's decision to engage in a preemptive war could be a plausible interpretation of citizens' rights, even if in the end it turns out to be based on mistaken empirical assumptions.[32] But this permission requires that the state in question responds to sufficiently robust evidence about a credible threat, and both the US and the UK failed to meet even this

violates #3, not democratic

---

[31] Stilz, "Collective Responsibility," 205.
[32] Stilz, "Collective Responsibility," 202.

standard.[33] As these examples suggest, Stilz's justification applies to a narrow set of cases, and does not cover the very cases that motivate her analysis.

The intentional citizenship justification, in contrast, accounts for these state wrongs as well. This is because, unlike the democratic authorization account, it does not prescribe a standard of what a legitimate state may do in its citizens' name. Instead, it suggests that when citizens intentionally participate in the state and perform their role in the maintenance of its corporate agency, they are liable for the outcome if this agent chooses to do wrong, and may be required to accept a nonproportional share of the burden of its remedial obligations.[34] It may be the case that the democratic authorization argument captures nonintentional citizens in sufficiently just states. But it has important limitations in comparison to the intentional participation account: it applies only to sufficiently democratic states, and even in them, only to cases where the wrongdoings they commit fall within the remit of what they may legitimately do in the name of their citizens.

Benefit from Wrongdoing

I now turn to examine three other factors that could in principle ground citizens' remedial obligations with regard to their state's wrongdoings. One such alternative is citizens' benefit from their state's wrongdoings. It is a fairly common view that agents who directly benefit from other people's wrongdoings ought to disgorge the tainted benefit, even if they have not solicited it.[35] This

---

[33] Endre Begby, "Collective Responsibility for Unjust Wars," *Politics* 32, no. 2 (2012): 104.

[34] Recall that, in chapter 4, I set some limits to this claim, which concerned the type of information citizens have on their state policies.

[35] See, for example, Daniel Butt, "On Benefiting from Injustice," *Canadian Journal of Philosophy* 37, no. 1 (2007): 129–52; Robert Goodin, "Disgorging the Fruits of Historical Wrongdoing," *American Political Science Review* 107, no. 3 (2013): 478–91; Christian Barry and David Wiens, "Benefiting from Wrongdoing and Sustaining Wrongful

principle could apply to the case of state wrongdoing, because if citizens benefited from their state's wrongdoing, they ought to disgorge these tainted benefits, regardless of the level of their personal blame. Their disgorged benefits should then be used to compensate the victims and to finance the state's other remedial obligations. Importantly, the beneficiary-pays principle captures both intentional and nonintentional citizens. Nonintentional citizens do not accept their citizenship status and perhaps resent the benefits their state bestows on them. But to the extent that they benefit from their state's wrongdoing, they too incur duties of disgorgement.

However, there are two problems with the deployment of the beneficiary-pays principle in the case of state wrongdoing. The first problem concerns the scope of the principle. As we just saw, the principle is limited to scenarios where the population of the state directly benefits from the wrongdoing in question. But this is often not the case. Consider again the examples I mentioned in the Introduction: the German reparation scheme for the crimes of the Nazis, the compensations paid by Iraq after its 1990 invasion of Kuwait, Argentina's and Chile's reparations to the victims of their human-rights violations, and Canada's reparations to its indigenous peoples. In none of these examples did a significant portion of the population benefit from the policies in question. Therefore, the beneficiary-pays principle could not justify a distribution of the burden among the population at large in these cases.

The second concern follows from this, and relates to the feasibility of a distribution scheme that is based on the

Harm," *Journal of Moral Philosophy*13, no. 5 (2016): 530–52. For critiques of this principle, see Robert Huseby, "Should the Beneficiary Pay," *Politics, Philosophy, Economics* 14, no. 2 (2015): 229–25; Carl Knight, "Benefiting from Injustice and Brute Luck," *Social Theory and Practice* 39, no. 4 (2014): 581–98. For a general review of the debate, see Avia Pasternak, "Benefiting from Wrongdoing," in *A Companion to Applied Philosophy*, ed. Kasper Lippert-Rasmussen, Kimberley Brownlee, and D. Coady (Oxford: Blackwells, 2016): 411–23.

beneficiary-pays principle. Given that this principle grounds the remedial duty of group members in their "tainted benefits," such beneficiaries' duties are capped at the level of the benefit they received. Once they have disgorged the benefit, they are no longer beneficiaries and therefore no longer under an obligation to the victims of the wrongdoing.[36] But this restriction raises the same problem for the benefit account as the one faced by the proportional blame-tracking distribution: a model that distributes the burden of the state's remedial obligations in light of their personal level of benefit needs to calculate that level of benefit. This task will be incredibly complex, especially given that the state offers a bundle of collective goods to its citizens, many of which are traceable to legitimate policies. Not only that, but it will not necessarily be the case that—even if it were possible to identify the tainted benefits—they would be sufficient to cover the full cost of compensation, rehabilitation, commemoration, and nonrepetition. As a matter of practice, then, it is not clear how the beneficiary-pays principle could ground a feasible scheme for the distribution of the state's remedial responsibilities.[37]

---

[36] All supporters of the principle agree on this cap. Elsewhere I have argued that if one is an "intentional beneficiary" (i.e., she welcomes or does not resist the benefit), she can be expected to contribute more than the benefit. But this observation does not assist us here, given that we are looking for a distribution model that does not require a distinction between intentional and nonintentional citizens. See Avia Pasternak, "Voluntary Benefits from Wrongdoing," *Journal of Applied Philosophy* 31, no. 4 (2014): 377–91.

[37] David Miller offers a different version of the beneficiary-pays principle in his discussion of cooperative groups. In these groups, members benefit from the group practices overall, and the benefits are distributed fairly between them. They therefore have a duty to accept an equal share of the group's remedial obligations (Miller, *National Responsibility*, 119, 131). But I don't agree that a fair share of the benefit of the group's activities is sufficient in itself to justify a nonproportional distribution. Consider a group that forces some people to join it against their will and then distributes the benefits between all participants on a fair basis. The coerced members may have a duty to disgorge these benefits, but given the coerced nature of the joint activity, we cannot expect them to accept a share of the burden that is not capped in this way. It follows, then, that this argument also requires a distinction between intentional and nonintentional citizens.

Capacity

A fourth factor that could ground citizens' liability to share the burden of their state's wrongdoing is a special capacity to do so. This idea is grounded in the fairly common intuition that if someone is in a position where she is able, more so than others, to address a serious wrong or harm, and when doing so is not very costly to her, she has a special obligation to act. Her obligation is stronger than the obligation of other people in the world who are not similarly positioned. A common example in this context is that of a group of bathers witnessing a child drowning at sea. In this scenario, the competent swimmers among the bathers have a duty to dive into the water to save the child. Those who cannot swim are clearly not under an obligation to act in this way, but they too may be under an obligation to assist however they can (call the emergency services and so on).

Does this fairly intuitive idea apply to the case of state wrongdoing, and can it justify a nonproportional distribution of the burden among the state's citizens? In responding to this question, we should first note that the capacity argument is typically used in contexts where a victim is in dire need and faces a threat to her life or to her other basic needs. Many state wrongdoings put their victims in dire need, but not all of them do. If the state commits a wrong that imposes more trifling burdens on its victims, our intuitions that anyone who can assist the victims should do so are far less clear-cut. But let's assume that the wrongdoing in question is a serious one. Here, as we saw in chapter 1, citizens' remedial obligations may involve various concrete tasks. They will need to contribute to the monetary resources required to pay out compensation, cover rehabilitation costs, and so on. Sometimes they will also need to initiate and support the required institutional policies and changes that will lead to the state meeting its remedial obligations. I think that it is plausible to suggest that at least in some states, and mainly in democratic states, citizens do have a special capacity, as a group, to influence their state's policies, and to ensure that it takes the necessary steps to comply with its remedial obligations. If the state initially refuses to accept its duties in this regard, then those citizens who have the ability to put effective pressure on state officials have a special obligation to do so.[38] The strength of this obligation will not be tied to their personal level of blameworthy contribution to the state wrongdoing, but to their ability to affect it, and in this sense it would be distinct from the blame-tracking model.[39]

However, similar conclusions do not apply when we turn to the citizens' obligation to accept a share of the monetary obligations that are created by the state's obligations of compensation, rehabilitation, commemoration, and nonrepetition. Here it may be the case that some citizens are particularly well placed to assist their state, given their personal level of wealth. But what grounds their obligation here is that they have the resources, rather than their membership in the state, and most citizens in most states will not be particularly well placed in this regard (whether or not they are intentional citizens). Indeed, notice that, in reality, the capacity argument places the obligation on anyone who has the resources to assist, and is not confined to the citizens of the wrongdoing state in particular. Put differently, the capacity argument identifies a basis for the nonproportional distribution of the state's monetary remedial responsibilities, but it does not support an *internal* nonproportional distribution, one that focuses on the state's citizens. In that sense it does not support the common intuition, with which we started in chapter 1, that there is something

[38] Notice that, as a matter of empirical contingency, even in democratic states it is probably less likely that nonintentional citizens would have the capacity for effective political influence, if they are oppressed citizens. See Michael Lipsky, "Protest in City Politics" (Chicago: Rand McNally, 1970); Douglas S. Massey and Nancy A. Denton, *American Apartheid: Segregation and the Making of the Underclass* (Cambridge MA: Harvard University Press, 1993).

[39] Cf. Lawford-Smith, *Not in Their Name*, 103. For a thoughtful analysis of the way in which intentional participation grounds duties of protest, see Jinyu Sun, "Political Obligations in Non-democracies: A Natural Duty Account of the Obligation to Resist" (PhD diss., University College London, 2019).

special about membership in the state, in light of which citizens are liable for their state's wrongdoing. The intentional participation account (as well as some of the other accounts I have discussed so far) is better placed to explain this intuition.

Associative Obligations

The final factor that could ground the citizens' duty to accept a nonproportional share of their state liabilities is their special associative obligations, or obligations of community. The starting point of this argument is the observation that relationships can create special obligations between their participants. On one version of this argument, these obligations are grounded in an intrinsic value of the relationship itself. Friendship is a common example here. As Joseph Raz explains, friendship is a relationship that revolves around mutual concern, and as such has an intrinsic value for its participants. To be a friend simply is to have, by the very nature of the relationship, reciprocal obligations that express our concern for our friends (for example, to dedicate time to them, or to assist them in their need). A person who fails to show concern by discharging these obligations is not a true friend.[40]

Some argue that associative obligations arise not just between the participants in intimate relationships such as friendship or family, but also in larger groups, and especially between citizens.[41] On this view, citizenship is a unique relationship between the members of a political community, where, as Andrew Mason puts it, each "is a member of a collective body in which they enjoy equal status with

---

[40] Joseph Raz, "Liberating Duties," Law and Philosophy 8, no. 1 (1989): 3–21.

[41] Ronald Dworkin, Law's Empire (London: Fontana, 1986), 195–202; John Horton, "In Defence of Associative Political Obligations, Part 1," Political Studies 54, no. 3 (2006): 427–43; John Horton, "In Defence of Associative Political Obligations, Part 2," Political Studies 55, no. 1 (2007): 1–19; Andrew Mason, "Special Obligations to Compatriots," Ethics 107, no. 3 (1997): 427–47; Yael Tamir, Liberal Nationalism (Princeton: Princeton University Press, 1993).

its other members."[42] To be an equal partner in the making of the collective body that governs our political life is intrinsically valuable for each participant. Understood in this moralized sense, citizenship generates special associative obligations between fellow citizens, including the obligation to obey the laws of the political community, and the duty to ensure that it continues to treat all its members as equals.

Can the claim that citizens have such political associative obligations help to ground their duty to accept a nonproportional share of their state's remedial obligations when it does wrong? I think the answer to this question could be affirmative for citizens who live in states where the political bond indeed has an intrinsic value for them. As we saw, these citizens have a special associative obligation to maintain and preserve their political bond. Suppose that their state advocated a policy that undermines this bond and discriminates against some of its citizens. It now turns to correct that wrong and repair the harm it had done. Its citizens have a special associative obligation to ensure that the equal status of all fellow citizens is restored, and therefore all of them ought to assist their state to fulfill its remedial obligations. This obligation will not depend on their personal association with the harm caused by their state or their personal blame for it. As we saw in chapter 1, if the state can target blameworthy citizens it ought to do so, but if a proportional distribution is infeasible, all citizens will have a duty to accept a nonproportional share of the burden, in order to preserve their valued relationship.

However, the political associative obligations argument has important limits. First, it is able to justify citizens' remedial obligations only with relation to domestic state injustices. After all, when the state commits a wrongdoing against people outside its borders, it is no longer the case that its citizens have a special relationship with the victims of the state harm, one which they have an obligation to maintain and preserve. Consider again the examples I mentioned earlier: while Canada, Chile, and Argentina were addressing wrongdoings that they had committed against their own citizens, Germany and Iraq were addressing wrongs that were committed primarily against other countries and individuals in the world. The claim that what grounds the citizens' duty to support their state's reparation schemes are their associative obligations does not apply to these latter cases. Here we would need to turn to alternative explanations, such as citizens' intentional participation.

And there is another important limitation on the scope of this argument. Recall that political associative obligations arise only in political settings where the civic relationship has an intrinsic value for the members of the state. Put differently, they need to be able to value their relationship to their fellow citizens, as fellow citizens. But as advocates of the idea of political associative obligations agree, it is not the case that the political bond between citizens is valuable in all types of states. Some, like Mason, argue that such obligations arise only in fully democratic states.[43] Others suggest that such obligations also arise in nondemocratic political communities, but they must cross a certain threshold of decency, and at the least secure their members' access to basic social goods.[44] Even if we accept this lower threshold, it remains the case that many states in the real world do not cross it, such as those highly authoritarian states in which, as we saw in the previous chapter, it is also the case that intentional citizenship is not prevalent. In that respect, both the intentional participation and associative obligations accounts rule out nonproportional distribution in similar types of regimes. The conclusions that these two accounts draw are similar also in the case of decent and democratic states. Here, too, the associative obligations account does not apply more broadly than the

---

[43] Mason, "Special Obligations." Ronald Dworkin advocates a similar line. See Dworkin, *Law's Empire*, 200.

[44] Horton, "In Defence, Part 2."

intentional participation account. Recall the two main categories of nonintentional citizens: citizens with secessionist sentiments and oppressed citizens. Both groups pose a problem for the associative obligations account as well. Citizens with strong secessionist aspirations reject their membership in their current state, and wish to secede into a different political entity. Put differently, such citizens do not accept that their membership in their current state has an intrinsic value for them. To the extent that the associative obligations account gives place to people's own evaluations of their relationship, it can scarcely apply to secessionist citizens.[45] The same problem arises with oppressed citizens in democratic states. As we saw in chapter 4, these are citizens who suffer from pervasive discrimination at the hand of the state and the political community. They do not accept their membership status in the state, given their wrongful marginalization. It is implausible to suggest that the state can demand that they accept an equal share of its remedial obligations to other citizens by evoking the intrinsic value of their membership in the state.[46]

That said, there is an important exception to my claim that oppressed citizens do not have a duty to accept a nonproportional share of the burden. I have in mind here, specifically, cases where the wrongdoing state is making a genuine effort to correct and repair the very relationship of oppression that these citizens suffer from. Consider, for example, states that are emerging from an era of authoritarian rule, as were Argentina in the 1980s and Chile in the 1990s. These states were struggling to establish democratic institutions and to create that intrinsic valuable bond between its

[45] For a careful discussion of the role that subjective identification plays in the associative obligations account see Horton, "In Defence, Part 2," 12–15.

[46] This is not to deny that oppressed citizens may have a duty to resist state oppression. But this duty would not be grounded in the intrinsic value of their membership in the state. For discussions of the oppressed's duties to resist injustice, see Shelby, "Justice, Deviance, and the Dark Ghetto"; Bernard R. Boxill, "Self-Respect and Protest," Philosophy & Public Affairs (1976): 58–69; Carol Hay, "The Obligation to Resist Oppression," Journal of Social Philosophy 42, no. 1 (2011): 21–45.

citizens. In order to achieve that goal, they needed to restore the bonds of trust between the state and the citizens, and to establish strong enough foundations of civic solidarity. Engaging in comprehensive compensation, rehabilitation, commemoration, and nonrepetition schemes were arguably necessary for such trust and solidarity to emerge. The citizens of such states, including those who suffered human rights violations at its hand, all have a duty to assist the state in completing these tasks, so that it can build a political community in which they can enjoy the intrinsic value of equal citizenship. I will return to such cases of rectifying historical injustices in chapter 7.

To sum up, I have examined in this section various accounts that could in principle justify a nonproportional distribution of the state's remedial obligations, as an alternative to the intentional participation account. As we saw, none of these accounts offers a fully satisfactory justification. The like-mindedness argument collapses into intentional participation. The democratic authorization argument applies only to a narrow category of state injustices. The benefit account requires complex calculations that renders it infeasible in real-world scenarios. The capacity argument does not limit the justification to the citizens of the wrongdoing state. Finally, the associative obligations argument applies only to domestic state injustices, and—like intentional participation—it does not ground the remedial obligations of nonintentional citizens (at least in some cases).

5.2 Distributing Responsibility in the State— A General Framework

We now have a comprehensive picture of the arguments that could justify the distribution of the state's remedial responsibilities among its citizens. Given the various limitations of each of these arguments, the conclusion that follows, I believe, is that we will not find a one-size-fits-all answer to the question of how states should distribute their remedial responsibilities among their citizens. Rather, we need a nuanced and context-specific approach that will be sensitive to the various factors in play in specific scenarios. I now turn to expand on this approach and the various considerations it needs to take into account. As we shall see, in states as we know them, the extent of intentional participation in the state is likely to play a decisive role in determining the appropriate distribution.[47]

Recall that in chapter 1, I highlighted the important role of blame in determining who should share the costs of wrongdoing. These observations lead to the conclusion that the first stage in the process of designing a morally acceptable distribution pattern requires that the policymakers examine whether a blame-tracking proportional distribution is feasible. After all, blame is a powerful source of remedial obligations, and fairness demands that those who are to blame for the state's wrongdoing should bear its costs. It therefore makes sense that the state (or the international community) will seek to identify at the least those agents within the state who are clearly and directly connected to the wrongdoing—if such agents indeed exist.[48] However, as I have argued throughout, typically a blame-tracking distribution will be infeasible on its own. All too often the costs of remedy will be too high to be borne only by those who are blameworthy, and the process of identifying blameworthy individuals beyond, perhaps, the most clear-cut cases is likely to be very burdensome and cost intensive.

At this point, those who design the distribution will need to determine whether a nonproportional distribution of the state's remedial responsibilities between its citizens is permissible. Here various factors should be taken into consideration. In the first instance, in democratic states, it may be the case that the state is able

---

[47] My context-sensitive and pluralist approach is inspired by David Miller's work on the sources of remedial obligations. See Miller, "Distributing Responsibilities."

[48] Recall that on the corporate moral agency thesis, it can be the case that a group does wrong without any of its members being blameworthy.

to show that its action, albeit clearly wrong, was a plausible interpretation of the citizens' rights (I suggested earlier that some preemptive wars, for example, could fall within this category). If that is
the case, then the state can demand that all its citizens—including
nonintentional citizens—will share in the burden, as the state is legitimately authorized to act in their name. Second, it may be the
case that the state's population is particularly well off, and therefore well placed, in light of its high level of resources, to assist their
state in discharging its remedial obligations (at least with regard to
its more serious wrongdoings). Third, it might be the case that at
least some citizens are clear beneficiaries of the state's wrongdoing,
and are liable to disgorge their benefits in compensation to the
victims. Finally, under some circumstances—and especially with
regard to internal injustices—associative obligations could justify
a nonproportional distribution among the population at large.[49] As
we saw in Section 5.1, I have not ruled out the possibility that these
factors could justify a nonproportional distribution among the citizenry. However, given the limitations I have pointed to, this will not
always, and perhaps even not often, be the case.

Policy designers should then turn to the intentional participation
framework. While the designers of the distribution scheme cannot
identify who is and who is not an intentional citizen, they can gauge
the extent of intentional participation in the state. In chapter 4,
I suggested various practical ways of doing this. In democracies,
attitude surveys and patterns of political participation can help to
serve this goal. In nondemocratic states, patterns of state repression, of civic participation, and of state manipulation should be
used to determine the scope of intentional citizenship.

Now, as we saw in chapter 4, in all states there will be some
nonintentional citizens. It therefore follows that a nonproportional
distribution is bound to have some "spillover" effect. But the size

---

[49] Recall that I suggested that this argument will not apply to nonintentional citizens,
unless they are required to address the very wrong that victimizes them.

of the group of citizens who will be unjustly burdened in this way by a nonproportional distribution will vary from state to state. When that group is relatively small, and the burdens that fall on it are not very high, proceeding with a nonproportional distribution will be overall a significantly less bad outcome than the available alternatives and, as such, permissible.

What are these alternatives then? One option with which we should compare the option of burdening the population of the wrongdoing state is that of foregoing compensation and rehabilitation efforts and leaving the costs with the victims. This could be the best possible solution in scenarios where the harm done to the victims is not very serious, or they have the capacity to absorb it, and where we have good reasons to think the majority of the population in the wrongdoing state consists of nonintentional citizens. In such scenarios the negative side effects of imposing the costs on the citizens of the wrongdoing state could be far worse than leaving the costs with the victims. In contrast, if we have good reasons to think that the vast majority of citizens in a given state are intentionally participating in it, and that only a small minority will be unjustly treated if the burden falls on the population at large, the conclusion is likely to be that extracting resources from the population as a whole is, overall, better than leaving the costs with the victims.

By and large, the empirical observations I made in chapter 4 suggest that in the democracies of the world, where the vast majorities of citizens are intentional participants, distributing the responsibility among the population at large is likely to be the recommended course of action. Some nonintentional citizens will be unjustly burdened, but especially if these burdens spread across the population at large, and as such remain relatively low for each nonintentional citizen, they are preferable to withholding compensation from the victims, given that the impact of doing so is likely to have much worse outcomes. In such cases a nonproportional distribution that is grounded in intentional participation is a model of distribution that is not costly to implement, that is justifiable to the vast majority of the population, and that generates the resources necessary for the state to meet its remedial obligations to its victims. Here it is worth recalling again the concerns about oppressed citizens who have a strong interest in not being associated with the state that wrongs them. These concerns can be met if the state (or the international community) publicly communicates that although it imposes the burden equally on all citizens, it recognizes that some citizens—and especially oppressed citizens—are burdened unfairly.[50]

Similar conclusions will apply in some nondemocratic states, if very large sections of their population are their intentional participants. In the majority of nondemocracies in the world, this is not the case. In such states, the distribution of liability to the population at large might be as unattractive as leaving the costs with the victims. Unfortunately, those who control the distribution patterns in such states are unlikely to be moved themselves by concerns about the burdens that fall on their populations. But given that these burdens are a foreseeable outcome of holding the state responsible, they should be taken into consideration by outside agents who are in a position to force a state to comply with its international responsibilities.[51]

[50] Is it possible that the model will not be feasible because the citizens of the state will not accept its implementation, on the grounds that it is not sufficiently sensitive to personal levels of blame? In response to this objection, notice first that the state should make some effort to assign higher shares of the burden to those who clearly share the blame. Furthermore, the state should be able to justify the distribution by highlighting the citizens' intentional participation. I have suggested that this is a sound basis for the distribution. Citizens may remain unreasonably unpersuaded by this argument. If that is the case, we would need to determine what is the best course of action, given these non-ideal conditions, and it is possible that they render a full compensation unachievable. I take it though that this scenario is unlikely in the real world. Typically, citizens do accept their obligation to share in the burden regardless of their level of personal fault. I thank Christian Barry for raising this objection.

[51] Cf. Lu, *Justice and Reconciliation*, 108–11. What should be done if a rogue state refuses to accept a justified pattern of distribution and imposes the burden on, say the oppressed citizens? The proceedings from such schemes will count as "tainted benefits," because they are sourced in wrongdoing. Even though the victims are entitled to compensation, they ought not accept compensation that is sourced in serious wrongdoing

There is one final alternative to resort to in such scenarios. This alternative is suggested by Cecile Fabre, in her discussion of the reconstruction of states in the aftermath of unjust wars. Fabre is wary of holding the unjust side in the war liable for these costs, because they will fall on citizens who are not necessarily able to bear it. She argues that in such scenarios the task of reconstruction can justifiably fall on third parties who were not involved in the conflict, but who have a general duty to ensure that all individuals in the world enjoy a decent standard of living and protection of their basic human rights. Fabre's suggestion can be broadened, and apply not just to the case of reconstruction in the aftermath of war, but also to costs that relate to other cases of state wrongdoings.[52] Whenever people are seriously harmed by a state, in a way that leaves them below the threshold of a decent standard of living, and if they cannot obtain compensation from the wrongdoing state because of the distributive impact on its citizens, they should be entitled to assistance from other states in the world, given those states' general duty of assistance to those whose basic needs are under threat. As Catherine Lu points out, an idea along these lines is already gaining international recognition and is institutionalized in the Trust Fund for Victims, which is part of the International Criminal Court. The Fund's "reparation mandate" is to implement "awards for reparations ordered by the Court against a convicted person."[53] But, the Fund can also complement the award of reparations when convicted individuals cannot meet the demands.[54] The Fund also has a complementary "assistance mandate" which uses other resources (voluntary contributions and private donations) in order

to others. In such cases alternative sources of compensation need to be found. The resources raised by the wrongdoing states may be used to try and alleviate the suffering of its citizens by channeling them back to them.

[52] Fabre, *Cosmopolitan Peace*, 168. Cf. Larry May, *After War Ends: A Philosophical Perspective* (Cambridge: Cambridge University Press, 2012), 194–95; Lu, *Justice and Reconciliation*, 240–44; Evans, *The Right to Reparation*, 230.

[53] https://www.trustfundforvictims.org/en/about/two-mandates-tfv.

[54] https://www.trustfundforvictims.org/en/about/legal-basis.

"to provide victims under Court jurisdiction with physical rehabilitation, psychological rehabilitation, and/or material support."[55] In short, the Fund uses international resources, collected from charitable donations, in order to address the needs of victims of crimes against humanity.

That said, there are limits to the protections that uninvolved agents can be expected to provide. It is commonly thought that this general duty of assistance is capped in important ways. In the international arena, uninvolved agents ought to ensure that all people, regardless of the country in which they live, enjoy a basic standard of living and the protection of their human rights.[56] When victims suffer serious harms from wrongdoing states, others in the world ought to help them. But it is far more controversial to suggest that uninvolved parties ought to come to their aid if the victims have suffered a minor harm or if they are themselves pretty well off and can easily absorb the harm. In such cases, it is more appropriate to leave the costs with the victims than to impose them on the nonintentional citizenry of the state, or on other uninvolved parties.

Let's conclude. I have discussed in this chapter the limitations of the intentional participation account as a basis for a nonproportional distribution of the burden, and those of various competing alternatives. The upshot of the analysis is that the way in which we hold states responsible, and how we distribute that responsibility to their citizens, must be context-sensitive and examine various considerations, including intentional participation. The precise answer to the question of how to distribute a

---

[55] https://www.trustfundforvictims.org/en/about/two-mandates-tfv.

[56] Versions of this position have been defended, for example, by Fabre, *Cosmopolitan Peace*, 3–4; Samuel Scheffler, *Boundaries and Allegiances: Problems of Justice and Responsibility in Liberal Thought* (Oxford: Oxford University Press, 2001); and Miller, *National Responsibility*. This threshold is adopted also by the Trust Fund for Victims. It focuses on restoring the dignity of victims and providing them with basic physical, emotional, and material assistance. See https://www.trustfundforvictims.org/en/what-we-do/programming-guiding-principles.

state's responsibility can be given only after an examination of the specifics of the case at hand. I have also suggested that, by and large, in democratic states, given that a high proportion of the population is intentionally participating in the state, that citizens have civic associative obligations, and that some of the states' wrongdoings are authorized by the citizens, it is likely to be overall justified to allow the costs of compensation to fall on citizens on a nonproportional basis. The same could be true for some nondemocratic states, if, for example, the scope of intentional participation in them is high. However, the empirical findings I explored in chapter 4 suggest that in most cases the citizens of nondemocracies will not be intentionally participating in their state. Here, those who design the compensation scheme will have to assess whether, overall, it is better to let the costs fall on the citizens of the wrongdoing state, on the international community, or on the victims of the wrongdoing.

In the next chapters, I turn to examine the pragmatic implementations of this nuanced approach to three instances in which states are held liable for their wrongdoings: state compensation schemes, state punishment, and state responsibility for its historical wrongdoings.

6

Distributing Responsibility—State Compensation and State Punishment

In the previous chapter, I concluded that the appropriate distribution of the state's remedial responsibilities depends on various contingent factors. These were the extent to which it is feasible to distribute the burden to members who are blameworthy for their contributions to the state's wrongdoing, the extent to which citizens as a whole are intentional participants in their state, the democratic legitimacy of the state and whether it's wrongdoing was a reasonable violation of the demands of morality and justice, whether citizens have special associative obligations to the victims of the state's wrongdoing, whether they benefited from the wrongdoing, and whether they have special capacities to address it. I also argued that—given all these considerations—by and large in democratic states a nonproportional distribution of the burden will typically be overall justified, while in most authoritarian states it typically will not.

In the current chapter, I turn to illustrate some of the action-guiding implications of this framework. Recall that in the Introduction I mentioned various contexts in which the problem of the distributive effect arises: in state officials' deliberations on how they should structure a compensation and reparation scheme and raise the resources to execute it, in citizens' deliberations on whether they should support their state's compensation scheme, and in international actors' design of their response to rogue states. In the current chapter, I focus on the third context. I use my

Responsible Citizens, Irresponsible States. Avia Pasternak, Oxford University Press. © Oxford University Press 2021. DOI: 10.1093/oso/9780197541036.003.0007

proposed framework to critically assess two instances of holding states remedially responsible for their international crimes.

The first instance is that of extracting compensation from delinquent states. While I support this practice in general, my account suggests that it must be sensitive to the regime type of the target state, and to the other relevant factors listed above. Ignoring such factors, and imposing the burden on the target state without sufficient attention to the subsequent harm to its citizens, can yield morally unacceptable results. I demonstrate this claim by examining, in Section 6.1, the 1991 United Nations Compensation Commission, a landmark scheme that extracted compensations from Iraq in the aftermath of the Gulf War. As we will see, its designers did not pay sufficient attention to Iraq's internal regime characteristics, nor to the scope of intentional citizenship within it, and imposed unjustified and serious burdens on most Iraqi citizens.

In Section 6.2, I turn to the question of punishing delinquent states—an idea that is gaining increasing support among scholars of international law. Here I review two prominent justifications of the idea that states, too, should be punished when they commit serious violations of international law. I then explore how the problem of the distributive effect of state punishment should shape the ways in which we punish criminal states.

6.1 State Compensation Schemes

The International Law Commission's Articles on State Responsibility is the core legal document that defines the content and scope of states' legal responsibilities for their international unlawful acts. This document includes a discussion of the compensatory obligations of states that have unlawfully harmed other states or individuals. The text addresses many thorny issues, including the definition of an international unlawful act, the identification of the injured parties, and the types of harm for which they may claim

damages. But, in line with the general outlook of public international law, it does not pay attention to a state's internal regime structure when it defines the scope of its compensatory responsibilities.
As James Crawford, who served as the Special Rapporteur of the
International Law Commission, explains, to be the appropriate
subject of legal rights and obligations, a state must have an effective
government. But the means by which it gains its effective control
over its population do not play a role in defining the scope of its international rights and obligations.[1]

This nondiscriminatory framework has been challenged in recent
scholarship. For example, advocates of the "odious debt doctrine"
argue that debts that were incurred by repressive governments, and
against the interests of their own populations, should not pass to
their democratic successors.[2] Others challenge the right of oppressive governments to trade in the natural resources of their country,[3]
or their right to exercise territorial sovereignty.[4] These accounts
share in common the idea that states' international legal rights and
responsibilities should be affected by their internal regime characteristics, and by the how they treat their own citizens. In a similar
vein, I argue that the internal political characteristics of a state can
also affect the way in which we hold it responsible for its unlawful
harms. I show this through an examination of the United Nation
Compensation Commission, established in the aftermath of Iraq's
1990 invasion of Kuwait, and which is considered to be an important milestone in the development of international legal practice.
In what follows, I first describe the scheme, and then explore Iraq's
regime characteristics at the time of its invasion of Kuwait and the

---

[1] Crawford, *The Creation of States*, 59. Cf. Brigitte Stern, "The Obligation to Make
Reparations," in *The Law of International Responsibility*, ed. James Crawford et al.
(Oxford: Oxford University Press 2010) 563–71.

[2] King, "Odious Debt: The Terms of the Debate."

[3] Wenar, "Property Rights and the Resource Curse."

[4] Stilz, "Nations, States and Territory."

scope of intentional participation within it. Finally, I assess the scheme in light of the framework I developed in chapter 5.

The UNCC Compensation Scheme

In the aftermath of the Gulf War and Iraq's defeat, the United Nations Security Council approved Resolution 687, which confirmed Iraq's liability for the losses it had caused during its military campaign in Kuwait. Resolution 687 also set up the United Nations Compensation Commission (UNCC), whose role was to process compensation claims against Iraq made by non-Iraqi individuals, corporations, and other states.[5] This ambitious UN-led process created, for the first time, an international forum for individuals to lay claims against states for harms suffered during an armed conflict.[6]

The UNCC defined six categories of claims against Iraq. The first three covered the most urgent claims, and were given priority hearings in the process: (1) claims submitted by individuals for having to flee Iraq or Kuwait as result of the war, (2) claims submitted by individuals for serious personal injury and death, and (3) claims submitted by individuals for property and financial losses of up to US$100,000. By the end of the process, the UNCC awarded a total of US$8.3 billion to claimants in these three groups. The other three categories included claims submitted by individuals for losses that exceeded US$100,000 and which amounted to a total of US$3.3 billion; claims submitted by corporations and to other private sector enterprises for losses to property and to business interests, which amounted to a total of US$26.3 billion; and claims

[5] John J. Chung, "The United Nations Compensation Commission and the Balancing of Rights between Individual Claimants and the Government of Iraq," *UCLA Journal Of International Law & Foreign Affairs* 10 (2005): 144–45.

[6] Evans, *The Right to Reparation*, 140; van Houtte, Das, and Delmartino, "The United Nations Compensation Commission."

submitted by governments and international organizations for the costs of evacuation of citizens and embassies, damage to their property, and damage to the environment, which amounted to a total of US$14.4 billion. In total, the UNCC awarded US$52.4 billion.[7]   *crazy!*

The UNCC was also authorized to determine the rate by which Iraq will have to pay these damages. In setting the payment rate, the UNCC considered Iraq's economic and financial capacities. At the time Iraq was the target of strict international trade sanctions. These sanctions, imposed by the UN between 1991 and 2003, restricted Iraq's oil exports—its main source of revenue—in order to prevent it from recovering its military capacities. Iraq was allowed to generate revenue from oil exports only for the purchase of basic foods, medicines, and other essential supplies. The UNCC was required to balance "between compensating the victims of Iraq's aggression and ensuring the current and future well-being of the Iraqi population."[8] It initially decided that 30 percent of the permitted Iraqi annual oil revenue should be directed toward the compensation scheme.[9] In 1999 a UN Humanitarian Panel Report raised concerns about Iraq's ability to supply even its population's most basic humanitarian needs while continuing to contribute to the scheme at this rate. The UNCC agreed to reduce Iraq's contribution to 25 percent of its annual oil revenue.[10] By 2005 the Commission concluded the claims processing. It was estimated that Iraq would complete the payments by 2021.[11]

---

[7] Data available at the UNCC website: https://uncc.ch/claims (last accessed April 2019).

[8] van Houtte, Das, and Delmartino, "The United Nations Compensation Commission," 363.

[9] This left Iraq with US$1 billion. Joy Gordon suggests that at that time Iraq needed three times this amount to meet the most basic needs of its population. Joy Gordon, *Invisible War: The United States and the Iraq Sanctions* (Cambridge, MA: Harvard University Press, 2010), 22–23.

[10] van Houtte, Das, and Delmartino, "The United Nations Compensation Commission," 364.

[11] "Iraq Resumes Payments of Gulf War Reparations to Kuwait," *Reuters*, April 20, 2018, https://www.reuters.com/article/us-mideast-crisis-iraq-kuwait-un/iraq-resumes-payments-of-gulf-war-reparations-to-kuwait-idUSKBN1HR26Q.

In designing this compensation scheme, the United Nations held the Iraqi state itself liable for the damage it had wrongfully inflicted; that is, Iraq was the corporate agent that failed to comply with its international obligations, and it was held to account for that failure. Yet the designers of the scheme were fully aware, and to an extent wary of the fact, that the scheme would have serious impact on ordinary Iraqis' lives. Indeed, given the situation in Iraq and the sanctions imposed on it, it was clear from the outset that the distribution of the burden among Iraqi citizens would not be proportional; that is, it would not be tailored to their personal involvement in their state and their contributions to its military campaign in Kuwait. As we saw, the UNCC gave some consideration to the humanitarian needs of the Iraqi population, and attempted to structure Iraq's payment rate so that it did not have too devastating an effect on its citizens at any point in time. But, in line with the common practice in public international law, the very fact that ordinary Iraqis would end up bearing the bulk of the burden for many years to come, and on a nonproportional basis, was not assumed, in itself, to be a serious obstacle to the scheme. And yet this very assumption is challenged once we examine Iraq's regime characteristics at the time.[12]

Intentional Citizenship in the Iraqi State

In order to assess the UNCC's structure, I will first examine the extent of intentional citizenship in Iraq during the period of its attack on Kuwait. At that time Iraq was ruled by the Ba'ath Party, which rose into power in 1968, thus bringing an end to the four decades

---

[12] Catherine Lu also offers a powerful critique of the UNCC, but her focus is on its debilitating impact on Iraq's ability to provide for its citizens in the aftermath of the war, rather than on the features of the Iraqi regime at the time of the invasion, and the subsequent liability of ordinary Iraqis for the crimes of their state. See Lu, *Justice and Reconciliation*, 231–33.

of bloody political struggles that had followed Iraq's emancipation from British imperial rule. Saddam Hussein, a key figure in the Ba'ath Party since its early days, became the *de facto* president of Iraq in 1979. Under his direction the party turned into a formidable organization that had complete control of the Iraqi state apparatus, and over all dimensions of political and civil life in Iraq.[13]

Recall that in chapter 4, I pointed to three factors that impact the extent of intentional participation in authoritarian states: the scope of civic participation, the level of state repression, and the type of information citizens have on their state policies. How did these factors play out in Iraq under Ba'ath Party rule? Let's examine first the extent of ordinary Iraqis' *civic participation* in their state. Recall Linz's distinction between "authoritarian" and "totalitarian" states. The former discourage political participation, and often are hardly present in ordinary citizens' lives. The latter encourage and even demand civic engagement. Iraq under Hussein's rule was clearly a totalitarian state.[14] Hussein himself declared it his "ambition to make all Iraqis in the country Ba'athists in membership and belief or in the latter only,"[15] and the main strategy of political control during his reign was "Ba'athification"—the attempt to generate loyalty to the regime by turning the Ba'ath Party into "the primary basis for political and social order and the supreme source for individual and collective identity."[16] Using a wide range of ideological

---

[13] Joseph Sassoon, *Saddam Hussein's Ba'th Party: Inside an Authoritarian Regime* (Cambridge: Cambridge University Press, 2011), 5.

[14] There is some disagreement around this question in the literature. The historian Joseph Sassoon, for example, argues that Iraq under Hussein was not a totalitarian state, because it did not have "any policy to transform the country and its economy into a centrally managed society," as did Russia under Stalin, for example (Sassoon, *Saddam Hussein's Ba'th Party*, 5). But as Sassoon's study clearly shows, and as others have argued, the Iraqi state did make considerable efforts to recruit the population and to engage it in active political participation. It aspired to "complete power over political power and thought" in Iraq (see also Aaron M. Faust, *The Ba'thification of Iraq: Saddam Hussein's Totalitarianism* [Austin: University of Texas Press, 2015], 7). In that respect, it had totalitarian aspirations, which were realized to a significant extent.

[15] Sassoon, *Saddam Hussein's Ba'th Party*, 46.

[16] Faust, *The Ba'thification of Iraq: Saddam Hussein's Totalitarianism*, 8.

and financial incentives, as well as formidable disincentives, the party reached impressive recruitment results. In 1986, for example, 10.27% of all Iraqis were Ba'ath Party members or affiliates (although the vast majority of these members and affiliates did not play an active role in it).[17]

Besides party affiliation, there were other forms of civic participation in the state. All male citizens over the age of eighteen were required to serve in the military for three years. Severe punishments were set for evaders and deserters. Citizens were also required to cast their vote in the general elections and in occasional referenda (though these did not offer meaningful political choices), and were expected to attend political rallies, meetings, and party-led social events. Public and private expressions of loyalty to the Ba'ath Party and adulations of Saddam Hussein himself were highly encouraged. Complying citizens were rewarded with medals, badges, and certificates, which were crucial for securing university places, housing, jobs, and pensions.[18]Clearly, then, the vast majority of Iraqi citizens were active participants in their state, and the state had a constant presence in their everyday lives.

But, as we saw in chapter 4, that Iraqis were *de facto* participating in their state does not yet imply that they were genuine intentional participants. The second factor that affects the scope of intentional participation is the level of *repression* the state deploys. Here there is much evidence to show that the Ba'ath Party used extreme levels of violence throughout its rule to secure civic compliance. Severe punishments were set for even the most minor expressions of political dissent, from capital punishment to amputations, torture, and long prison sentences.[19] For example, the punishment for insulting the president in public was life imprisonment and full confiscation of one's property. The family members of dissenters were treated

---

[17] See Sassoon, *Saddam Hussein's Ba'th Party*, 52.

[18] Sassoon, *Saddam Hussein's Ba'th Party*, 211.

[19] Sassoon, *Saddam Hussein's Ba'th Party*, 199.

as "guilty by association," and they too were punished accordingly.[20] The regime also often resorted to indiscriminate, collective punishments for political dissent, especially against ethnic and geographical groups that it found harder to penetrate and control.[21]

Another central repressive means regularly deployed by the Iraqi state was the collection of information on its citizens.[22] Iraqi citizens were required to regularly report to the state on their work, their health, and their daily activities. Not only that, but "almost every citizen was forced to be a watchdog and informer for the regime." Not reporting a "suspicious" act, even by a family member, was itself a crime.[23] These practices instilled a culture of fear and distrust among many sections of the population, and made political opposition far harder to organize.[24]

Finally, the third factor to consider when we assess ordinary Iraqis' participation in their state relates to the type and level of *information* they had about their state and its policies. The Iraqi state regularly lied to and manipulated its citizens. It had complete control over the printed press and other media and used censorship abundantly.[25] Given the lack of communication with the outside world, its citizens had no access to alternative sources of information. They were routinely fed false news and false rumors initiated by government agents, including on the spread of opposition to the state and the existential threats it faced.[26] They were also exposed, from a very young age, to intense methods of mass indoctrination,

---

[20] Sassoon, *Saddam Hussein's Ba'th Party*, 218.
[21] Blaydes, *State of Repression*, 50–51.
[22] Sassoon, *Saddam Hussein's Ba'th Party*, 112–14, 22–26.
[23] Sassoon, *Saddam Hussein's Ba'th Party*, 127.
[24] As Lisa Blaydes emphasizes, the Iraqi state's success in controlling its population was not uniform across the country. Some groups, distanced from the central administration by geography, culture, and language, managed to maintain higher levels of communal solidarity, and also displayed higher levels of political resistance (Blaydes, *State of Repression*, 81–82.)
[25] Sassoon, *Saddam Hussein's Ba'th Party*, 62–63.
[26] Sassoon, *Saddam Hussein's Ba'th Party*, 117, 27.

and the compulsory state education system, the media, and the cinema instilled in them a personality cult of Saddam Hussein.[27]

Despite these extraordinary levels of state repression and manipulation, some Iraqi citizens nevertheless engaged in civic resistance, or they remained noncompliant to an extent. Noncompliance came in many forms: refusal to serve in the army, or defection;[28] refusal to denounce family members, or to submit reports to the security services on the behavior of employees;[29] and spreading political jokes and political rumors that contradicted state propaganda.[30] At times, the population even resorted to more open forms of resistance, such as the wave of public protests that spread across Iraq in 1991 (and which was heavily suppressed by the regime).[31] At the same time, as the historian Joseph Sassoon points out, it remained the case that many Iraqis did not take part in such acts of protest and "voluntarily wanted to be part of the system."[32] These Iraqis, we can presume, who were Hussein's supporters, genuinely perceived themselves as willing contributors to his rule and to the maintenance of their state under his control. Should we conclude that they were intentional participants in their state? The framework I developed in the previous chapters suggests that the answer to this question, in many cases, is negative. For, as we saw in chapter 3, we should be very wary of treating as intentional participants citizens whose political outlooks were heavily shaped, from an early age, by intense indoctrination; who were routinely lied to and manipulated by their state and had no access to alternative sources of information

[27] Sassoon, *Saddam Hussein's Ba'th Party*, 61–68.
[28] For analysis of rates of draft dodging in Iraq, see Blaydes, *State of Repression*, chapter 10.
[29] Sassoon, *Saddam Hussein's Ba'th Party*, 221.
[30] Blaydes, *State of Repression*, 196.
[31] Blaydes, *State of Repression*, 86–88. Blaydes also suggests that resistance to the regime was more widespread in some areas (e.g., northern Iraq) and among some ethnic or religious groups (Iraqi Kurds and Shi'as).
[32] Sassoon, *Saddam Hussein's Ba'th Party*, 53.

about its policies; and who faced dire consequences if they refused to comply with their state's orders. It may well be the case that the Ba'ath Party succeeded in "forcing the majority of individuals to adjust their values in order to survive," and in doing so it turned them into accepting citizens.[33] But the process by which their preferences were formed was itself extremely manipulative and highly coercive. Genuine intentional participation requires that one not only accepts one's membership status, but also that one will not reject the process by which one grew to accept it. We have every reason to assume that even Iraqi regime supporters would have resisted, upon reflection, the ways in which they were led to hold their beliefs. I submit, then, that—despite their expressions of support and their compliance—we should not view the majority of Iraqi citizens under Saddam Hussein's rule as intentional citizens of their state.

Distributing Responsibility in Iraq

As we saw earlier, the UNCC allowed the burden of compensation to fall on the Iraqi population at large, by using Iraq's revenue from its oil exports as its main source of income. My framework suggests that before turning to such a nonproportional distribution model, the designers of the scheme ought to have considered targeting funds from individuals who were themselves clearly blameworthy for Iraq's violations of international law—not in the least Saddam Hussein and his family members, who had accumulated vast personal wealth during his reign. Perhaps at least some of the scheme's costs could have been funded in this way.

However, let's assume that these resources—even if they were extracted—would not have been sufficient to cover the full cost of the compensation scheme. As we saw in chapter 5, to justify the

[33] Sassoon, *Saddam Hussein's Ba'th Party*, 226.

imposition of the remainder of the burden on ordinary Iraqis, various factors ought to have been examined. I have already shown that the majority of the Iraqi population were nonintentional citizens. What about the other factors?

Let's consider first Iraqi citizens' *benefit* from their state's wrongful policies. As we saw in chapter 5, distribution of the burden in light of benefit is problematic in itself, but these complexities aside, it is also not the case that Hussein's decision to invade Kuwait benefited ordinary Iraqis. It is commonly thought that the invasion was the result of Hussein's gross miscalculation of Western states' response to an act of international aggression, which perhaps resulted from his paranoid and megalomaniac personality.[34] Whatever Hussein's motives were, the invasion had a predictably devastating effect on most ordinary Iraqis. There is no official data on Iraqi casualties in the Gulf War, but one widely cited study suggests that civilian deaths were in the low thousands, and combatant deaths in the area of 26,000.[35] In addition to these direct casualties, the ensuing US-led military campaign against Iraq, the goal of which was to force Iraq to withdraw from Kuwait, inflicted serious damage on the country's infrastructure, including the destruction of its electricity grids and water purification, sewage, and telecommunications systems. The overall cost of the damage was estimated at US$190 billion. This damage had devastating humanitarian consequences, including dire shortages of food and medical supplies, sharp rises in child mortality, and the collapse of the Iraqi economy.[36] Clearly, then, benefit from state wrongdoing cannot serve to justify the imposition of the burden of compensation on ordinary Iraqi citizens.

---

[34] For an analysis, see Efraim Karsh and Inari Rautsi, "Why Saddam Hussein Invaded Kuwait," *Survival* 33, no. 1 (1991): 18–30.

[35] Beth Daponte, "A Case Study in Estimating Casualties from War and Its Aftermath: The 1991 Persian Gulf War," *Medicine & Global Survival* 3, no. 2 (1993): 57–66.

[36] Gordon, *Invisible War*, 21–22.

A second potential justification for a nonproportional distribution of the burden among citizens is their special capacity to assist their state in discharging its own remedial duties. Clearly, ordinary Iraqis were not particularly well placed in 1991 to assist their state in meeting its monetary compensatory obligations. In the years that followed the war, most Iraqis experienced a sharp drop in their income (with average GDP per capita shrinking by over 75 percent from 1989 levels), and did not have access even to the most basic provisions. They certainly did not have the special capacity to assist their state in discharging its remedial duties.

Finally, what about Iraqi citizens' associative obligations? As we saw in chapter 5, this argument could explain why all the citizens of a wrongdoing state have a duty to assist it in addressing a wrongdoing that mars their political solidarity and equal citizenship. But this argument does not apply to the compensation Iraq paid to the victims of Saddam's war. The UNCC did not aim to address the wrongs the Iraqi state committed against its own citizens, or to influence Iraq's internal regime structure. Furthermore, it was open only to complaints submitted by non-Iraqi citizens, companies, and governments, with whom Iraqis as such did not have special associative political relations that could ground an associative duty of care.[37]

We can conclude, then, that the UNCC's working assumption, according to which Iraq's compensatory liabilities should have fallen on the Iraqi population at large and on a nonproportional basis, did not have a solid normative foundation. It remains the case that the Iraqi state itself was responsible for its decision to invade Kuwait, and yet the design of the UNCC meant that the burden of the state's remedial obligations foreseeably fell on its oppressed citizens, who were not liable for it. These conclusions do not diminish the urgency of the claims put forward by the victims of the Iraq's

[37] van Houtte, Das, and Delmartino, "The United Nations Compensation Commission," 354.

aggression, many of whom incurred very serious harms. But the urgency of these claims does not imply that it was Iraqi citizens' special duty to address them.

I mentioned in chapter 5 two alternatives to the path the designers of the UNCC took. The first was to turn to the international community, which has the obligation at the least to assist those victims who were in dire need, so that their ability to secure their basic human rights was not endangered. The UNCC's differentiation between different type of claims, and its working assumption that claims brought forward by refugees and claims for loss of life and limb should be given top priority, laid the foundation for determining what types of claims should be funded by the international community (perhaps through an institutional mechanism similar to the Trust Fund for Victims). Whichever of these urgent needs could not have been met through targeting blameworthy agents within Iraq should have fallen on countries with more resources, whose populations were not as impoverished as the Iraqi population at the time.

This solution would have left many victims' claims unsatisfied. For example, claims made by other states for costs of evacuations, or claims made by business corporations for property and financial losses, could not be straightforwardly covered by an international fund, if we accept that such a fund should only be used to meet victims' basic needs. At this point the designers of the UNCC would have faced a difficult question: Should they leave these costs with such victims, or should they impose them on Iraqi citizens? In both scenarios, uninvolved, innocent third parties would have incurred the price. But clearly the Iraqis felt the financial impact much more strongly than these relatively wealthy victims would have. Given the relative capacities of the two parties, I submit that the preferred route of action would have been to leave the costs of harm in these less urgent categories with the victims. To be clear, this solution does not suggest that the claimants were liable for the costs of the harm caused to them. It only suggests that transferring the costs to Iraq's citizens would not be a satisfactory solution either. The overall balance of considerations suggests that they ought to fall on the agents who are more capable of absorbing them.

As I noted earlier, the UNCC is a typical example of the current practice in public international law, which does not consider internal regime structure as a relevant factor in determining the scope of states' remedial obligations. My analysis suggests that this practice should be replaced by a much more discriminatory framework, which takes into account the state's internal structure. Here one can raise the objection that this alternative framework ends up letting authoritarian states off the hook, even when they have committed very serious atrocities. It leaves the costs of what they had done with their victims, or foists it on the international community. Would this scheme not create perverse incentives for authoritarian states to deepen the oppression of their populations, so that they are not held to account for their wrongdoings?

My response to this objection is that the framework I offer here does not let authoritarian *states* as such off the hook. It remains the case that the state is liable for what it has done. However, given states' peculiar corporate nature and regime structure, it also remains the case that the state may not distribute these costs in whatever way it sees fit, regardless of the moral cost of that distribution. Those who design a compensation scheme from the outside need not deny the liability of rogue states, but they should take steps to ensure that this liability is managed fairly. It is clear that individuals who hold positions of power in authoritarian states share the blame for its wrongdoings, and it is they who should be targeted in the first instance, carrying whatever portion of the burden their assets and wealth allows them to. Indeed, if the prospect of suffering personal losses rather than passing the buck to the citizenry was more real for rogue state leaders, they would have more incentives to ensure that intentional citizenship in their state is more widespread. A clear implication of my analysis, then, is that the international community must devise better ways for extracting and confiscating

resources from rogue state leaders. For in the absence of such effective mechanisms, it becomes impossible to hold authoritarian states
liable without imposing the burden on their populations, who are
themselves the victims of their wrongdoings, and who have no special relation to their state's crimes, thus giving such states little in-
centive to reform.

6.2 Punishing States

I now turn to assess the implications of my framework for the idea
of state criminal punishment. For the purpose of this discussion
I'll define punishment as an intentional imposition of a burden
in response to a legal offense by an entity with the legitimate authority to do so.[38] While we commonly associate punishment
with the imposition of burdens on individual offenders, most domestic jurisdictions also subject corporate entities to criminal
prosecutions and legal punishments.[39] In contrast, current practice
in public international law does not recognize the criminal liability
of states, and does not subject them to criminal prosecutions. The
Articles on States Responsibility do not assign criminal liability to
states, and the International Court of Justice only has the mandate
to prosecute individuals within a state for the commission of international crimes.

However, in recent years several legal scholars and philosophers
have challenged this restriction and called for the introduction of
criminal proceedings against states, especially in cases of crimes
against humanity.[40] Some also suggest that public international and

[38] H. L. A. Hart, *Punishment and Responsibility: Essays in the Philosophy of Law*
(Oxford: Clarendon Press, 1970), 5.

[39] For discussion, see Celia Wells, *Corporations and Criminal Responsibility*
(Oxford: Oxford University Press, 2001); William Wringe, *An Expressive Theory of
Punishment* (London: Palgrave MacMillan 2016), chapter 7.

[40] See, for example, Mark Drumbl, "Collective Responsibility and Postconflict Justice,"
in *Accountability for Collective Wrongdoing*, ed. Tracy Isaacs and Richard Vernon
(New York: Cambridge University Press, 2011): 23–60; Anthony F. Lang Jr., "Crime

domestic laws are moving in the direction of incorporating states' criminal liabilities.[41] It is therefore worth considering what shape the practice of punishing states should take, if the idea of holding states criminally liable should ever materialize.

All adherents of state punishment take as their starting point the assumption that states are corporate moral agents, which—as we saw in chapter 1—are distinct from their members. As corporate moral agents, states are the appropriate targets of punishment, though supporters of this idea disagree on the general justification of such punishment. These disagreements reflect a deeper disagreement in philosophical and legal scholarship on the very purpose of legal punishment. Rather than review that ongoing debate in detail, I will focus here on two popular defenses of legal punishment. I will first suggest that on both views the expansion of criminal accountability to the state itself is plausible. I will then turn to discuss how the distributive effect should shape the practice of state punishment from each of these perspectives.

Punishing States: The Expressive and the Duty-to-Victims Accounts

The first justification of legal punishment I will mention here, which is probably the most influential in the current literature, focuses on its expressive functions. It suggests that the imposition of punishment by a public authority is justified because it is

and Punishment: Holding States Accountable," *Ethics and International Affairs* 21, no. 2 (2007): 239–57; David Luban, "State Criminality and the Ambition of International Criminal Law," in *Accountability for Collective Wrongdoing*, ed. Tracy Isaacs and Richard Vernon (New York: Cambridge University Press, 2011), 61–91; Tanguay-Renaud, "Criminlizing the State"; Wringe, *An Expressive Theory of Punishment*, chapter 8; Richard Vernon, "Punishing Collectives: States or Nations?," in *Accountability for Collective Wrongdoing*, ed. Tracy Isaacs and Richard Vernon (New York: Cambridge University Press, 2011), 287–306.

[41] See discussions in Drumbl, "Collective Responsibility and Postconflict Justice"; Lang, "Crime and Punishment."

necessary for the communication of the community's condemnation of the crime.[42] This justification has been used to justify the
punishment of corporate agents in general, and of states in particular.[43] The claim here is that there are important expressive values
to the imposition of punishment on criminal states by a legitimate
international authority. States are powerful entities that control
vast resources and have efficient propaganda machines, and they
often use these to obscure or downplay their violations of international law, both to their own populations and to the world at large.
Holding states criminally accountable exposes the true nature of
their actions, and communicates, to their victims, to their citizens,
and to other states in the world, the international community's condemnation. It will also send a powerful message that despite their
enormous resources, and their ability to mobilize populations and
generate feelings of attachment and loyalty, states are not above
individuals in a normative sense. Indeed, failing to punish states
might send the opposite message, that states do deserve some kind
of moral immunity.[44]

A second influential justification of legal punishment is
advocated by Victor Tadros. It suggests that punishment is justified
not so much in light of the messages it communicates, but rather
in light of its deterring impact on future perpetrators, and on the
ensuing duties that fall on wrongdoers when they commit a crime.
As Tadros explains, agents who commit a wrongdoing incur the en-
forceable obligation, owed to their victims and to their community
at large, to do what they can to prevent their future selves and other
people from committing such crimes. Given that punishment has
a deterring effect, incurring the costs of punishment is a way for

[42] See, for example, Joel Feinberg, "The Expressive Function of Punishment," *Monist*
49, no. 3 (1965): 397–423.

[43] Lang, "Crime and Punishment"; Luban, "State Criminality"; Avia Pasternak,
"Cosmopolitan Justice and Criminal States," *Journal of Applied Philosophy* (2018);
Vernon, "Punishing Collectives: States or Nations?"

[44] Cf. Luban, "State Criminality."

a wrongdoer to discharge these obligations of nonrepetition. A legitimate authority is therefore justified in imposing the burdens of punishment on offenders.[45]

This account of the purpose of legal punishment can easily be extended to corporate agents in general, and to states in particular. On this view, as institutional moral agents, states ought to look after their own populations and at the least not violate the basic rights of other populations in the world. When they violate these duties, they owe it to their victims and to the international community to ensure that they and other states will not commit such violations again. Suffering the costs of punishment—a setback to their corporate interests imposed by a legitimate authority—could be a way of discharging this duty, if it deters them and other states (or other types of agents in the world) from committing future international crimes.[46] Therefore, the international community is justified in imposing such costs on rogue states.

The Distributive Effect of Collective Punishment

I have argued so far that the idea of punishing states is compatible with both the expressive and the duty-to-victims justifications of legal punishment. However, once we turn to the practicalities of punishing states, we are likely to face, once again, the problem of the distributive impact on the rogue state's population. Consider the suggestion that state punishment should take the form of

---

[45] Tadros, *The Ends of Harm*, chapter 12.

[46] I am putting to the side here the question of whether corporate punishment has a deterring effect in general, and on states in particular. As Mark Drumbl points out, in the absence of criminal state sanctions, we have very little empirical information on their deterring impact (Drumbl, "Collective Responsibility and Postconflict Justic", 59). Cleary, if state punishment has no deterring effect then it cannot be justified on the duties to victims view.

punitive fines or punitive trade sanctions.[47] These measures may well express the international community's condemnation of the crime, and perhaps may deter other states from committing similar crimes. But they will also have a detrimental distributive effect on the target state's citizens, who do not necessarily share the blame for their state's crimes.

In what follows I will examine three strategies for dealing with this problem.[48] The first two strategies seek to minimize the distributive effect of state punishment. But their deployment risks undermining the very purposes of punishing states. The third strategy incorporates the idea of intentional citizenship, and suggests that the distributive effect of state punishment can be justified to intentional citizens, and sometimes to nonintentional citizens as well.

According to the first strategy, the solution to the distributive effect of state punishment is for the international community to develop procedures for holding states criminally liable without imposing a burdensome punishment on them. This strategy flows from existing expressive accounts of punishment. For example, in his influential expressive defense of legal punishment, Joel Feinberg invokes the idea that, instead of the use of hard treatment, a community might be able to devise "an elaborate public ritual" that will be sufficient to "express in the most solemn way the community's condemnation of a criminal for his dastardly deed."[49] David Luban expands on this idea. He argues that—given the distributive effect—the core of the process of holding states criminally liable should not be the imposition of punishment (as

---

[47] See, e.g., Tanguay-Renaud, "Criminlizing the State." This idea follows the practice in domestic criminal law, which typically imposes financial sanctions on criminal corporations. See discussion in Bucy, "Corporate Criminal Liability."

[48] I borrow parts of the discussion in the next paragraphs from Pasternak, "Cosmopolitan Justice and Criminal States."

[49] Feinberg, "The Expressive Function of Punishment," 420. Cf. Jeffrie Murphy and Jean Hampton, *Forgiveness and Mercy* (Cambridge: Cambridge University Press, 1990), 126.

it is in domestic courts). Rather, the core should be the trial it-self—the public process of truth-finding and of condemnation, in which "the full dimensions of the human catastrophe [are] dis-played to the world patiently, step by step, for all to see."[50] This proposal echoes existing domestic practices that were developed in the context of postconflict and transitional justice, where the function of public proceedings against perpetrators is not so much to impose punitive sanctions but to serve as a "theater of ideas" where large questions of collective memory and even na-tional identity are engaged."[51] In the same spirit, Luban suggests, the public process of holding states criminally liable can remain "purely declaratory," and yet still serve important expressive goals, such as putting the state itself in the dock and challenging ideologies and political narratives that grant states immunity from moral scrutiny.[52]

Luban's proposal offers a ready solution to the problem of the distributive effect, as no punishment is distributed to the citizens of rogue states. But this solution also comes with a price. The ob-vious problem it faces is that it can only offer a declaratory condem-nation of criminal states, even in cases where it can be shown that the state has ordered the commission of very serious violations of human rights. Mere condemnations of the perpetrator by a crim-inal court are clearly an improvement over the existing status quo, where no legal forum exists even for that specific purpose. And yet it is far from clear that declarations alone can indeed serve as a se-rious enough deterring factor for future wrongdoers (as required by Tadros's view), or that they are able to communicate the seri-ousness of the crime, per the expressive view. Indeed, as we saw, one of the expressive goals of criminal prosecutions against states is to deflate the "fetishism of the nation state."[53] But this goal will be

50 Luban, "State Criminality," 73–74.
51 Mark Osiel, *Mass Atrocity, Collective Memory and the Law* (New Brunswick, NJ: Transaction Publishers, 1999), 3 (cited in Luban, "State Criminality," 74.)
52 Luban, "State Criminality," 90.
53 Luban, "State Criminality."

undermined if serious wrongdoings that are committed by states are met with declaratory condemnations only, while in the case of individual offenders they are met with far more burdensome punishments.

The second strategy to address the distributive effect advocates the punishment of states, but in a way that will harm only their interests, and not the interests of their citizens. William Wringe, for example, argues against the imposition of punitive damages on states, precisely because they have "spillover effects" on citizens. Instead, he advocates "status measures" against states, such as cultural boycotts, the downgrading of their status and participation rights in international organizations, and setting limits on their rights to diplomatic representation.[54] To this list one may add measures that could in fact benefit the state's citizens in the long run. I take the lead here from existing practices of corporate punishment in domestic settings. Typically, these involve not only punitive damages, but also monitoring and probatory terms and mandated structural and leadership changes to the organization.[55] We can envision parallel measures imposed on delinquent states, such as requiring regime change, changes to the government, or the introduction of human rights compliance mechanisms. Such measures will set back the state's own interests, in the sense that they will restrict its capacity to make autonomous decisions and have full control over its own internal processes. But they may well end up benefiting the state's population, particularly if they help to prevent internal human rights violations.

I agree with Wringe that deploying such measures is a useful strategy for addressing the distributive effect problem. However, this solution faces remaining challenges. Firstly, as a matter of practice, some of the measures that Wringe proposes cannot be

[54] Wringe, *An Expressive Theory of Punishment.* Cf. Erskine, "Kicking Bodies and Damning Souls," 286.

[55] For discussion, see Bucy, "Corporate Criminal Liability." Cf. Wells, *Corporations and Criminal Responsibility,* 37–38.

contained at the state level without having a negative impact on the citizens. Consider, for example, cultural boycotts. These are likely to have serious detrimental effects on many citizens within the boycotted state, including sportspersons, artists, academics, or people whose income relies on tourism. Perhaps then we ought to further restrict the types of punishment that may permissibly be imposed on states to include only measures that have very little negative, if not a beneficial, effect on the citizenry. These may include limiting the state's rights to diplomatic representation, or enforcing a system for monitoring the state's compliance with human rights standards. But a lingering concern remains as to whether these limited responses will be sufficiently serious, given the type of international crimes that states will typically find themselves being held criminally liable for (e.g., genocide, war crimes, mass violations of human rights). A punitive response that amounts to merely a downgraded status in international organizations, or the revocation of diplomatic rights, or even subjection to external monitoring regimes, might seem like a mere slap on the wrist. Like Luban's proposal, it can undermine both the expressive and the deterrence goals of the punishment.

These concerns do not imply that the second strategy should be abandoned. As many recent commentators on legal punishment note, when we design a proportionate punishment, we must take into account its impact not only on the direct perpetrator, but also on those individuals who surround him and depend upon him (such as his family members).[56] In a similar way, the impact on the state's citizens, as I have argued throughout, must be taken into account. Furthermore, punishing states using these limited measures is likely to be able to serve the goals of punishment better than not punishing them at all. And yet the framework I developed in the previous chapters suggests that, at least sometimes, we may impose on delinquent states more serious punishments despite their

---

[56] Fabre, *Cosmopolitan Peace*, 192–93; Tadros, *The Ends of Harm*, 356–59.

distributive effect, because these state's citizens have a duty to accept a nonproportional share of such burdens.

Consider first intentional citizens. Let's assume that the wrongdoing state in question is a democratic state, and that most of its citizens are its intentional participants. These citizens have a duty to accept a share of their state's remedial duties, which include, as we saw in earlier chapters, and as confirmed by Tadros's account, duties of nonrepetition. And they may well also include, as suggested by the expressive account of punishment, duties of "satisfaction"—namely, accepting measures that bring satisfaction to their victims beyond monetary and rehabilitative needs, including prosecuting perpetrators and accepting the state's own responsibility.[57] Per the expressive view, to satisfy its victims, the criminal state ought to accept the costs of punishment as a way of recognizing its moral blame and the wrongness of its crimes. On the duties to victims view, the state ought to accept the burdens of punishment as a way of preventing the commission of such wrongs in the future. On either account, incurring the burden of punishment is part of the remedial responsibilities that fall on a delinquent state as result of its wrongdoing. It follows then that its intentional citizens may have a duty to accept a share of the costs, as participants in their state's activities. As before, if there is a way to distribute these costs only among the citizens who also share moral blame, this route should be adopted. But if it's not possible (given feasibility constraints), then all intentional citizens have a duty to accept a nonproportional share of the burden—e.g., in the form of being unable to attend sports events, academic conferences, and so on. Here it is important to remember that the fact that intentional citizens end up with a nonproportional share of the burden is not a form of direct punishment on them. After all, these citizens have not necessarily committed any wrongdoing in participating in their state's activities. They do not incur direct duties to the victims to

<hr/>

[57] Evans, *The Right to Reparation*, 45.

publicly communicate that they have acted wrongly or to prevent future wrongs against them. Rather, the burdens they ought to bear are entailed from their membership in the state and their duty to assist it to meet its own remedial obligations. An important implication of this strategy, then, is that if punitive damages are inflicted upon a state, those who inflict them should be careful not to communicate a message of condemnation to the citizens of the state— even if the burdens end up falling on them.[58]

What about nonintentional citizens? Based on the conclusions I drew in Section 6.1, we might be led to think that—if the rogue state has features similar to those of Iraq in the early 1990s—the international community ought not impose serious punishments on it that will have a negative distributive effect on its citizens. But this is not necessarily the right conclusion. Recall that it can be the case that even the nonintentional citizens of a rogue state have a capacity-based duty to accept the burdens of their state's remedial obligations, if doing so prevents a serious wrong or harm. Here it can be argued that, at least when the wrongdoing state commits serious violations of human rights, failing to punish it would constitute a serious wrong indeed. On the expressive view, failing to punish such a state will constitute a failure to send a clear message of condemnation of the atrocity. On the duties to victims view, failing to punish the state may end up failing to prevent that state, as well as other states, from committing similar atrocities in the future. At least in the case of grave international crimes, then, imposing more than a trifling burden on the wrongdoing state is a moral imperative. Now, assume that—given the limitations of international law—it is foreseeable that these more serious burdens will have a negative effect on the population of the target state, and on a nonproportional basis. Assuming that the burdens that fall on

[58] Cf. Avia Pasternak, "The Distributive Effect of Collective Punishment," in *Collective Wrongdoing*, ed. Richard Vernon and Tracy Isaacs (New York: Cambridge University Press, 2011), 210–30.

each individual citizen are not very great in themselves, they may be overall justified, as these nonintentional citizens find themselves in the position that, in incurring these burdens, they help to prevent a very serious wrong. Even if they are not especially connected to their state and its wrongdoing, they can have a general duty, grounded in people's more general duties to prevent a wrong, to accept a share of the burden.[59]

One concern that could arise here is that this strategy paves the way for the imposition of very serious costs on the citizens of a delinquent state. Perhaps, it could be argued, we may also imprison intentional citizens as a way of communicating the wrongness of the actions of their state. In his defense of criminal liability against states, Richard Vernon addresses this concern by distinguishing the "political identity" of citizens from their other identities, and arguing that the punishment of states may only restrict citizens' political participation rights, but not their other liberties. In this way the state punishment affects citizens only as members of their state. For that reason, imprisoning citizens is impermissible, but limiting their state's autonomy in a way that will undermine their democratic influence is.[60] However, a lingering concern with this answer is that it can be quite hard to identify punitive measures that only restrict citizens' political liberties. For example, as Vernon concedes, punitive fines on the state cannot be justified because they strike citizens "in the generic capacity as consumers of private or public goods."[61] Vernon's strategy then risks leaving us very few options of permissible punishment, which again will not be sufficient to serve the very goals of punishment.

---

[59] My argument here bears resemblance to Cecile Fabre's defense of international trade sanctions. Fabre argues that such sanctions harm both the citizens of the target and of the sanctioning state, but that both groups may have a duty to incur these costs, given the sanctions' deterring and symbolic values. See Cécile Fabre, *Economic Statecraft: Human Rights, Sanctions, and Conditionality* (Cambridge, MA: Harvard University Press, 2018), chapter 3.

[60] Vernon, "Punishing Collectives: States or Nations?," 304.

[61] Vernon, "Punishing Collectives: States or Nations?," 305.

A more promising route for limiting the costs that may fall on citizens as participants in their state is simply to point out that the costs that fall on them must take into account the nature and magnitude of their involvement in their state. Given that many intentional citizens commit no wrongdoing in participating in their state, and even if their complicity is wrongful, then, as we saw in chapter 3, their level of wrongdoing is often very low, it is simply very unlikely that imposing very serious costs on them—such as imprisonment—will be appropriate. Furthermore, unlike monetary fines, prison sentences have an inherently condemning quality to them. While we can effectively tax a person without condemning her, it is hard to see how we can imprison a person without her experiencing herself as the target of condemnation and reproach. Finally, citizens often have dependents of their own, and their well-being should also be taken into account. These various considerations suggest that we ought to limit the type of costs that may reasonably fall on ordinary citizens. These should be costs that do not have an essential condemning quality, and should not undermine their ability to discharge their own duties of care.[62] On this account, punitive damages can be justified, but mass arrests cannot.

To sum up, as with the case of state compensation schemes, the practice of punishing states can have important beneficial effects on the victims of a state's wrongdoing, but also on potential future victims. But punishing a state comes with a moral cost, in the sense that it negatively affects the state's citizens. These costs will have to be balanced against the expected benefits of the act. Citizens who are intentional participants in their state have a duty to accept a nonproportional share of the burden. When the majority of citizens are not intentional citizens, the burden could also be justified on them, as long as the crime for which their state is being punished is a serious one, and the impact on them is not severe. Going back to the example of Iraq, my analysis suggests that were

[62] Cf. Tadros, *The Ends of Harm*, 358.

the international community to punish Iraq for its illegal invasion of Kuwait, it would have to do it with great care. Given the general level of destitution of the Iraqi population, and the lack of intentional citizenship in Iraq, it would probably have had to resort to the more symbolic forms of punishment. On the other hand, were the international community to punish the United States for its 2003 invasion of Iraq, it would have been permissible to impose punitive fines and other types of punishment that would have affected its population.

Let's conclude. In this chapter I have examined the pragmatic implications of the framework I offered for assessing the distributive effect. This framework called for a case-by-case analysis of the specific circumstances under which the state committed a wrongdoing, and of the relationship of its citizens to that wrong and to their membership in the state. Existing international law, I have suggested, uses too blunt an instrument when it treats states as black boxes and ignores the impact that state responsibility practices have on the citizens of the delinquent state. Deploying this process will undoubtedly be far more complex than what we currently do, but it will also avoid imposing further harms on populations who are often themselves the victims of their state's policies.

7

Intentional Citizenship and Historical Wrongs

So far in the book I have examined the distribution of state responsibility for present-day wrongdoings. However, it is often the case that states are asked to address wrongs they committed in the past, before many (if not all) their present-day citizens were alive. For example, the vast majority of German citizens in the early 2000s— when Germany was still paying reparations to Holocaust victims— were not alive when the Nazis ruled over Germany. Similarly, Canada's racist policies against the children of First Nations and their families, for which it started paying reparations in 2008, were committed before the lifetime of many contemporary Canadian citizens. And as we saw in the last chapter, Iraq is still paying into the UNCC scheme for a war it initiated almost thirty years ago.

These fairly common cases present a fresh challenge to the question of the distribution of responsibility in the state: Why should current generations be encumbered with the burden of repairing the wrongs of the past?[1] In this chapter I address this question using the intentional participation framework. At first glance, this

---

[1] I am setting aside some of the important questions that are extensively debated in the rich literature on historical wrongs, such as the "nonidentity problem"—which concerns whether the descendants of victims of historical wrongs can plausibly make reparative demands in the present, given that they would not have existed had the original wrong not occurred. Various solutions have been offered to this problem and in what follows I assume it can be shown that present-day generations are owed reparations for wrongs committed against their forefathers. For a review of this question, and the solutions, see Melinda Roberts, "The Nonidentity Problem," in *The Stanford Encyclopedia of Philosophy*, ed. Edward N. Zalta (Stanford: Stanford University, 2019), https://plato.stanford.edu/archives/sum2019/entries/nonidentity-problem/.

noah

Responsible Citizens, Irresponsible States. Avia Pasternak, Oxford University Press. © Oxford University Press 2021. DOI: 10.1093/oso/9780197541036.003.0008

framework hardly seems applicable to historical wrongs. How can a present-day citizen be participating in policies that were implemented even before she was born? I argue in response that intentional participation in the state can in fact ground present-day citizens' duty to accept a nonproportional share of the burdens of their state's remedial responsibilities even for its historical wrongdoings. However, in line with the framework I developed in chapters 4 and 5, I also argue that the state's regime structure and its treatment of its citizens at the time it committed the wrongdoing will affect the scope of its citizens' liabilities, at that time and in the future. Put differently, the distribution of liability for past state wrongs must consider the relationship between the citizens and their state—both in the past and in the present.

The chapter proceeds as follows. I begin, in Section 7.1, with a brief exploration of the position, common in both political theory and practice, that present-day states should be held to account for wrongs they committed in the past. I then turn to show that the intentional participation framework justifies the distribution of the state's liability of the state for its past among present-day citizens.

In Section 7.2, I turn to address a challenge to my state-centered approach to historical responsibility. This challenge, raised by David Miller, suggests that when we anchor responsibility for the past in the identity of the *state*, we are unable to hold present-day citizens responsible for wrongs that were committed by states that no longer exist. For that reason, Miller proposes, we should anchor responsibility for the past in the *nation*—the entity that precedes the state and survives state identity changes. I argue in response that present-day states are liable for the wrongs committed by their predecessors even in the case of state dissolution. However, I also argue that this passage of responsibility must take into account the nature of the regime in both the predecessor and the successor states. Both states should be structured in a way that allows for the nonproportional distribution of the burden in them.

[Handwritten margin note: But could argue nation is there b/c of state]

Section 7.3 turns to examine the more common scenarios of internal regime change. Here I challenge the perceived view in public international law and practice, according to which a regime change does not affect the way in which we hold a state responsible for its wrongdoings, and which suggests that present-day governments remain accountable for the wrongs committed by their predecessor, even if their country has gone through a fundamental regime change. In contrast, I argue that if a predecessor regime was highly oppressive, even the intentional citizens of its successor may not be expected to incur its remedial obligations. This conclusion has worrying implications, especially with regard to present-day democratic governments' duties to address the plight of the victims of their brutal predecessors. In Section 7.4, I examine other justifications for these duties.

7.1 Intentional Participation in Wrongs of the Past

What grounds the liability of present-day generations for the wrongs committed in the past, and before their lifetime? One common answer to this question focuses on the continuous identity of the corporate agents that committed or were complicit in such wrongdoings: firms, universities, churches, and states. Let's assume, for example, that state A engaged in a genocidal war against state V at time T. In the aftermath of this war, state A incurs the familiar range of remedial obligations to the victims of its aggression: duties of compensation, reparation, rehabilitation, and nonrepetition. But let's assume that state A refused to address these duties—perhaps because it was victorious, or perhaps because there was no international body in place to enforce them. Decades pass, and we are now in time T1. State A has gone through various internal changes. One generation of its citizens has been replaced by another, and its old government personnel—those who orchestrated the war—are no longer in power. And yet, despite the passage of time, the key elements that make it state A remain the same. It has the same name, the same flag, and the same territory; it is governed by the same general internal principles; it is recognized—by itself, by its population, and by public international law—as state A.[2] At time T1 it remains the perpetrator of the atrocities committed at time T, and continues to owe remedial obligations to the victims (or to their descendants).[3]

The idea that perpetrator states owe reparations in light of what they did in the past is fairly common in the philosophical literature on responsibility for past wrongs.[4] It is also common in political practice. For example, the CARICOM Reparations Commission, whose mission is to establish the case for payment of reparations to Caribbean nations for historical wrongs associated with the transatlantic slave trade, takes current European states to be the principals addressees of its demands, *inter alia*, given their status as the "legal bodies that instituted the framework for developing and sustaining these crimes."[5] On the CARICOM Reparations Commission's view, this fault-based liability does not wane with time if the corporate agents in question retain their core corporate legal identity.

However, as we saw in the previous chapters, a challenge to this approach is that if we hold a state liable for its actions, its citizens will pay a price. In the case of historical wrongs this challenge is

---

[2] Crawford, *The Creation of States*, 667; Erskine, "Assigning Responsibilities."

[3] As I noted in footnote 1 I am setting aside the question of how the passage of time affects the content of a perpetrator state's remedial obligations. I assume that even if the original victims no longer exist, it may well be the case that their descendants are owed compensation.

[4] See, for example, Chandran Kukathas, "Who? Whom? Reparations and the Problem of Agency," *Journal of Social Philosophy* 37, no. 3 (2006): 338; Daniel Butt, *Rectifying International Injustice* (Oxford: Oxford University Press, 2008), chapter 6; James S. Fishkin, "Justice between Generations: Compensation, Identity, and Group Membership," *Nomos* 33 (1991): 95; Richard Vernon, "Against Restitution," *Political Studies* 51, no. 3 (2003): 544.

[5] See http://caricomreparations.org/caricom/caricoms-10-point-reparation-plan/. The commission grounds its claims in the fact that the ex-colonial powers are still liable for their previous wrongdoings, and in their position as "custodians of criminally accumulated wealth."

more formidable, given that the crimes were committed before the current generation of citizens and policymakers were alive, or committed when they were only children. It is therefore impossible to distribute this burden to them on a blame-tracking proportional basis, as those who committed the crimes are no longer among them.

So on what basis should the responsibility be distributed among present-day citizens? One answer to this question focuses on the benefits that present-day citizens derive from their state's historical wrongs.[6] For example, in the context of the question of Britain's responsibility for its complicity in the transatlantic slave trade, it has been argued that given that contemporary British citizens are benefiting to this day from the riches accumulated by the British Empire through the slave trade, they can be expected to share the burden of compensation to contemporary Caribbean nations.[7]

However, as I argued in chapter 5, while the beneficiary-pays principle does ground the duties of beneficiaries to disgorge a tainted benefit in compensation to the victims, it runs into difficulties when we apply it to mass-scale wrongdoings, and especially to mass-scale historical wrongs. First, there are many cases of historical wrongs from which very few, if any, contemporary individuals directly benefit. Moreover, as I suggested in chapter 5, this approach caps the disgorgement duties of present-day citizens

[handwritten margin note: Beneficiary pays]

---

[6] Daniel Butt, "Repairing Historical Wrongs and the End of Empire," *Social & Legal Studies* 21, no. 2 (2012): 227–42; Miller, *National Responsibility*, 153.

[7] A version of this claim appears, for example, in the celebrated BBC documentary *Britain's Forgotten Slave Owners*, which was produced in collaboration with University College London (see https://www.bbcstudios.com/case-studies/britains-forgotten-slave-owners/). It also appears, for example, in the open letter to the British prime minister David Cameron from the chair of the CARICOM Reparations Commission, Sir Hillary Beckles, asking that he lend his support to a program of reparative justice between the two countries: "You are, Sir, a prized product of this land and the bonanza benefits reaped by your family and inherited by you continue to bind us together like birds of a feather." See "Britain Has Duty to Clean Up Monumental Mess of Empire, Sir Hilary Tells Cameron," *The Jamaica Observer*, September 28, 2015, http://www.jamaicaobserver.com/news/Britain-has-duty-to-clean-up-monumental-mess-of-Empire--Sir-Hilary-tells-Cameron_19230957.

at the level of benefit they derive from the past wrongful act. Calculating how much they benefited, especially from wrongs committed in the distant past, is bound to be incredibly complex and fraught with disagreements.[8] Can we turn then to the intentional participation approach in order to justify a nonproportional distribution of the burden?[9]

To answer this question, let's go back to the case of state A. Assume that the citizens of state A at time T1 are intentionally participating in their state. As such, they are the inclusive authors of a wide range of its policies. As I noted before, the application of the intentional participation framework to state A's past wrong seems problematic. For how can the citizens be the inclusive authors of policies that were committed before they were born? Intentional participation requires that one intends to play a role toward the successful production of a collective outcome. The citizens of state A at time T1 cannot plausibly be intending to contribute to policies that were executed before their lifetime. We cannot stretch the intentional participation framework so that it would also cover past state acts.[10]

However, while the citizens of state A at time T1 are not participating in policies that were executed in time T, their participation in their state at time T1 does connect them to their state's past wrongs, and justifies their duty to accept a share of their state's liability for it. The starting point of my argument here is Daniel Butt's observation that a perpetrator's wrongdoing is not necessarily confined to the original wrong itself. Consider again state A. At time T it inflicted wrongful suffering on the citizens of state V.

---

[8] Cf. Kukathas, "Who? Whom? Reparations and the Problem of Agency," 339. For other problems with the approach in the context of mass historical injustices see Lu, *Justice and Reconciliation*, 149–54.

[9] For reasons I discussed in chapter 5, I don't think the capacity or democratic authorization arguments are likely to apply to many cases of historical wrongs either. I return to the associative obligations argument later in the chapter.

[10] This point is raised in Janna Thompson, "Collective Responsibility for Historic Injustices," *Midwest Studies in Philosophy* 30, no. 1 (2006): 156–57.

But it then commits a further wrongdoing by refusing to address their plight. Put differently, at time T1, state A *perpetuates* the harm it imposed on its victims at time T. In acting in this way, it commits a "further injustice" against them (or against their descendants): it leaves open the wounds that it inflicted, which are unlikely to close by themselves.[11] In doing so, it may well compound the original harm to the victims (or their descendants), as its impact may grow over time. Finally, the refusal communicates state A's ongoing disrespect and disregard of state V's citizens' equal moral status, and of the validity of their demands.

Now, as we saw, at time T1 the citizens of state A are not participating in the original wrongdoing that their state committed, namely the genocidal war against state V. But at time T1 they are participating in state A's ongoing failure to comply with its original duties, and with its perpetuation of its victims' suffering. The only way to address *that* further wrong is for state A to acknowledge its failure and offer adequate remedy to the victims (or their descendants), in the form of compensation, reparation, rehabilitation, and nonrepetition (adjusted to the nature of the harm they suffer in the present, given state A's ongoing failures). Refusing to do so constitutes a wrong at time T1, and the citizens of state A, at time T1, are participating in *that* wrongdoing. It is therefore justified to impose on them a nonproportional distribution of the burden, per the intentional participation view.

This account can help to explain the duty of current generations of citizens to share in the burden of reparation schemes for past wrongdoings, such as those advocated by the CARICOM Reparations Commission. For example, given that Britain was heavily complicit in the transatlantic slave trade, it should have addressed the plight of those it had seriously harmed through its actions, and it bears these remedial responsibilities to this very day.

---

[11] Butt, *Rectifying International Injustice*, 177. Cf. Barry and Wiens, "Benefiting from Wrongdoing and Sustaining Wrongful Harm."

The citizens of Britain today did not participate in the slave trade. But many of them are the intentional participants in a state that has continually failed to comply with its obligations to its past victims and perpetuated their suffering. According to the CARICOM Commission, the way to repair this wrong is to transfer resources to present-day Caribbean nations. Assuming this is indeed a plausible way to discharge Britain's historical remedial responsibilities, the vast majority of present-day British citizens can be expected to share these costs, as intentional participants in their state.

7.2 State Succession and the Transfer of Liability

I have argued that citizens of present-day states can be expected to share the burden of addressing their state's past wrongs, given their state's continuous identity over time. David Miller offers a critique of this approach, arguing that focusing on the state as the bearer of responsibility for historical wrongs implies that when a state ceases to exist, and is replaced by another, no present-day agent is responsible for past wrongs.[12] Miller suggests that this pitfall can be avoided if we shift our focus to the responsibility of the nation, which is more basic than that of the state, and which survives changes in the identity of the institutions that govern the nation.

I am less confident than Miller that the nation is the type of corporate entity that we can hold responsible for its past and present actions.[13] That said, although cases of state succession are not very common in reality, they do pose an interesting challenge to the view that revolves around the identity of the state as an agent responsible for its past. What should this approach say for cases of state

---

[12] Miller, *National Responsibility*, 111. Cf. Jeff Spinner-Halev, *Enduring Injustice* (Cambridge: Cambridge University Press, 2012), 80–84.

[13] I elaborate on this in Pasternak, "Mobs, Firms and Nations."

succession? The existing international legal practice does not offer a unified view on this question. As one scholar of the public international law of succession notes, "if there is one common theme running through all recent literature on the law of state succession it is that the subject is largely confused and resistant to simple exposition."[14] Among the range of positions on this problem, we find— at one end of the spectrum—the "clean slate view," which suggests that there should not be any transfer of liabilities from a state to its successor, given the change in the personal identity of the state. At the other end we find "the successor liability view," according to which *all* liabilities should transfer from a predecessor state to its successor.[15] Both extremes prove to be unattractive, given their lack of attention to the specific circumstances in which one state is replaced by a new entity (e.g., by dissolution, merger, or annexation) and the liabilities that are involved (e.g., government debts, liabilities that result from treaties, or compensatory liabilities that result from wrongdoing). Surely these factors will shape the transfer of liability in specific instances.[16]

As before, my concern here is with one group of liabilities that might pass from one state to its successor: the range of remedial obligations that flow from state wrongdoing. To simplify matters, I will also focus only on one type of state succession, where I think it is the most difficult to justify the transfer of liability from one state to the next: succession through dissolution, where one state is dissolved, and is then replaced by a new state entity. This specific type of state succession has received scattered attention in legal practice, and courts have offered different and inconsistent rulings

[14] Matthew C. Craven, "The Problem of State Succession and the Identity of States under International Law," *European Journal of International Law* 9, no. 1 (1998): 143.

[15] For a review of the various legal positions on succession, see Matthew C. Craven, *The Decolonization of International Law* (Oxford: Oxford University Press, 2007), 29–52.

[16] Ian Brownlie, *Principles of Public International Law*, 6th ed. (Oxford: Oxford University Press, 2003), 83–84; Craven, "The Problem of State Succession," 148–49; Andrea Zimmermann, "State Succession in Treaties," in *Max Planck Encyclopedia of Public International Law*, ed. Rüdiger Wolfrum (Oxford: Oxford University Press, 2007).

in relevant cases, so for the purposes of the discussion here, I'll leave aside the legal debates, and focus on the normative considerations that flow from the intentional participation framework.[17] Could this framework justify the distribution of the burden to present-day citizens even in cases of state dissolution, or is Miller right to argue that state dissolution creates a gap and leaves the claims of victims unanswered?

When answering this question, it is worth examining how domestic jurisdictions address a similar problem. Business corporations routinely change their legal identity through mergers and acquisitions. These constant changes make it hard for criminal and civil courts to establish their legal liabilities over time and to hold them responsible for their past actions. One commonly deployed solution to this problem treats a new corporate entity as a "mere continuation" of its predecessor if the new corporate entity shares some core features with its predecessor. For example, this would be the case if it uses the predecessor's facilities or employees, if it has a similar organizational structure, or if in general it has a "substantial similarity to the predecessor."[18] In such cases, the new entity is required to assume the compensatory liabilities of the former body.

Could a similar solution be applied to the case of state dissolution? Imagine a scenario where a new state bears great similarity to its predecessor: it has the same territory, the same population, a very similar constitution, and perhaps even the same personnel occupying key offices. In such a case, it would be plausible to suggest that there has not been a substantial change in the identity of the

---

[17] For a review of the legal cases, see Michael John Volkovitsch, "Righting Wrongs: Towards a New Theory of State Succession to Responsibility for International Delicts," *Columbia Law Review* 92, no. 8 (1992): 2162–214. Zimmermann, "State Succession in Treaties."

[18] Mihailis E. Diamantis, "Corporate Essence and Identity in Criminal Law," *Journal of Business Ethics* 154, no. 4 (2019): 955–66; John H. Matheson, "Successor Liability," *Minnesota Law Review* 96 (2011): 371–422; Marie T. Reilly, "Making Sense of Successor Liability," *Hofstra Law Review* 31 (2002): 745–94.

state. The successor state is a mere continuation of its predecessor. As such, it remains liable for its predecessor's wrongdoings, and its intentional citizens can be expected to incur a nonproportional share of the burden. However, while this solution is conceptually sound, in practice, cases of mere continuation in state dissolution are unlikely to occur. Typically, a new state will have a new name, a new constitution, and a new government.[19]

However, even though successor states are rarely the mere continuation of their predecessors, it doesn't follow that they do not inherit their predecessors' remedial obligations. After all, successor states do inherit the full range of natural and artificial resources that their predecessor controlled, and they use them to execute their own, new, agenda. As Miller himself notes in his discussion of individuals' responsibility for the past, in both common and Roman law jurisdictions, agents who inherited wealth are liable for the obligations their predecessor should have addressed when they were alive.[20] This basic principle may well apply to corporate agents as well. A successor state that inherits, or assumes the right to, the resources of its predecessor, is also liable for its predecessor's obligations. Had the predecessor state paid the debts it owed to its victims, the new state would not have the same level of resources to control. It is therefore liable to addresses these liabilities, using the resources it inherited, which should have been transferred to the victims of its predecessor. The compensatory liabilities of a successor state can pass over to its successor even if the latter does not bear a resemblance to the former, as long as the latter takes over the former state's resources. As we saw in the previous section, if the successor state refuses to address these outstanding obligations, it

[19] Perhaps some cases of decolonization—if one agrees they count as cases of state dissolution—could fall under the mere continuation thesis, if there was very little change to the administration and legal structure of the country (e.g., some cases of decolonization of the Commonwealth). For discussion, see Volkovitsch, "Righting Wrongs," 2202.

[20] Miller, *National Responsibility*, 149–50. Miller does not attempt to use this framework to explain the transfer of liability between states or nations over time.

is perpetuating the victims' suffering, thus committing a separate wrong against them. Its intentional citizens, down the generational lines, are participating in that wrong, and as such can be expected to share the burden of undoing it.

This solution helps to address Miller's own critique that state succession creates, in general, responsibility gaps for past wrongs. However, this solution remains vulnerable to a more restricted version of Miller's critique (and one that his own account of *national* responsibility is vulnerable to as well). Recall the framework I proposed in chapter 5 for the distribution of responsibility in the state. As we saw there, the way we hold states responsible for their wrongdoings should be sensitive to the costs that fall on their citizens, and to the relationship between the citizens and their state. As I now turn to show, this framework may limit the scope of citizens' liability not just for what their state does in the present, but also diachronically, with regard to the responsibilities it inherits from its predecessor.

To see this, consider the case of state C. At time T it was ruled by a highly oppressive regime—perhaps not unlike the one that ruled over Iraq throughout the 1980s and 1990s. Under the control of this authoritarian government, state C engages in an unjust war. Time passes, and at time T1—perhaps as result of the war—state C is dissolved and is replaced by a different state, state D. Does D incur remedial obligations to the victims of its predecessor's unjust war? To answer this question, we first need to look more closely at C's remedial responsibilities at time T, given the distributive effect. Recall that, as I argued in chapter 5, various factors determine how state C's responsibility should have been distributed among its citizens at time T: Was a blame-tracking distribution feasible? Were they intentional participants in their state? Did they authorize their state to act as it did? Did they have a special capacity to address the plight of the victims? Did they benefit from the wrongdoing or have special associative obligations to the victim? Let's assume (as arguably was the case in Iraq in the 1990s) that none of these factors would have justified a nonproportional distribution of the burden at time T. As I argued in chapter 5, this conclusion has important implications for how we would have held C remedially liable at time T, given the adverse effect on its already oppressed citizens. In such cases, C's obligations should have been discharged through the use of the international community's resources, and sometimes even absorbed by the victims themselves. If that is indeed the case, then it follows that—*per* the inheritance argument—state D does not inherit these liabilities. After all, it would no longer be the case that at time T1, D inherited from C resources that it should have used at time T in order to comply with its compensatory obligations. For in such cases, the liability (or the portion of it that could not be apportioned by a blame-tracking distribution) should have been transferred to agents outside state C.[21]

Similar conclusions apply in cases where a predecessor state is replaced by one that is highly oppressive. Let's assume that state E committed a wrong at time T and then dissolved and was replaced by state F. State E was the type of state where a nonproportional distribution of the burden of the state's liabilities was justified— perhaps because it was ruled by a fairly benign regime and the vast majority of its citizens were intentional participants in their state. State E should straightforwardly compensate its victims at time T, and distribute the burden between its citizens. And yet it refuses to do so, and in time is replaced by state F, a highly authoritarian state. Are the citizens of state F liable for the burden of compensation to the victims of their predecessor? As we saw in Section 7.2, they would be, if they are participating in state F and in its perpetuation of the victims' plight. But if they are not intentional

---

[21] One might argue that the relevant benchmark against which we should measure state D's liabilities is one where state C was not controlled by an abusive regime, and could have been held corporately liable despite the distributive effect. But the problem with this line of argument is that, presumably, were state C not controlled by the abusive regime, it would not have committed the wrongdoings in question. Therefore, this counterfactual also cannot explain the duties that fall on state D.

participants in their state, and are neither benefiting from its refusal to accept its predecessor's obligations nor in a special position to assist, there is no solid basis for the claim that they ought to accept a nonproportional share of the burden of their state's continued failure to address the obligations that it inherited.

To conclude the discussion here, the framework I developed in chapter 5 applies not only synchronically, to wrongdoings states commit in the present, but also diachronically, to the responsibilities they inherit from the past. The context-sensitive approach requires that we examine whether the distribution of the responsibility to the state citizens would have been justified at the time it committed the wrongdoing, in order to determine whether it passes on to a successor state. If it was not, then it is no longer the case that present-day citizens should pay for the crimes committed in the past.[22]

7.3 Regime Change and the Transfer of Liability

As I noted earlier, cases of state succession are not very common in the real world. Barring intense periods of international political turmoil (such as the aftermath of the First World War, the end of the colonial era, or the collapse of the Soviet Union), only rarely do old members leave, or new members join, the international community

---

[22] As I mentioned earlier, Miller suggests that, given the gaps in the continuous identity of the state, we should revert to the idea of *national* responsibility, where the nation, rather than the state, is held responsible for its past wrongdoings. However, his idea of national responsibility cannot solve the particular problem I have identified here. After all, Miller is also reluctant to use this framework in cases where a nation is controlled by a highly oppressive regime. For, as he explains, in the absence of democratic procedures, it can "be difficult to establish how far the population as a whole is implicated in support for the activities in question" (Miller, *National Responsibility*, 127.) It follows then that on his account, too, present-day co-nationals would not inherit the liabilities for crimes that were committed by a nation-state that was highly oppressive, given that we cannot attribute its actions to the nation.

of states. Far more common are internal state transformations, which—though they do not constitute a change in the identity of the state as such—give it a very different character. Common examples here are revolutionary transitions from autocratic to democratic regimes (like those that swept over South America in the 1980s), or regime changes that are imposed on the losing side in the aftermath of a war (e.g., the division and regime change imposed on Germany in the aftermath of World War II, or the transformation of Iraq after the Second Gulf War).

I noted in the previous section that international and domestic jurisdictions do not have a unified approach to the question of the transfer of state liabilities in cases of succession. The picture is different in cases of internal regime changes. Here the dominant position is that with regime change, "the international legal personality of the state remains intact, state succession has not occurred, and the state remains responsible for the obligations entered by the predecessor government on behalf of the state."[23] Not only are new regimes expected to accept their predecessor's obligations in the international arena, this principle also applies to domestic obligations as well. Newly established democratic governments often initiate reparative schemes to the victims of their dictatorial predecessors. This was common practice, for example, across the new democratic regimes of South America in the 1980s and 1990s. As the Chilean government explained in 1991, when it initiated its reparation scheme, the new administration owed these reparations as an expression of "the recognition and responsibility that may be owed by the State."[24]

However, as I now turn to argue, it is far from straightforward to justify the distribution of responsibility to the citizens of states that

[23] Tai-Heng Cheng, "Why New States Accept Old Obligations," *University of Illinois Law Review* (2011): 36. Cf. Crawford, *The Creation of States*, 678–79.

[24] Cited in Elisabeth Lira, "The Reparations Policy for Human Rights Violations in Chile," in *The Handbook of Reparations*, ed. Pablo de Greiff (Oxford: Oxford University Press, 2008), 58.

committed past atrocities and then gone through regime change. The problem here is not, as Jeff Spinner-Halev argues, that the very continuous identity of the state is put under question when it has gone through an internal regime change.[25] One reason to resist the change of identity view is that typically the new regime and the citizens of the state do not challenge the continuous identity of their state, but instead regard themselves as members of the same institutional agent despite the structural changes it underwent.[26] Instead, the challenge here is similar to the one I raised with regard to state succession, and pertains to the nature of the regime at the time the wrongs were committed. To see this challenge, consider now state G, which is controlled, at time T, by a highly oppressive regime. State G commits an atrocity at time T. Our already familiar framework points to the set of factors we should examine in order to determine how its remedial liabilities should have been distributed at time T. Assume, that—given the extent of oppression in state G and the lack of widespread intentional citizenship in it—the majority of citizens are not liable for a nonproportional share of their state's remedial obligations. Assume also that the final balancing of the various considerations at hand leads to the conclusion that imposing the burden on them is a worse option than imposing the burden on the international community and on the victims. As we saw in chapter 6, this description fits the situation in Iraq in the 1990s, for example.

Now let's assume that state G has gone through a radical regime change. Following a democratic revolution, a new government

[25] Spinner-Halev, *Enduring Injustice*, 81.

[26] Consider the case of Venezuela. Spinner-Halev questions its continuous identity, given that it has had twenty-four different constitutions since 1811. But the continuity of the Venezuelan state has not been challenged by these successive Venezuelan governments, nor by Venezuelans themselves, who continue to commemorate the 5th of July, 1811—the date Venezuela first got its independent state status—as the national Independence Day. For a discussion of the continuous identity of the state from the perspective of political theory, see Sean Fleming, *Leviathan on the Leash* (PhD diss., Cambridge University 2018), chapter 4.

is put in place. This government rewrites the constitution of the country and rules in accordance with democratic principles. Time passes, and the citizens of state G, given the change in the nature of their regime, become intentional participants in their state. They are the inclusive authors of its policies and liable for its wrongdoings in the way I described in chapter 3. Are these citizens also liable to accept a share of the burden of the remedial obligations state G incurred at time T? I submit that the answer to this question is negative. After all, at time T, state G was not the type of corporate entity that could have distributed its liability to its population at large. Given the range of balancing considerations, at time T that burden should not have passed on to its subjects. But if that is the case, then why should its citizens become liable for this burden at time T1? It remains the case that these citizens were not the intentional participants in the past regime's policies, and their democratic government at time T1 is not perpetuating the wrongs done to the victims. These victims' demands from time T should have been met by the international community, and/or should have been absorbed by them. State G changed its character at time T1, but this does not mean that we may ignore its past treatment of its citizens when we determine the scope of its present-day liabilities.

My core claim, then, is that states may demand that their citizens accept a nonproportional share of the burdens of their liability only when their treatment of their citizens, *at the time at which they commit the wrongdoing,* meets certain standards. When that is not the case, then neither they, nor the international community, nor their victims can demand that the state's citizens will absorb the costs of the state's crime, regardless of their personal involvement in it. This conclusion has important action-guiding implications. Consider again the case of the UNCC, which I discussed in the previous chapter. I argued there that it was wrong to hold Iraqi citizens liable in the immediate aftermath of the First Gulf War for the crimes of their regime. My argument suggests that it is also wrong to demand that contemporary Iraqi citizens continue to contribute to the UNCC to this day, thirty years after the original wrongdoing. In the course of these thirty years, Iraq has attempted to become a democratic state, and let's assume—if only for the sake of argument—that intentional citizenship in contemporary Iraq is prevalent. Even if that were the case, present-day Iraqis are not liable for the wrongs committed by the regime that oppressed the previous generation. The burdens of compensation for the crimes of that regime should have been allocated to those agents who were better able to absorb them, at the time. They should not be imposed on the generations of ordinary Iraqis to come.

We will reach different conclusions, however, in cases of regime change where in both stages the citizens were liable for a nonproportional share of the burden. Consider, for example, a democratic transition from a fairly benign authoritarian regime. Given the low levels of state repression and manipulation deployed by the authoritarian regime, it is reasonable to assume that the vast majority of its citizenry, by and large, were intentionally participating in their state. In such a case, the distribution of the state's liability among the population at large and on a nonproportional basis at time T is uncontroversial. If the state fails to comply with these duties at time T, then at time T1 it will be perpetuating the plight of the victims, and its citizens at time T1 will be participating in that wrong and liable for the costs.

I noted earlier that public international law does not commonly treat regime change as a cause for reconsidering a state's international obligations. However, as I briefly mentioned in chapter 5, the claim that a state's internal structure should affect the content of its international obligations appears elsewhere in the literature. The version of this claim that is most relevant to the question of responsibility for past wrongs appears in the discussions around states' "odious" debts. Odious debts are incurred by a dictatorial state without the consent of the population, and not for the benefit of the population (e.g., in order to ensure their ongoing subjugation). Furthermore, their creditor issues the loan despite being aware of the nature of the regime and the purpose of the loan.[27] It is commonly agreed that odious debts do not pass on to successor states in cases of state *succession*.[28] But there is far greater controversy around them in cases of regime change. While the common view is that odious debts do pass on to successor regimes, there is growing support for the view that they should not. Indeed, the doctrine of odious debt was evoked with regard to the debts that were incurred by Saddam Hussein's regime. In the aftermath of its 2003 invasion of Iraq, the US administration pushed forward the view that the successor democratic government in Iraq was not liable for the previous regime's debts, under the doctrine of odious debt. According to some accounts, this pressure played a role in Iraq's creditors' acceptance of an 80 percent reduction in Iraqi debt obligations.[29]

One fairly common argument in favor of the doctrine of odious debt points to the gap between the interests of the regime and those of its subjects in dictatorial states. This argument is advanced, for example, by Alexander Nahum Sacks, whose work shaped the development of the doctrine:

When a despotic regime contracts a debt, not for the needs or in the interests of the state . . . this debt is odious for the population of the entire state, this debt does not bind the nation, it is a debt of the regime, a personal debt contracted by the power that contracted it and consequentially it falls with the demise of that power.[30]

---

[27] King, "Odious Debt: The Terms of the Debate," 632.

[28] Cheng, "Why New States Accept Old Obligations," 40. See discussion of the development of the legal debate around this issue in King, "Odious Debt: The Terms of the Debate."

[29] For discussion, see Jai R. Massari, "The Odious Debt Doctrine after Iraq," *Law and Contemporary Problems* 70, no. 4 (2007): 139–56.

[30] Sacks, *Les Effets des Transformations De Etats*, 157–58; cited in Jeff King, *The Doctrine of Odious Debt in International Law: A Restatement* (Cambridge: Cambridge University Press, 2016), 52. King goes on to develop a different defense of the odious debt doctrine, according to which it is sufficient that the debt was incurred with the knowledge of the creditor and that its purpose is serious violations of *jus cogens*. His

Sacks's argument rests on the intuition that if a repressive government incurs a debt against the interests of its population, it may not transfer that debt to that population, and it also may not pass it on to its democratic successor. If the creditors cannot get their money back from those who wrongfully took the loan (i.e., on a proportional basis), the debt ought to be forgiven, or absorbed by the lenders.[31] My argument suggests that the same logic should apply to compensatory obligations: given that the population of a state controlled by an oppressive regime is not properly participating in the state's wrongful policies (and assuming no other factors tie them to that wrongdoing), demanding that they pay for its policies is unjustified.

To conclude, the starkly different treatment that cases of state succession and state regime change receive in international public law ought to be reconsidered. In both cases, and regardless of whether the original state retains its corporate identity, if at the time it commits a wrongdoing the state is an oppressive corporate agent, which rules over a population that is not genuinely participating in its actions, then the liabilities that its government acquires on its behalf cannot justifiably pass on to the present or the future citizens of that state.

7.4 Meeting Victims' Demands

I have argued so far that on the intentional participation framework, contemporary citizens are not liable for a nonproportional share of the burden of their state's wrongdoings, when these were committed at a time when their state was highly oppressive. Who is responsible for addressing the victims' demands then? When

account draws on the doctrine of complicity and the prohibition on lenders to assist in the commission of serious human rights violations.

[31] Cf. Cheng, "Why New States Accept Old Obligations."

it comes to state debts, adherents of the odious debt doctrine are content to leave the monetary loss with the lenders, given that they knew, or should have known, the nature of the state to which they issued the loan and the purpose for which it was intended. But the picture is different in the case of remedial obligations, where the monetary and other claims are made not by bad-faith creditors, but by innocent victims (or their descendants) who merely found themselves in harm's way.

As we saw in chapter 5, there can be other agents, besides the current population of the wrongdoing state, who could be expected to assist the victims. In the first instance, there can be agents outside the state who share the blame for the state's historical wrongdoings, and who should incur the burdens of compensation in light of their complicity. This idea was proposed, for example, by the South African Truth and Reconciliation Commission, which addressed the atrocities committed by the apartheid regime. The Commission recommended that funding for the reparations scheme should be sought, *inter alia*, from the Swiss government and Swiss banks, given their financial support and complicity in the crimes of the South African apartheid regime.[32] Assuming these agents are corporate agents, whose identity stretches over time, their obligation to assist victims of wrongdoings can stretch well into the future. Furthermore, even if blameworthy agents cannot be identified, we can implement the idea of a "universal compensation scheme," which I mentioned in chapter 5. Such a scheme, which Cecile Fabre suggests should be used to fund war reparations, can also be used to address the claims of individuals and communities who were harmed in the past by repressive regimes and states that no longer exist.

---

[32] Christopher Colvin, "Overview of the Reparations Program in South Africa," in *The Handbook of Reparations*, ed. Pablo de Greiff (Oxford: Oxford University Press, 2008), 199.

Clearly, these proposals require a radical shift in the way we distribute responsibility for state wrongdoing at present. At least at present, targeting agents outside the state is likely to present difficult pragmatic challenges, *inter alia*, given the absence of enforcement mechanisms.[33] While, as I mentioned before, a scheme along the lines of the universal compensation scheme has emerged at the international level, it is currently limited to cases of contemporary wrongdoings and only to addressing the needs of victims who are in dire need. Indeed, as things currently stand, it is the case that successive governments accept the reparatory obligations of their authoritarian predecessors. This is typically the case with internal reparations schemes, such as those that were implemented by South Africa, Chile, and Argentina in the 1990s. Going back to the list of sources of remedial obligations I examined in chapter 5, there is one claim which could help to justify the spread of the burden of these internal reparation schemes on the population at large. I have in mind here the claim that as participants in an intrinsically valuable political relationship, citizens have associative political obligations, which can include the duty to accept a nonproportional share of the state's remedial obligations, even if they have not intentionally participated in that state.

As applied to the case of historical wrongs, the idea is that past injustices—such as those committed by a brutal regime against citizens who dared to resist it, or by a genocidal regime against persecuted minorities—threaten the ability of a newly established democratic polity to restore the bonds of trust and solidarity among its citizens. Measures of state compensation, rehabilitation, and commemoration, and efforts to ensure nonrepetition, may be needed in order to increase the trust of all citizens—including those who were oppressed by the regime—in the new political institutions

---

[33] Indeed, the Truth and Reconciliation Commission's proposal to target outside agents was not implemented. The South African government took upon itself the duty of reparation, but, *alia*, due to its lack of resources, many victims' claims remained unsatisfied. See discussion in Colvin, "Overview of the Reparations Program in South Africa."

of their state and to help eliminate civil strife.[34] In such scenarios, all citizens will have the duty, grounded in their political associative obligations, which themselves are generated from the intrinsic value of their newly established democratic bond, to ensure that their state is able to secure solidarity, trust, and equal membership between them, and to deepen their mutual democratic ties. These associative duties exist regardless of citizens' intentional citizenship or degree of involvement in the state's crimes, and the burdens can be distributed among citizens on a nonproportional basis.

But notice that, as I argued in chapter 5, the associative obligations argument does not apply to all cases of historical wrongs. It applies specifically to scenarios where the valuable political bond between citizens is threatened given the persistence of past wrongs. When past wrongs do not adversely affect the contemporary relationships between citizens, or when the wrongs were done to people who are not members of the state, and where the descendants of victims and of wrongdoers are not engaged in an intrinsically valuable relationship they have a special duty to preserve, then we need an alternative justification for the distribution of the burden on a nonproportional basis among the wrongdoing state's citizens. As I have suggested, it may well be the case that such an argument cannot be found.

One possible objection to this conclusion is drawn from Janna Thompson's work. Thompson argues that citizens of contemporary states have a duty to share their state's remedial obligations, even with regard to external past wrongs, given their duty "to

---

[34] On the corrosive impact of historical injustices on citizens' trust in their state, see Spinner-Halev, *Enduring Injustice*, 74–79. On the role of reparations as restoring trust and solidarity in transitional societies, see Pablo de Greiff, "Justice and Reparations," in *The Handbook of Reparations*, ed. Pablo de Greiff (Oxford: Oxford University Press, 2008), 452–76. Cf. Chandran Kukathas, "Responsibility for Past Injustice: How to Shift the Burden," *Politics, Philosophy & Economics* 2, no. 2 (2003): 173–74. But for a more skeptical view of the positive correlation between transitional justice measures and successful democratic transition, see Tricia D. Olsen, Leigh A. Payne, and Andrew G. Reiter, "The Justice Balance: When Transitional Justice Improves Human Rights and Democracy," *Human Rights Quarterly* 32, no. 4 (2010): 980–1007.

support the operation of their [state's] morally reliable practices and institutions."[35] In her view, the morally reliable state is one whose policies seek to track justice and which corrects its ways and compensates those it harms when it commits a moral error.[36] All people have a strong interest in living under morally reliable institutions, and therefore we all have a duty to support a state that seeks to remedy its past wrongs and increase its moral reliability, regardless of our subjective attitudes to it.[37]

However, I am not persuaded that Thompson's argument indeed shows that citizens have a duty to accept a share of the burden of their state's remedial obligations with regard to its tainted past, especially in cases of regime change. On Thompson's account, it needs to be the case that a state's past mistakes affect its moral reliability in the eyes of the world and in the eyes of its citizens in the present. But why should this be the case, if the state has gone through a fundamental regime change? The state is already doing a lot to demonstrate that it no longer abides by the same odious ideology of its predecessor, by setting up a new constitution, replacing those who stand at its head, and so on. Its character today is already very different from what it was in the past, and it need not be the case that it ought to also pay compensation for the past just in order to show its moral reliability. As I suggested above, paying compensation can be required of it, however, as a way of restoring its citizens' democratic associational bonds.[38]

It is time to conclude. I have offered in this chapter an analysis of citizens' liability for their state's wrongdoing across time, and through changes in the identity or character of the state. In the simple straightforward case—where a democratic state maintains its identity and character over time—it is fairly easy to show that present-day intentional citizens can be expected to share the cost

---

[35] Thompson, "Collective Responsibility for Historic Injustices," 162.
[36] Thompson, "Collective Responsibility for Historic Injustices," 162–63.
[37] Thompson, "Collective Responsibility for Historic Injustices," 164–66.
[38] Miller, *National Responsibility*, 145–46.

of what their state had done, even in the distant past. However, in reality we face messier scenarios, where states go through radical character and even identity changes. I have argued, in line with the framework I offered earlier in the book, that the political characteristics of the state that committed the wrong, at the time it committed the wrong and at present, affect the obligations of its present-day citizens. When the state is one that oppressed its citizens, so that by and large they are not its intentional citizens, and have not benefited from the wrongdoing or had a special capacity to address it, that state may not pass its liabilities on to them on an equal basis at the time it did the wrong. When a new state is born out of struggle against such an oppressive predecessor, or where the population of a state is freed from the yoke of such an authoritarian regime, it does not inherit the predecessor's liabilities, and therefore the new generation of citizens will not be particularly well placed to address the plight of the victims of past wrongs. That said, I argued that when addressing the wrongs of the past it is necessary, in order for the state to be able to function as a democratic polity, that its current citizens will have a duty to assist it in doing so.

Conclusions

My goal in this book was to answer the question, "Should citizens pay for their state's wrongdoings?" I approached this question from the position that states are moral agents in themselves, and as such are responsible for their own actions. It is the state, in the first instance, that owes duties of compensation, rehabilitation, reparation, and nonrepetition to the victims of its wrongdoings, or to their descendants. And yet, given the corporate nature of the state, these forward-looking responsibilities will have a foreseeable distributive impact on the state's members. In order to fully justify the practice of holding states responsible, we need to be able to justify its impact on their citizens.

Throughout the book I contrasted two leading approaches to this problem. The first suggests that the distributive effect of the state's responsibility on its members is justified to the extent that it tracks these members' own faulty contributions to their state's wrongdoings. Such proportional distribution, which is likely to target key policymakers and policy enactors within the state, is intuitively attractive. And yet real-world states rarely, if ever, adopt it. Instead, they typically let the burdens of their liabilities fall more or less equally on the population at large. One reason for the proportional distribution's lack of popularity, I suggested in chapter 1, is that it is impracticable. In particular, it is costly, and can be ineffective in generating sufficient resources to address the state victims' needs. Given these concerns, is the state justified in turning to its population at large and demanding that it accepts a nonproportional distribution of the burdens of its own wrongdoings?

Responsible Citizens, Irresponsible States. Avia Pasternak, Oxford University Press. © Oxford University Press 2021. DOI: 10.1093/oso/9780197541036.003.0009

My first task in this book was to develop a fresh justification for a nonproportional distribution of the burden, one that applies to real-world citizens and could be used in real-world states. My justification revolved around the claim that citizenship is not merely a status, but also involves acting together, with other citizens, in the state. As I explained in chapter 2, the starting point of this argument is the view that collective action involves, at a minimum, agents who act with a participatory intention; that is, agents who see themselves as contributing to the realization of a collective end. I argued (in chapter 3) that this general formulation applies to citizens in their states. When citizens perform their various roles in their state—from paying taxes to obeying the law, voting, etc.—they also see themselves as contributing to the maintenance of their state as a corporate agent, with the ultimate legal and political authority over the territory in which they live. These citizens are therefore taking part in their state's activities, and even in activities or policies they disagree with or are unaware of. Our collective participation in our state's policies, I suggested, renders us the inclusive authors of a very wide range of our state's policies. Excluded from the account are only policies that are hidden from us by the state in a deep sense, and policies that the state deceives us about. Under normal circumstance, and in the absence of deep secrets and lies, we are the inclusive authors of all our state policies.

The idea of intentional citizenship, I argued, explains why citizens can be expected to accept a nonproportional share of the state's remedial obligations for its wrongdoing, if a blame-tracking distribution proves to be impracticable. For, as I explained in chapter 2, when people choose to act with others, they willingly give up control over the outcomes of the shared endeavor, accepting that they will be credited if their joint endeavor leads to beneficial outcomes, and burdened if it does not. Taking part in a collective act *ipso facto* commits us to a potential share of the consequences of the shared activity. This insight suggests, then, that when citizens take part in their state's activities, they become part of the group of individuals who may be called upon to assist the state in answering for the wrongs it committed.

However, there is an important caveat to this moral demand. I argued that it applies only to group members who *accept* their membership status in their group. People accept their membership in a group if they are not alienated from it and do not see it as forced on them against their will. Put differently, people are the genuine authors of their participatory intentions, to the extent that they do not resist these intentions or the process through which they were formed. When they are the genuine authors of these intentions, they are liable for the consequences of their group's actions. Applied to the case of citizens, then, this caveat suggests that intentional citizens should not be alienated from their state. They might not have a viable option to leave their state, or to refuse participation in it, but they nevertheless do not view it as an alien and coercive force in their lives. Crucially, it is essential that their attachment to their state is not gained through extreme coercion and manipulation, so that when they reflect on their participation in the state, and the processes that shaped their attitudes to it, they do not experience a sense of alienation and resistance.

After having described the contours of intentional citizenship, I proceeded to examine to what extent this idea applies to real-world citizens, in real-world states. I proposed that we can gauge the answer to this question by looking at existing cross-national surveys on people's attitudes to their state and their national identity. Analyzing some of the questions that appear in surveys such as the World Values Survey, the Eurobarometer, and the Afrobarometer, I concluded that intentional citizenship is fairly prevalent in democratic states, where samples of vast majorities of the population express attachment to their membership in their state. But I also pointed to groups of citizens within democratic states to which the model of intentional citizenship does not seem to apply. These groups included, mainly, citizens who belong to secessionist groups and citizens who are themselves marginalized by their state.

What about the citizens of nondemocratic states? Given that attitude surveys do not always offer reliable data on citizens' political beliefs in such states, I turned to more general authoritarian regime typologies in order to identify the factors that affect the scope of intentional citizenship in them. My final conclusion, in chapter 4, was that in most nondemocracies, it is unlikely that genuine intentional citizenship will be prevalent among the population at large. And yet, there are some nondemocratic states in which, given the low levels of repression they use, or their reliance on generally shared comprehensive doctrines, intentional citizenship can be more common.

I thus reached the conclusion that the intentional participation justification for the nonproportional distribution of the state's responsibility applies to many citizens in many states in the world. But not to all of them. In chapter 5, I turned to examine other possible justifications for the distribution of the state's responsibility on an equal basis, including the claim that citizens authorize their state to act in their name, that citizens benefit from their state's actions, that citizens are best placed to address their state's victims' needs, and that citizens' political associative obligations generate the obligation to share the burden equally. While I did not rule out any of these factors as a plausible explanation for why citizens should pay for their state's wrongdoings, I also showed that, in reality, none of these arguments applies across the board—to all types of states, and/or to all types of state wrongdoing.

Based on these insights, I turned to the second task of this book, which was to develop a general framework for the appropriate distribution of the state's responsibilities among its population. Here, my core proposal was that we should not expect the same pattern of distribution to be right for all cases of state wrongdoing. Given the great variety of regime types we have in the world, as well as the very different circumstances that surround states' wrongdoings, and their varying levels of impacts on their victim and on the state's own citizens, we must adopt a context-sensitive, pluralist framework that picks up considerations that are salient to the case at hand. In chapter 5, I mapped the various considerations that ought to be taken into account. I argued that policymakers who design the distribution should proceed in several steps. First, they should examine whether a blame-tracking proportional distribution of the burden is practicable, at least for a portion of the burden overall. Next, they need to examine whether a nonproportional distribution of the burden (or what remains of it) to the citizens at large is permissible. Here various factors will play a role. In most states, the vast majority of the population will be intentionally participating in their state, and liable for the burden for that reason. But other factors can play a role as well: that citizens authorized their state to act as it did, that they benefited from its wrongdoing, that they are particularly well-placed to address it, or that they have special associative obligations to its victims. I acknowledged that, in all likelihood, in real-world states, some citizens will not be captured by any of these arguments. However, the size of this group of citizens, to which none of these arguments apply, will greatly vary across states. By and large, in democratic states, this group is likely to be very small. In nondemocratic states, on the other hand, it is likely to include the majority of the population. The policymakers in question will need to decide on the best course of action, given the size of this group and the likely impact of the distribution on it. In states where intentional citizenship is prevalent, and equal distribution can be justified to the vast majority of the population, proceeding with a nonproportional distribution will be overall a significantly less bad outcome than the available alternatives. On the other hand, in states where citizens are not genuine intentional participants, and where none of the other factors apply, we are likely to conclude that the burden ought to stay with the victims, or be absorbed by the international community.

In chapters 6 and 7, I turned to examine some of the practical implications of this framework. My core suggestion here was that my framework calls for a revision of public international law, which currently ignores the way in which states' liabilities for their past and present wrongdoings are distributed within the state. In chapter 6, I showed this with regard to the extraction of compensations from delinquent states. I critically examined the landmark United Nations Compensation Scheme, which was imposed on Iraq in the aftermath of its invasion of Kuwait. I argued that, given the extraordinary levels of political oppression in the Iraqi State, it was wrong to design the compensation scheme in a way that meant that the burden fell on ordinary Iraqis. Given the high moral costs of imposing the burden on the Iraqi population, the designers of the scheme should have looked for alternative sources of revenue, and even should have left some of the costs with the victims. Finally, I examined the implications of my framework for the increasingly popular view in public international law that states should also be punished for their wrongdoings.

In chapter 7, I turned to examine the implications of my framework for the practice of holding states responsible for their historical wrongdoings. Here I argued that present-day citizens, who are intentional participants in their state, are liable for a nonproportional share of their state's obligations even with regard to wrongdoings that were committed before their lifetimes. Not only that, I suggested that even in cases of state succession, where the identity of the state has changed, the intentional citizens of a successor state may be liable for the wrongdoings committed by a predecessor state.

However, I also set some important restrictions on the passage of state responsibility across time. I suggested that, per the intentional participation account, contemporary citizens are liable for their state's historical wrongs (or for their predecessor state's historical wrongs) only when that state's internal regime structure was so that, at the time it committed the wrongdoing, it was justified, at that time, to pass its liabilities to its citizens. When that is not the case, present-day citizens should not be expected to bear the burdens of the past. Put differently, I argued that the extent of intentional citizenship in the state affects the distribution of the state's corporate liabilities not just in the present, but also in the future. This restriction, I argued, has important implications for how we hold states responsible in cases of regime change, and especially in transitions from authoritarian to democratic regimes. After all, newly established democratic regimes often initiate reparation schemes to address the wrongs committed by their predecessors, and the costs of such schemes are distributed among the population at large. This distribution cannot always be justified on an intentional participation framework. That said, it could sometimes be argued that all citizens, including the victims of a former oppressive regime, have a duty, which flows from their political associative obligations, to assist their state in restoring democracy, equal citizenship, and trust in the state. This suggestion is compatible with my more general claim that we should not assume there is a single answer to the questions of whether, and why, citizens should pay for their state's wrongdoing. The answers to these questions require careful engagement with the specific circumstances at hand, and may change in light of them.

In the Introduction, I mentioned three groups to whom the discussion in this book is of relevance: decision-makers in the international bodies that hold states responsible for their international wrongs; policymakers within states, who design the scheme of distribution within the state; and ordinary citizens, who need to decide whether to lend their support to such schemes when offered the choice to do so. What lessons, then, might each of these groups draw from the analysis I provided here?

Let's look at the international arena first. Here two core recommendations emerge from the discussion. The first is that international policymakers ought to take into consideration, in their dealing with delinquent states, the relationship between these states and their citizens. It is wrong to assume that citizens, just by virtue of being citizens, are somehow liable for what their state does, purportedly, in their name. In that respect, not all states are equal. This fact does not imply that, in the final balance, it will necessarily be the case that the costs of authoritarian states' wrongdoings ought to be directed away from their populations. But international policymakers owe it to the citizens of such states to give careful consideration to the fact that these citizens were uninvolved in their state's crimes, and communicate their recognition of that fact.

The second recommendation I should highlight here is that, given the difficulty in justifying the distributive effect on the citizens of oppressed regimes, the international community ought to devise better ways of extracting and confiscating resources from those who are in control of such states, and who orchestrate their wrongdoings. For in the absence of such effective mechanisms, it becomes impossible to hold authoritarian states liable without imposing the burden on their populations, who are themselves the victims of their wrongdoings and who have no special relation to their state's crimes.

As for policymakers within the state, my analysis suggests that the current practice, prevalent in most states of the world, that the effect of the state's wrongdoing should by default be distributed to the population at large, is problematic. This is so especially given that there is no principled objection to the view that those agents within the state who most clearly share the blame for its wrongdoing should be the ones who carry the burden of that wrong. The state then owes it to its citizens at large a justification for why it chooses to ignore this view, and to not deploy a blame-tracking model of distribution. I suggested that in many real-world cases the state will be able to justify a resort to an equal distribution, and yet the option of a blame-tracking distribution needs to be explored before we resort to equal distribution. Not only that, it is also important that the state deploys the right argument in defense of equal distribution. As we saw throughout this book, sometimes the state should be able to point to the fact of citizens' participation in the state as the source of their obligation to assist it in discharging its obligations. But not all state citizens are participating in their state in this way, and public reason demands that they are offered an alternative justification, or that the state acknowledges the fact that there is no such justification to give.

As for state citizens, my analysis suggests that for many citizens in the world, being a citizen implies sharing responsibility for what one's state does. I suspect that many citizens in the world already accept this claim, given the sense of pride that many citizens report experiencing when their state performs well, as well as the uneasiness, moral discomfort, and shame they feel when it does wrong. My analysis tapped into and justified these moral sentiments. It demonstrated the connection between citizens and their state policies, one that exists despite the fact that most citizens, even in democracies, play a marginal role in their state's decision-making processes. Importantly, this connection remains even when citizens disagree with their state's policies. As long as we see ourselves as part of our state, and intend to contribute to its ability to rule over us, we are genuine members of our state, and liable for the outcome of the collective endeavor we, ultimately, choose to be part of.

APPENDIX

National Identity Surveys

Table A.1 How attached do you feel to your country? Eurobarometer (2005)*

Country	Very attached	Fairly attached	Very attached + fairly attached
Poland	66	31	97
Greece	78	19	97
Finland	63	33	97
Cyprus	74	23	97
Portugal	65	31	97
Denmark	80	16	97
Ireland	71	25	96
Turkey	85	11	96
Bulgaria	79	17	96
Hungary	77	19	96
Slovenia	61	34	95
Croatia	71	25	95
Malta	67	27	94
Austria	60	33	94
Romania	63	30	93
Sweden	61	32	93
France	57	35	93
Italy	53	39	92
Estonia	55	37	92
Luxembourg	54	37	91
Latvia	62	28	90

Table A.1 Continued

Country	Very attached	Fairly attached	Very attached + fairly attached
Lithuania	51	39	90
Spain	53	36	90
Czechia	41	49	90
United Kingdom	47	40	88
Germany	38	49	87
Slovakia	42	45	86
Netherlands	40	43	83
Belgium	43	38	82

As percent of all respondents.
*Data drawn from: https:// ec.europa.eu/ COMMFrontOffice/ publicopinion/ index. cfm/ Chart/ getChart/ themeKy/ 26/ groupKy/ 158

Table A.2 How attached do you feel to your country? Eurobarometer (2014)*

Country	Very attached	Fairly attached	Very attached + fairly attached
Greece	77	20	97
Portugal	59	38	97
Slovakia	53	43	96
Bulgaria	73	23	96
Denmark	84	12	96
Iceland	68	28	96
Poland	58	38	95
Malta	73	21	95
Sweden	63	32	95
Finland	64	30	95
Austria	60	34	94
Albania*	74	20	94
Ireland	65	28	94
Germany	50	43	93
Cyprus	66	27	93
Estonia	57	36	93
Slovenia	53	39	92
France	57	35	92
Luxemburg	52	40	92
Romania	56	36	92
Italy	50	41	92
Latvia	70	21	91
Lithuania	55	35	90
Hungary	57	33	90
UK	54	34	88
Czechia	36	52	88
Croatia	55	32	87
Montenegro	63	23	87
Netherlands	41	45	86
Belgium	38	46	84

Table A.2 Continued

Country	Very attached	Fairly attached	Very attached + fairly attached
Spain	49	34	83
Serbia	49	32	81
Turkey*	49	30	79

As percent of all respondents.

*Data drawn from https:// ec.europa.eu/ COMMFrontOffice/ publicopinion/ index. cfm/ Chart/ getChart/ themeKy/ 26/ groupKy/ 158 countries with (*) were defined as partly- free by the Freedom House for that year See Freedom in the World 2014 (Freedom House). Available online at: https:// freedomhouse.org/ sites/ default/ files/ 2020- 02/ Freedom_ in_ the_ World_ 2014_ Booklet.pdf

Table A.3 I see myself part of [Country].* World Value Survey Waves 5+6, countries defined as Free by the Freedom House

Country	Strongly agree	Agree	Agree + strongly agree
Ghana	76	24	100
Trinidad and Tobago	84	15	99
Estonia	61	37	98
Finland	73	26	99
Peru	47	50	97
Poland	52	45	97
Sweden	57	40	97
Norway	75	22	97
Uruguay	42	54	96
Australia	45	50	95
Canada	45	51	95
Taiwan	30	65	95
Slovenia	35	60	95
Cyprus	69	26	95
Tunisia	68	26	94
Chile	41	52	93
United States	44	50	93
Hungary	62	31	93
Netherlands	18	75	93
Brazil	42	50	93
South Korea	25	68	93
Italy	48	45	92
Argentina	38	53	91
India	65	26	91
Japan	24	67	91
Switzerland	42	48	90

Table A.3 Continued

Country	Strongly agree	Agree	Agree + strongly agree
Bulgaria	54	36	89
Spain	50	39	89
South Africa	46	41	86
Serbia and Montenegro	48	38	86
Germany	39	47	86
Romania	41	44	85
Andorra	23	62	84

As percent of all respondents.
*This data is drawn from http://www.worldvaluessurvey.org/wvs.jsp

Table A.4 I see as myself part of [Country].* World Value Survey Waves 5+6, countries defined as Partly Free by the Freedom House

Partly-free countries	Strongly agree	Agree	Strongly agree + agree
Georgia	81	18	98
Zimbabwe	64	35	98
Armenia	75	23	98
Nigeria	62	36	98
Mexico	49	48	97
Morocco	66	31	97
Philippines	55	42	97
Indonesia	50	47	97
Ecuador	72	25	96
Moldova	52	45	96
Mali	80	16	96
Malaysia	51	43	94
Kyrgyzstan	80	14	94
Singapore	31	63	93
Colombia	33	60	93
Pakistan	62	30	92
Turkey	60	31	91
Ukraine	52	37	89
Hong Kong	23	66	89
Kuwait	58	29	87
Lebanon	32	45	77

As percent of all respondents.
*This data is drawn from http://www.worldvaluessurvey.org/wvs.jsp

Table A.5 I see myself as part of [Country].* World Value Survey Waves 5+6, Countries defined as 'not free' by the Freedom House

Unfree countries	Strongly agree	Agree	Strongly agree + agree
Qatar	92	8	100
Rwanda	76	23	99
Uzbekistan	96	3	99
Jordan	84	14	98
Egypt	71	27	98
Iran	56	41	97
Viet Nam	52	45	97
Libya	77	19	97
Kazakhstan	85	12	97
Thailand	52	44	96
Burkina Faso	67	28	96
Azerbaijan	78	17	95
Yemen	62	33	95
Ethiopia	57	37	94
Zambia	65	29	94
Algeria	64	29	92
Russia	64	28	92
Palestine	42	49	91
Belarus	60	29	89
China	36	52	88
Bahrain	38	39	77

As percent of all respondents.
*This data is drawn from http://www.worldvaluessurvey.org/wvs.jspTable A.6

Table A.6 How close do you feel to your country?* ISPP (1995)

Country	Very close	Close	Sum
Hungary	80	17	96
Japan	60	35	95
Norway	52	43	94
Australia	61	33	94
Poland	55	39	94
New Zealand	56	38	94
Slovenia	49	44	93
Bulgaria	72	21	93
Ireland	54	39	93
Czech R	48	44	92
Austria	56	35	91
Spain	43	47	90
Slovakian Rep	42	48	89
Italy	43	45	88
Netherlands	28	59	87
Latvia	41	45	86
Sweden	33	50	83
Russia	42	40	82
East Germany	28	54	81
USA	35	46	81
West Germany	24	55	79
Canada	35	40	75
Great Britain	24	47	71
Philippines	22	46	68

As percent of all respondents.
*Data drawn from https://www.gesis.org/en/issp/modules/issp-modules-by-topic/national-identity/1995

Table A.7 How close do you feel to your country?* ISPP (2003)

Country	Very close	Close	Close + very close
Hungary	75	22	97
New Zealand	62	34	95
Slovenia	47	48	95
Israel Jews	80	15	94
Bulgaria	66	28	94
Ireland	54	39	93
Austria	60	33	93
Portugal	52	41	93
Australia	51	42	93
Poland	45	48	93
Switzerland	41	51	92
Denmark	56	36	92
Finland	48	44	92
Chile	58	34	92
Japan	49	43	92
Spain	44	47	91
France	57	34	91
Czech Republic	39	51	90
Slovakia	40	50	90
Uruguay	56	33	90
United States	52	37	90
Norway	43	46	90
South Africa	61	27	88
Venezuela	59	28	87
Canada	47	39	87
Sweden	41	45	87
Philippines	36	49	85
Korea (South)	40	44	84

Table A.7 Continued

Country	Very close	Close	Close + very close
Germany-West	26	58	84
Taiwan	32	50	82
Germany-East	24	56	80
Netherlands	29	50	80
Latvia	28	52	79
Great Britain	34	45	79
Israel Arabs	26	43	69
Russia	26	41	67

As percent of all respondents.
*Data drawn from: https://www.gesis.org/issp/modules/issp-modules-by-topic/national-identity//

Table A.8 Ethnic or national identity? Afro Barometer wave 6 (2014/15)*

Country	I feel equally [R's Country] and (R's ethnic group)	I feel more [R's Country] than (R's ethnic group)	I feel only [R's Country]	Total
Ghana*	51	11	34	96
Burundi (R5)	8	16	71	95
Tanzania	24	12	58	94
Zambia*	59	7	27	93
South Africa*	22	8	62	92
Madagascar	19	23	49	91
Sierra Leone	44	14	33	91
Côte d'Ivoire	47	5	39	91
Kenya	40	12	38	90
Mauritius*	60	6	24	90
Cameroon	41	10	39	90
Lesotho	58	2	29	89
Botswana*	66	4	19	89
Namibia*	44	6	38	89
Benin*	30	11	47	88

Niger	16	16	56	88
Zimbabwe	29	7	51	87
Zimbabwe	34	15	38	87
Malawi	48	3	36	87
Burkina Faso	36	13	37	86
Senegal*	32	6	47	85
Liberia	59	10	16	85
Togo	31	8	46	85
Zambia	50	5	29	84
Mali	34	6	44	84
Mozambique	18	14	53	84
Cape Verde*	50	19	14	83
Uganda	50	11	20	81
Nigeria	33	11	37	81

As percent of all respondents.

* The data is drawn from https://www.afrobarometer.org/ Countries with (*) were defined as Free by the Freedom House for that year. See *Freedom in the World 2014* (Freedom House). Available online at: https://freedomhouse.org/sites/default/files/2020-02/Freedom_in_the_World_2014_Booklet.pdf

Bibliography

Abdel-Nour, Farid. "National Responsibility." *Political Theory* 31, no. 5 (2003): 693–716.

Abdel-Nour, Farid. "Responsible for the State: The Case of Obedient Subjects." *European Journal of Political Theory* 15, no. 3 (2016): 259–75.

Ali, Sundas, and Anthony Heath. *Future Identities: Changing Identities in the UK—The Next 10 Years*. London: Government Office for Science, 2013.

Barry, Christian, and David Wiens. "Benefiting from Wrongdoing and Sustaining Wrongful Harm." *Journal of Moral Philosophy* 13, no. 5 (2016): 530–52.

Beerbohm, Eric. *In Our Name: The Ethics of Democracy*. Princeton: Princeton University Press, 2012.

Beetham, David. *The Legitimation of Power*. London: Macmillan International Higher Education, 2013.

Begby, Endre. "Collective Responsibility for Unjust Wars." *Politics* 32, no. 2 (2012): 100–108.

Billig, Michael. *Banal Nationalism*. London: SAGE, 1995.

Blaydes, Lisa. *State of Repression: Iraq under Saddam Hussein*. Princeton: Princeton University Press, 2018.

Boxill, Bernard R. "Self-Respect and Protest." *Philosophy & Public Affairs* 6, no. 1 (1976): 58–69.

Bratman, Michael. *Faces of Intention: Selected Essays on Intention and Agency*. Cambridge: Cambridge University Press, 1999.

Bratman, Michael. *Shared Agency*. Oxford: Oxford University Press, 2014.

"Britain Has Duty to Clean Up Monumental Mess of Empire, Sir Hilary Tells Cameron." *The Jamaica Observer*, September 28, 2015. http://www.jamaicaobserver.com/news/Britain-has-duty-to-clean-up-monumental-mess-of-Empire--Sir-Hilary-tells-Cameron_19230957.

Brownlie, Ian. *Principles of Public International Law*. 6th ed. Oxford: Oxford University Press, 2003.

Buchanan, Allen. "Theories of Secession." *Philosophy & Public Affairs* 26, no. 1 (1997): 31–61.

Bucy, Pamela H. "Corporate Criminal Liability: When Does It Make Sense." *American Criminal Law Review* 46 (2009): 1437–57.

Butt, Daniel. "On Benefiting from Injustice." *Canadian Journal of Philosophy* 37, no. 1 (2007): 129–52.

Butt, Daniel. *Rectifying International Injustice*. Oxford: Oxford University Press, 2008.

Butt, Daniel. "Repairing Historical Wrongs and the End of Empire." *Social & Legal Studies* 21, no. 2 (2012): 227–42.

Cane, Peter. *Responsibility in Law and Morality*. Oxford: Hart, 2002.

Cassesse, A. "International Law in a Divided World." Oxford: Oxford University Press, 1986.

Chang, Eric, and Miriam A. Golden. "Sources of Corruption in Authoritarian Regimes." *Social Science Quarterly* 91, no. 1 (2010): 1–20.

Cheibub, José Antonio, Jennifer Gandhi, and James Raymond Vreeland. "Democracy and Dictatorship Revisited." *Public Choice* 143, no. 1–2 (2010): 67–101.

Cheng, Tai-Heng. "Why New States Accept Old Obligations." *University of Illinois Law Review* 2011 (2011): 1–51.

Child, Richard. "Should We Hold Nations Responsible? David Miller, National Responsibility and Global Justice." *Res Publica* 15, no. 3 (2009): 195–202.

Christenson, Gordon A. "Attributing Acts of Omission to the State." *Michigan Journal of International Law* 12, no. 2 (1990): 312–70.

Christiano, Thomas. *The Constitution of Equality: Democratic Authority and Its Limits*. Oxford: Oxford University Press, 2008.

Christman, John. *The Politics of Persons*. Cambridge: Cambridge University Press, 2009.

Chung, John J. "The United Nations Compensation Commission and the Balancing of Rights between Individual Claimants and the Government of Iraq." *UCLA Journal of International Law & Foreign Affairs* 10 (2005): 141–78.

Coffee, John C., Jr. "'No Soul to Damn: No Body to Kick': An Unscandalized Inquiry into the Problem of Corporate Punishment." *Michigan Law Review* 79 (1981): 386–460.

Collins, Stephanie. "Distributing State Duties." *Journal of Political Philosophy* 24, no. 3 (2016): 344–66.

Colonomos, Ariel, and Andrea Armstrong. "German Reparations to the Jews after World War II: A Turning Point in the History of Reparation." In *The Oxford Handbook of Reparations*, edited by Pablo de Greiff, 390–419. Oxford: Oxford University Press, 2006.

Colvin, Christopher. "Overview of the Reparations Program in South Africa." In *The Handbook of Reparations*, edited by Pablo de Greiff, 177–214. Oxford: Oxford University Press, 2008.

Cooper, David E. "Collective Responsibility (a Defense)." In *Collective Responsibility: Five Decades of Debate in Theoretical and Applied Ethics*, edited by Larry May and Stacey Hoffman, 35–46. Lanham, MD: Rowman & Littlefield, 1991.

Copp, David. "The Collective Moral Autonomy Thesis." *Journal of Social Philosophy* 38 (2007): 369–88.

Copp, David. "The Idea of a Legitimate State." *Philosophy & Public Affairs* 28, no. 1 (1999): 3–45.

Craven, Matthew C. *The Decolonization of International Law.* Oxford: Oxford University Press, 2007.

Craven, Matthew C. "The Problem of State Succession and the Identity of States under International Law." *European Journal of International Law* 9, no. 1 (1998): 142–62.

Crawford, James. *The Creation of States in International Law.* 2nd ed. Oxford: Oxford University Press, 2006.

Crawford, James. *The International Law Commission's Articles on State Responsibility: Introduction, Text and Commentaries.* Cambridge: Cambridge University Press, 2007.

Crawford, James, and Jeremy Watkins. "International Responsibility." In *The Philosophy of International Law,* edited by Samantha Besson and John Tasioulas, 283–98. Oxford: Oxford University Press, 2010.

Cudd, Ann. *Analyzing Oppression.* Oxford: Oxford University Press, 2006.

Dan-Cohen, Meir. "Sanctioning Corporations." *Journal of Law and Policy* 19, no. 1 (2010): 15–43.

Daponte, Beth. "A Case Study in Estimating Casualties from War and Its Aftermath: The 1991 Persian Gulf War." *Medicine & Global Survival* 3, no. 2 (1993): 57–66.

Davenport, Christian. "State Repression and Political Order." *Annual Review of Political Science* 10 (2007): 1–23.

Davenport, Christian. "State Repression and the Tyrannical Peace." *Journal of Peace Research* 44, no. 4 (2007): 485–504.

de Greiff, Pablo. "Justice and Reparations." In *The Handbook of Reparations,* edited by Pablo de Greiff, 452–76. Oxford: Oxford University Press, 2008.

Delmas, Candice. *A Duty to Resist: When Disobedience Should Be Uncivil.* Oxford: Oxford University Press, 2018.

Dewey, John. "The Historic Background of Corporate Legal Personality." *Yale Law Journal* 35, no. 6 (1926): 655–73.

Diamantis, Mihailis E. "Corporate Essence and Identity in Criminal Law." *Journal of Business Ethics* 154, no. 4 (2019): 955–66.

Drumbl, Mark. "Collective Responsibility and Postconflict Justice." In *Accountability for Collective Wrongdoing,* edited by Tracy Isaacs and Richard Vernon, 23–60. New York: Cambridge University Press, 2011.

Dworkin, Ronald. *Law's Empire.* London: Fontana, 1986.

Dworkin, Ronald. *Sovereign Virtue: The Theory and Practice of Equality.* Cambridge, MA: Harvard University Press, 2000.

Eley, Geoff. "Hitler's Silent Majority? Conformity and Resistance under the Third Reich (Part Two)." *Michigan Quarterly Review* 42, no. 3 (2003).

Erskine, Toni. "Assigning Responsibilities to Institutional Moral Agents: The Case of States and Quasi States." *Ethics and International Affairs* 15, no. 1 (2001): 67–86.

Erskine, Toni. "Kicking Bodies and Damning Souls: The Danger of Harming 'Innocent' Individuals While Punishing 'Delinquent' States." In *Accountability for Collective Wrongdoing*, edited by Tracy Isaacs and Richard Vernon, 261–86. New York: Cambridge University Press, 2011.

Evans, Christine. *The Right to Reparation in International Law for Victims of Armed Conflict*. Cambridge: Cambridge University Press, 2012.

Ezrow, Natasha M., and Erica Frantz. *Dictators and Dictatorships: Understanding Authoritarian Regimes and Their Leaders*. New York: Continuum International, 2011.

Fabre, Cecile. *Cosmopolitan Peace*. Oxford: Oxford University Press, 2016.

Fabre, Cecile. *Cosmopolitan War*. Oxford: Oxford University Press, 2012.

Fabre, Cecile. *Economic Statecraft: Human Rights, Sanctions, and Conditionality*. Cambridge, MA: Harvard University Press, 2018.

Faust, Aaron M. *The Ba'thification of Iraq: Saddam Hussein's Totalitarianism*. Austin: University of Texas Press, 2015.

Feinberg, Joel. "Collective Responsibility (Another Defense)." In *Collective Responsibility: Five Decades of Debate in Theoretical and Applied Ethics*, edited by Larry May and Stacey Hoffman, 53–76. Lanham, MD: Rowman & Littlefield, 1991.

Feinberg, Joel. "The Expressive Function of Punishment." *Monist* 49, no. 3 (1965): 397–423.

Fine, Sarah, "Refugees, Safety and a Decent Human Life" *Proceedings of the Aristotelian Society* 119, no. 1 (2019): 25–52.

Fishkin, James S. "Justice between Generations: Compensation, Identity, and Group Membership." *Nomos* 33 (1991): 85–96.

Fleming, Sean. *Leviathan on the Leash*. PhD diss., Cambridge University, 2018.

Frankfurt, Harry. "Alternate Possibilities and Moral Responsibility." *Journal of Philosophy* 66, no. 23 (1969): 829–39.

Frankfurt, Harry. "The Faintest Passion." In *Necessity, Volition and Love*, 95–107. Cambridge: Cambridge University Press, 1998.

Frankfurt, Harry. "Freedom of the Will and the Concept of a Person." *Journal of Philosophy* 68, no. 1 (1971): 5–20.

Frantz, Erica, and Natasha M. Ezrow. *The Politics of Dictatorship: Institutions and Outcomes in Authoritarian Regimes*. Boulder, CO: Lynne Rienner, 2011.

Freeman, Mark. *Necessary Evils: Amnesties and the Search for Justice*. Cambridge: Cambridge University Press, 2009.

French, Peter. *Collective and Corporate Responsibility*. New York: Columbia University Press, 1984.

Gellately, Robert. *Backing Hitler: Consent and Coercion in Nazi Germany*. Oxford: Oxford University Press, 2002.

Gerschewski, Johannes. "The Three Pillars of Stability: Legitimation, Repression, and Co-optation in Autocratic Regimes." *Democratization* 20, no. 1 (2013): 13–38.

Gilabert, Pablo, and Holly Lawford-Smith. "Political Feasibility: A Conceptual Exploration." *Political Studies* 60 (2012): 809–25.

Gilbert, Margaret. "Collective Wrongdoing: Moral and Legal Responses." *Social Theory and Practice* 28, no. 1 (2002): 167–87.

Gilbert, Margaret. *A Theory of Political Obligation: Membership, Commitment, and the Bonds of Society.* Oxford: Clarendon Press, 2006.

Gilbert, Margaret. "Walking Together: A Paradigmatic Social Phenomenon." *Midwest Studies in Philosophy* 15, no. 1 (1990): 1–14.

Goodin, Robert. "Apportioning Responsibilities." *Law and Philosophy* 6, no. 2 (1987): 167–85.

Goodin, Robert. "Disgorging the Fruits of Historical Wrongdoing." *American Political Science Review* 107, no. 3 (2013): 478–91.

Goodin, Robert. *Utilitarianism as a Public Philosophy.* Cambridge: Cambridge University Press, 1995.

Gordon, Joy. *Invisible War: The United States and the Iraq Sanctions.* Cambridge, MA: Harvard University Press, 2010.

Green, Leslie. *The Authority of the State.* Oxford: Oxford University Press, 1990.

Guemba, José Maria. "Economic Reparations for Grave Human Rights." In *The Handbook of Reparations*, edited by Pablo de Greiff, 22–51. Oxford: Oxford University Press, 2006.

Gutmann, Amy, and Dennis F. Thompson. *Democracy and Disagreement.* Cambridge, MA: Belknap Press of Harvard University Press, 1996.

Hart, H. L. A. *Punishment and Responsibility: Essays in the Philosophy of Law.* Oxford: Clarendon Press, 1970.

Hay, Carol. "The Obligation to Resist Oppression." *Journal of Social Philosophy* 42, no. 1 (2011): 21–45.

Hayner, Priscilla B. *Unspeakable Truths: Facing the Challenge of Truth Commissions.* New York: Routledge 2002.

Hess, Kendy. "If You Tickle Us . . . How Corporations Can Be Moral Agents without Being Persons." *Journal of Value Inquiry* 47, no. 3 (2013): 319–35.

Hindriks, Frank. "The Freedom of Collective Agents." *Journal of Political Philosophy* 16, no. 1 (2008): 165–83.

Hjerm, Mikael. "National Identities, National Pride and Xenophobia: A Comparison of Four Western Countries." *Acta Sociologica* 41, no. 4 (1998): 335–47.

Hodgson, Geoffrey M. "What Are Institutions?" *Journal of Economic Issues* 40, no. 1 (2006): 1–25.

Honoré, Tony. *Responsibility and Fault.* Oxford: Hart, 1999.

Horton, John. "In Defence of Associative Political Obligations, Part 1." *Political Studies* 54, no. 3 (2006): 427–43.

Horton, John. "In Defence of Associative Political Obligations, Part 2." *Political Studies* 55, no. 1 (2007): 1–19.

Huseby, Robert. "Should the Beneficiary Pay." *Politics, Philosophy, Economics* 14, no. 2 (2015): 209–25.

"Iraq Demands America, Britain Pay Reparations for 2003 Invasion." *The New Arab* January 19, 2017. https://english.alaraby.co.uk/english/news/2017/1/19/iraq-demands-america-britain-pay-reparations-for-2003-invasion.

"Iraq Resumes Payments of Gulf War Reparations to Kuwait." *Reuters* April 20, 2018. https://www.reuters.com/article/us-mideast-crisis-iraq-kuwait-un/iraq-resumes-payments-of-gulf-war-reparations-to-kuwait-idUSKBN1HR26Q.

Isaacs, Tracy. *Moral Responsibility in Collective Contexts*. Oxford: Oxford University Press, 2011.

Isaacs, Tracy. "Collective Moral Responsibility and Collective Intention." *Midwest Studies in Philosophy* 30, no. 1 (2006): 59–73.

Jaspers, Karl. *The Question of German Guilt*. New York: Fordham University Press, 2000.

Jubb, Robert. "Contribution to Collective Harms and Responsibility." *Ethical Perspectives* 19, no. 4 (2012): 733–64.

Jubb, Robert. "Participation in and Responsibility for the State." *Social Theory and Practice* 40, no. 1 (2014): 51–72.

Kagan, Shelly. "Causation and Responsibility." *American Philosophical Quarterly* 25, no. 4 (1988): 293–302.

Kailitz, Steffen. "Classifying Political Regimes Revisited: Legitimation and Durability." *Democratization* 20, no. 1 (2013): 39–60.

Karsh, Efraim, and Inari Rautsi. "Why Saddam Hussein Invaded Kuwait." *Survival* 33, no. 1 (1991): 18–30.

Kershaw, Ian. *The Nazi Dictatorship: Problems and Perspectives of Interpretation*. London: Bloomsbury, 2015.

King, Jeff. *The Doctrine of Odious Debt in International Law: A Restatement*. Cambridge: Cambridge University Press, 2016.

King, Jeff. "Odious Debt: The Terms of the Debate." *North Carolina Journal of International Law and Commercial Regulation* 32, no. 4 (2006): 605–67.

Klein, Naomi. "Why Is War-Torn Iraq Giving $190,000 to Toys R Us?" *The Guardian*, October 16, 2004. http://www.guardian.co.uk/world/2004/oct/16/iraq.comment.

Knight, Carl. "Benefiting from Injustice and Brute Luck." *Social Theory and Practice* 39, no. 4 (2014): 581–98.

Köllner, Patrick, and Steffen Kailitz. "Comparing Autocracies: Theoretical Issues and Empirical Analyses." *Democratization* 20, no. 1 (2013): 1–12.

Kukathas, Chandran. "Responsibility for Past Injustice: How to Shift the Burden." *Politics, Philosophy & Economics* 2, no. 2 (2003): 165–90.

Kukathas, Chandran. "Who? Whom? Reparations and the Problem of Agency." *Journal of Social Philosophy* 37, no. 3 (2006): 330–41.

Kutz, Christopher. "Acting Together." *Philosophy and Phenomenological Research* 61, no. 1 (2000): 1–31.

Kutz, Christopher. "Causeless Complicity." *Criminal Law and Philosophy* 1 (2007): 289–305.

Kutz, Christopher. "The Collective Work of Citizenship." *Legal Theory* 8, no. 4 (2002): 471–94.

Kutz, Christopher. *Complicity: Ethics and Law for a Collective Age.* Cambridge: Cambridge University Press, 2000.

Kutz, Christopher. "Secret Law and the Value of Publicity." *Ratio Juris* 22, no. 2 (2009): 197–217.

Lang, Anthony F., Jr. "Crime and Punishment: Holding States Accountable." *Ethics and International Affairs* 21, no. 2 (2007): 239–57.

Lawford-Smith, Holly. *Not in Their Name: Are Citizens Culpable for Their States' Actions?* Cambridge: Cambridge University Press, 2019.

Lee, Ian B. "Corporate Criminal Responsibility as Team Member Responsibility." *Oxford Journal of Legal Studies* 31, no. 4 (2011): 755–81.

Lepora, Chiara, and Robert Goodin. *On Complicity and Compromise.* Oxford: Oxford University Press, 2013.

Levitsky, Steven, and Lucan Way. "The Rise of Competitive Authoritarianism." *Journal of Democracy* 13, no. 2 (2002): 51–65.

Linz, Juan J. *Totalitarian and Authoritarian Regimes.* Boulder, CO: Addison-Wesley, 1985.

Lippert-Rasmussen, Kasper. "Responsible Nations: Miller on National Responsibility." *Ethics and Global Politics* 2, no. 2 (2009): 109–30.

Lipsky, Michael. "Protest in City Politics." Chicago: Rand McNally, 1970.

Lira, Elisabeth. "The Reparations Policy for Human Rights Violations in Chile." In *The Handbook of Reparations*, edited by Pablo de Greiff, 57–101. Oxford: Oxford University Press, 2008.

List, Christian. "The Logical Space of Democracy." *Philosophy & Public Affairs* 39, no. 3 (2011): 262–97.

List, Christian, and Philip Pettit. Group Agency. Oxford: Oxford University Press, 2011.

Lu, Catherine. *Justice and Reconciliation in World Politics.* Cambridge: Cambridge University Press, 2017.

Luban, David. "State Criminality and the Ambition of International Criminal Law." In *Accountability for Collective Wrongdoing*, edited by Tracy Isaacs and Richard Vernon, 61–91. New York: Cambridge University Press, 2011.

MacKinnon, Rebecca. "Liberation Technology: China's 'Networked Authoritarianism.'" *Journal of Democracy* 22, no. 2 (2011): 32–46.

Mason, Andrew. "Special Obligations to Compatriots." *Ethics* 107, no. 3 (1997): 427–47.

Massari, Jai R. "The Odious Debt Doctrine after Iraq." *Law and Contemporary Problems* 70, no. 4 (2007): 139–56.

Massey, Douglas S., and Nancy A. Denton. *American Apartheid: Segregation and the Making of the Underclass.* Cambridge, MA: Harvard University Press, 1993.

Matheson, John H. "Successor Liability." *Minnesota Law Review* 96 (2011): 371–422.

May, Larry. *After War Ends: A Philosophical Perspective.* Cambridge: Cambridge University Press, 2012.

May, Larry. *The Morality of Groups: Collective Responsibility, Group-Based Harm, and Corporate Rights.* Notre Dame, IN: University of Notre Dame Press, 1987.

May, Larry. *Sharing Responsibility.* Chicago: University of Chicago Press, 1992.

McCrone, David, and Frank Bechhofer. *Understanding National Identity.* Cambridge: Cambridge University Press, 2015.

Miller, David. "Collective Responsibility and Global Poverty." *Ethical Perspectives* 19, no. 4 (2012): 627–48.

Miller, David. "Distributing Responsibilities." *Journal of Political Philosophy* 9, no. 4 (2001): 453–71.

Miller, David. *National Responsibility and Global Justice.* Oxford: Oxford University Press, 2007.

Miller, David. "A Response." *Critical Review of International Social and Political Philosophy* 11, no. 4 (2008): 553–67.

Miller, David. "Review: *A Theory of Political Obligation* by Margaret Gilbert." *Philosophical Quarterly* 58, no. 233 (2008): 755–57.

Miller, David, and Sundas Ali. "Testing the National Identity Argument." *European Political Science Review* 6, no. 2 (2014): 237–59.

Mills, Charles W. *The Racial Contract.* Ithaca, NY: Cornell University Press, 2014.

Munro, Robrert. *Should Citizens Pay for the Costs of Their State's Unjust Actions? Defending an Individualist Moral Responsibility-Based Account of Liability.* PhD diss., Manchester University, 2015.

Mokrosinska, Dorota. "The People's Right to Know and State Secrecy." *Canadian Journal of Law & Jurisprudence* 31, no. 1 (2018): 87–106.

Mokrosinska, Dorota. "Why States Have No Right to Privacy, but May Be Entitled to Secrecy: A Non-consequentialist Defense of State Secrecy." *Critical Review of International Social and Political Philosophy* 23, no. 4 (2020): 415–444.

Møller, Jørgen, and Svend-Erik Skaaning. "Autocracies, Democracies, and the Violation of Civil Liberties." *Democratization* 20, no. 1 (2013): 82–106.

Morris, Herbert. *An Essay on the Modern State.* Cambridge: Cambridge University Press, 1998.

Murphy, Jeffrie, and Jean Hampton. *Forgiveness and Mercy*. Cambridge: Cambridge University Press, 1990.

Nussbaum, Martha. "Introduction." In *Responsibility for Justice*, by Iris Marion Young. IX–XXV. Oxford: Oxford University Press, 2013.

Oberman, Kieran. "Immigration as a Human Right" in *Migration in Political Theory: The Ethics of Movement and Membership*, edited by Sarah Fine and Lea Ypi, 33–51. (Oxford, Oxford University Press).

Olsen, Tricia D., Leigh A. Payne, and Andrew G. Reiter. "The Justice Balance: When Transitional Justice Improves Human Rights and Democracy." *Human Rights Quarterly* 32, no. 4 (2010): 980–1007.

Osiel, Mark. *Mass Atrocity, Collective Memory, and the Law*. New Brunswick, NJ: Transaction Publishers, 1999.

Parrish, John. "Collective Responsibility and the State." *International Theory* 1, no. 1 (2009): 119–54.

Pasternak, Avia. "Benefiting from Wrongdoing." In *A Companion to Applied Philosophy*, edited by Kasper Lippert-Rasmussen, Kimberley Brownlee, and D. Coady, 411–23. Oxford: Blackwell 2016.

Pasternak, Avia. "Cosmopolitan Justice and Criminal States." *Journal of Applied Philosophy* 36, no. 3 (2018): 366–374.

Pasternak, Avia. "The Distributive Effect of Collective Punishment." In *Collective Wrongdoing*, edited by Richard Vernon and Tracy Isaacs, 210–30. New York: Cambridge University Press, 2011.

Pasternak, Avia. "From Corporate Moral Agency to Corporate Moral Rights." *The Law & Ethics of Human Rights* 11, no. 1 (2017): 135–59.

Pasternak, Avia. "The Impact of Corporate Tasks Responsibilities: A Comparison of Two Models." *Midwest Studies in Philosophy* 38, no. 1 (2014): 222–31.

Pasternak, Avia. "Limiting States' Corporate Responsibility." *Journal of Political Philosophy* 21, no. 4 (2013): 361–81.

Pasternak, Avia. "Mobs, Firms and Nations—A Critique of David Miller's Account of Collective Responsibility." In *Political Philosophy, Here and Now: Essays in Honour of David Miller*, edited by Daniel Butt, Sarah Fine, and Zofia Stemplowska. Oxford: Oxford University Press, forthcoming.

Pasternak, Avia. "Sharing the Costs of Political Injustice." *Politics, Philosophy, Economics* 10, no. 2 (2011): 188–210.

Pasternak, Avia. "Voluntary Benefits from Wrongdoing." *Journal of Applied Philosophy* 31, no. 4 (2014): 377–91.

Patten, Alan. "Democratic Secession from a Multinational State." *Ethics* 112, no. 3 (2002): 558–86.

Pettit, Philip. "Groups with Minds of Their Own." In *Socializing Metaphysics: The Nature of Social Reality*, edited by Frederick F. Schmitt, 167–93. Lanham, MD: Rowman & Littlefield, 2003.

Pettit, Philip, and David Schweikard. "Joint Actions and Group Agents." *Philosophy of the Social Sciences* 36, no. 1 (2006): 18–39.

Pierik, Roland. "Collective Responsibility and National Responsibility." *Critical Review of International Social and Political Philosophy* 11, no. 4 (2008): 465–83.

Pozen, David E. "Deep Secrecy." *Stanford Law Review* 62 (2009): 257–339.

Raz, Joseph. *The Authority of Law: Essays on Law and Morality*. Oxford: Clarendon Press, 1979.

Raz, Joseph. "Liberating Duties." *Law and Philosophy* 8, no. 1 (1989): 3–21.

Reicher, Stephen, Russell Spears, and S. Alexander Haslam. "The Social Identity Approach in Social Psychology." In *The SAGE Handbook of Identities*, edited by Mararet Wetherell and Chandra Talpade Mohanty, 45–62. London: SAGE, 2010.

Reilly, Marie T. "Making Sense of Successor Liability." *Hofstra Law Review* 31 (2002): 745–94.

Roberts, Melinda. "The Nonidentity Problem." In *The Stanford Encyclopedia of Philosophy*, edited by Edward N. Zalta (Stanford, CA: Stanford University, 2019). https://plato.stanford.edu/archives/sum2019/entries/nonidentity-problem/.

Rönnegard, David. *The Fallacy of Corporate Moral Agency*. Dordrecht: Springer, 2015.

Rotberg, Robert I., and Dennis Thompson, eds. *Truth v. Justice: The Morality of Truth Commissions*. Princeton: Princeton University Press, 2000.

Sangiovanni, Andrea. "Structural Injustice and Individual Responsibility." *Journal of Social Philosophy* 49, no. 3 (2018): 461–83.

Sassoon, Joseph. *Saddam Hussein's Ba'th Party: Inside an Authoritarian Regime*. Cambridge: Cambridge University Press, 2011.

Satz, Debra. "What Do We Owe the Global Poor?" *Ethics and International Affairs* 19, no. 1 (2005): 47–54.

Scheffler, Samuel. *Boundaries and Allegiances: Problems of Justice and Responsibility in Liberal Thought*. Oxford: Oxford University Press, 2001.

Schweikard, David, and Hans Bernhard. "Collective Intentionality." In *The Stanford Encyclopedia of Philosophy*, edited by Edward N. Zalta (Stanford, CA: Stanford University, 2013). https://plato.stanford.edu/archives/sum2019/entries/collective-intentionality/.

Segovia, Alexander. "Financing Reparations Programs." In *The Handbook of Reparations*, edited by Pablo de Greiff, 651–73. Oxford: Oxford University Press 2006.

Shapiro, Scott. "Massively Shared Agency." In *Rational and Social Agency: The Philosophy of Michael Bratman*, edited by Manuel Vargas and Gideon Yaffe, 258–89. Oxford: Oxford University Press, 2014.

Shelby, Tommie. *Dark Ghettos: Injustice, Dissent, and Reform*. Cambridge MA: Harvard University Press, 2016.

Shelby, Tommie. "Justice, Deviance, and the Dark Ghetto." *Philosophy & Public Affairs* 35, no. 2 (2007): 126–60.

Spinner-Halev, Jeff. *Enduring Injustice.* Cambridge: Cambridge University Press, 2012.

Spiro, Peter. "A New International Law of Citizenship." *American Journal of International Law* 105, no. 4 (2011): 694–746.

Stargardt, Nicholas. *The German War: A Nation under Arms, 1939–1945.* London: Hachette UK, 2015.

Stern, Brigitte. "The Obligation to Make Reparations." In *The Law of International Responsibility,* edited by James Crawford, Alain Pellet, Simon Olleson, and Kate Parlett, 563–71. Oxford: Oxford University Press 2010.

Stewart, James "Complicity," in *The Oxford Handbook of Criminal Law,* ed. Markus D. Dubber and Tatjana Hömle (Oxford: Oxford University Press, 2014).

Stilz, Anna. "Collective Responsibility and the State." *Journal of Political Philosophy* 19, no. 2 (2011): 190–208.

Stilz, Anna. *Liberal Loyalty: Freedom, Obligation, and the State.* Princeton: Princeton University Press, 2009.

Stilz, Anna. "Nations, States and Territory." *Ethics* 112, no. 3 (2011): 572–601.

Stilz, Anna. "The Value of Self-Determination." *Oxford Studies in Political Philosophy* 2 (2016): 98–127.

Sun, Jinyu. *Political Obligations in Non-democracies: A Natural Duty Account of the Obligation to Resist.* PhD diss., University College London, 2019.

Tadros, Victor. *The Ends of Harm: The Moral Foundations of Criminal Law.* Oxford: Oxford University Press, 2011.

Tajfel, Henri. *Differentiation between Social Groups: Studies in the Social Psychology of Intergroup Relations.* London: Academic Press, 1978.

Tamir, Yael. *Liberal Nationalism.* Princeton: Princeton University Press, 1993.

Tanguay-Renaud, Francois. "Criminalizing the State." *Criminal Law and Philosophy* 7, no. 2 (2013): 255–84.

Theiss-Morse, Elizabeth. *Who Counts as an American?: The Boundaries of National Identity.* Cambridge: Cambridge University Press, 2009.

Thompson, Dennis F. "Democratic Secrecy." *Political Science Quarterly* 114, no. 2 (1999): 181–93.

Thompson, Janna. "Collective Responsibility for Historic Injustices." In *Midwest Studies in Philosophy* 30, no. 1 (2006): 154–68.

Tollefsen, Deborah. *Groups as Agents.* Cambridge: Polity Press, 2015.

Tyler, Tom R. *Why People Obey the Law.* Princeton: Princeton University Press, 2006.

Valentini, Laura. "Correction and (Global) Justice." *American Political Science Review* 105, no. 1 (2011): 205–20.

van Houtte, Hans, Hans Das, and Bart Delmartino. "The United Nations Compensation Commission." In *The Oxford Handbook of Reparations,* edited by Pablo de Greiff, 321–89. Oxford: Oxford University Press, 2006.

Vernon, Richard. "Against Restitution." *Political Studies* 51, no. 3 (2003): 542–57.

Vernon, Richard. "Punishing Collectives: States or Nations?" In *Accountability for Collective Wrongdoing*, edited by Tracy Isaacs and Richard Vernon, 287–306. New York: Cambridge University Press, 2011.

Viehoff, Daniel. "Legitimacy as a Right to Err." In *Political Legitimacy*, edited by Jack Knight and Melissa Schwartzberg, 174–200. New York: New York University Press, 2019.

Volkovitsch, Michael John. "Righting Wrongs: Towards a New Theory of State Succession to Responsibility for International Delicts." *Columbia Law Review* 92, no. 8 (1992): 2162–214.

Walker, Nigel. *Why Punish?* Oxford: Oxford University Press, 1991.

Wall, Edmund. "The Problem of Group Agency." *Philosophical Forum* 31, no. 2 (2000): 187–97.

Walzer, Michael. *Just and Unjust Wars: A Moral Argument with Historical Illustrations*. 2nd ed. New York: Basic Books, 1992.

Wells, Celia. *Corporations and Criminal Responsibility*. Oxford: Oxford University Press, 2001.

Wenar, Leif. "Property Rights and the Resource Curse." *Philosophy and Public Affairs* 36, no. 1 (2008): 2–32.

Wendt, Alexander. "The State as Person in International Theory." *Review of International Studies* 30, no. 2 (2004): 289–316.

Wertheimer, Alan. *Coercion*. Princeton: Princeton University Press, 1987.

Wigell, Mikael. "Mapping 'Hybrid Regimes': Regime Types and Concepts in Comparative Politics." *Democratization* 15, no. 2 (2008): 230–50.

Wintrobe, Ronald. "The Tinpot and the Totalitarian: An Economic Theory of Dictatorship." *American Political Science Review* 84, no. 3 (1990): 849–72.

Wringe, William. *An Expressive Theory of Punishment*. London: Palgrave Macmillan, 2016.

Yack, Bernard. "The Myth of the Civic Nation." *Critical Review* 10, no. 2 (1996): 193–211.

Young, Iris Marion. "Responsibility and Global Labor Justice." *Journal of Political Philosophy* 12, no. 4 (2004): 365–88.

Young, Iris Marion. *Responsibility for Justice*. Oxford: Oxford University Press, 2011.

Zimmermann, Andrea. "State Succession in Treaties." In *Max Planck Encyclopedia of Public International Law*, edited by Rüdiger Wolfrum. Oxford: Oxford University Press, 2007.

Index

For the benefit of digital users, indexed terms that span two pages (e.g., 52–53) may, on occasion, appear on only one of those pages.